our

D0625456

Breaking Boundaries:
Women in Higher Education

Edited by

Louise Morley and Val Walsh

Taylor & Francis
Publishers since 1798

UK	Taylor & Francis Ltd, 1 Gunpowder Sq., London EC4A 3DE
USA	Taylor & Francis Inc., 1900 Frost Road, Suite 101, Bristol, PA 19007

First published 1996

A Catalogue Record for this book is available from the British Library

ISBN 0 7484 0519 4
ISBN 0 7484 0520 8 (pbk)   19018959

Library of Congress Cataloging-in-Publication Data are available on request

Series cover design by Amanda Barragry

Typeset in 10/12 pt Times
by Best-set Typesetter Ltd., Hong Kong

Printed in Great Britain by SRP Ltd, Exeter

Contents

Contents

WHEN
(Women in Higher Education Network)

WHEN is a national network spanning all sectors of Higher Education in the UK. It brings together academics, administrators, students and support staff from all disciplines and at all levels in HE. Its aim is to further the position of women in HE and change the climate of HE to one where all women can reach their full potential.

WHEN offers all women teaching, learning and working in HE the opportunity to share information and to network for example via its annual conference. It aims to raise awareness and share good practice on a broad range of issues which women in HE have themselves identified as important.

WHEN was set up in 1988 at the University of Cambridge. It has also been based at the University of Nottingham and at the University of Central Lancashire.

WHEN has initiated a series of books with Taylor & Francis Publishers beginning with *Changing the Subject: Women in Higher Education*, edited by Sue Davies, Cathy Lubelska and Jocey Quinn. These publications combine selected conference papers and are a good opportunity for women to get their research published and share their knowledge.

For more information and membership details contact:

Jacquie Melia
Centre for Health Studies
University College Salford
Frederick Road
Salford M6 6PU

Tel/Fax: (0161) 745 3332
Email: Jacqueline melia@ucsalf.ac.uk

Introduction

Louise Morley and Val Walsh

This edited collection contains multiple readings and interpretations of women's engagement with higher education as academics, researchers and students. Chapters demonstrate and examine processes of equity and change, in relation to organizational culture, curriculum development, knowledge production, and the needs and contributions of diverse women. Black women, disabled women, Irish women, mothers and older women, and women in male-dominated disciplinary locations such as management education, theorize and share experiences. In so doing they document and challenge the often implicit obstacles to equality and feminism in the academy.

Attention is given to organizational, intellectual and emotional processes influencing women's participation and well-being in higher education. Connections and separations are demonstrated between location in dominant organizations of knowledge production and women's inner worlds. Themes include analysis of the effectiveness of policies for equality, and the resulting need to analyse the implementation gap, that is, the vast discrepancy between policy intention, text and gendered practices. Power is theorized differently by writers, some represent it as property, with zero sum qualities, believing that it has to be redistributed, and is accessible to women in higher education, if successfully decoded. Others perceive power as so deeply sedimented in organizational, social and interpersonal relations, that policies for change seem naive and based on a rationalist connection between intervention and outcome. In this analysis changes in higher education need to come from a variety of sources. Employment and recruitment of women as staff and students is important, but so too is a critical appraisal of the services delivered, for example feminist epistemology, pedagogy, curriculum development and management.

The analysis of women's presence in organizations can often degenerate into essentialized notions of critical mass theory, viewing a causality between women's underrepresentation numerically, and horizontal and vertical segregation. As Currie and Kazi (1987, p. 88) indicated, 'Merely adding women to the academy will not radicalize knowledge as power relations extend beyond the power of men over women'. Breaking boundaries involves naming barriers to women's participation in higher education, as well as testifying to the consequences of power relations based on social class, 'race', sexualities, age, disabilities, and ethnicities. It is always a challenge to engage intellectually and politically with issues of difference, without being open to allegations of tokenism and further marginalization. This collection includes discussion on disability, deafness, Irishness, motherhood, 'race' and age, firstly, because of the quality of the writing, and also in recognition that debates on feminism and organizational change are often partial, situated and exclusionary. Diversity is understood as both change agent and goal, within feminism as well as the academy.

Methodological pluralism is exemplied by the various ways in which contributors have sought to elicit, analyse and interpret data. Some studies rely on unmediated accounts of empirical evidence, while others draw heavily on case studies, autobiography, literature and feminist theory. Reflexive accounts of the research process and deliberations about legitimacy and location suggest that women are challenging patriarchal boundaries of knowledge production. Furthermore, there are endeavours to move beyond modernist bipolarities in methodologies, with feminist research a synonym for good practice, and to subject feminist research itself to critical rigour and reflection. Contributors demonstrate that rethinking roles and demarcations also involves disclosure within research and pedagogic practice, and this involves risks as well as opportunitites.

Underpinning these chapters, however, is a central irony: whereas the university is traditionally viewed as a social institution which celebrates differentiation of forms of thought, difference remains within dominant patriarchal paradigms, with the result of gender and other structures of inequality being oppositionally located. So, while higher education claims to be in the business of promoting understanding, critical reflection and reflexive social inquiry, it often lacks an understanding and a critique of itself (Barnett, 1993). Higher education is a pivotal institution in society and the consequences of women's underrepresentation in positions of authority have wider and more serious resonances for issues of equity, social justice and participation in public life. Currently higher education functions as a structure for reproducing power relations, rather than challenging them.

The academy has been depicted as intellectuals segregated into their separate 'tribes and territories' (Becher, 1989), forming non-communicating cognitive groupings. A key question relates to how counter-hegemonic discourses such as feminism can be inserted into higher education and make a difference to cultures, employment and knowledges. It is evident that interventions and analysis are strong, and yet change agents often act in isolation in organizational and intellectual contexts characterized by fragmentation. The new market values in higher education, with an emphasis on managerialism, regulation and measurement, such as quality assurance and performance indicators, exacerbates the pressure for standardized uniformity. So, while some chapters assert the ineffectiveness of organizational policies for equality, others analytically relate these failures to wider changes in public policy.

Over the last thirty years, feminists in the academy have developed an extensive and substantial body of research, pedagogy and knowledge, much of it framed as counter-hegemonic, anti-oppressive practice. This is a considerable historical achievement. This collection makes it clear that there is still much to be done before the academy is a safe and welcoming environment for women, and provides examples of how women are sustaining these feminist struggles at every level, with energy, determination and creativity.

Some chapters in this book are papers presented at the 1994 Women in Higher Education Conference at the University of Central Lancashire; others were specially commissioned for the book.

Christine Heward argues that the notion of a professional career as an upward progress through a hierarchy developed in the nineteenth century. At this time, the career route from public school to Oxbridge into a successful career in the professions and government was institutionalized. Heward observes that between 1910 and 1960 women dominated initial teacher education, proving themselves able managers of large, mixed institutions of higher education. Strongly institutionalized hegemonic masculinities excluded women from universities in the UK for six hundred years. While women have increased their presence in the undergraduate population steadily this century, their admission has been confined to the lower echelons of the academic profession. Heward illustrates how self-confidence in intellectual ability, self-advertisement in making a reputation and networking, privilege men and disadvantage women. Within academic subject communities and subcultures, these effects cumulate so that the careers of men and women diverge, with men being promoted and women languishing in the lowest grades throughout their careers. She concludes that equal opportunities policies introduced since the Sex Discrimination Act in 1975 have proved ineffectual in challenging this occurrence.

Meg Maguire indicates how, until recently, age has been neglected and absent from much feminist analysis. In her chapter she ensures that age is included and not ignored in the complexity of social relations of power which marginalize and position women as 'other'. Focusing on ageism in higher education, she has chosen to consider two categories of women: those who work as teachers and 'mature' women students who are regulated through the nomenclature 'non-traditional'. Via illustrative empirical work and feminist theory, her intention is to allow for 'a more meaningful exploration of difference, which will eventually reinforce women's collective efforts to bring about change' (Morley, 1992, p. 524). The essential point is that ageist/sexist constructions which are normalized in educational discursive practices need to be revealed if they are to be displaced.

Liz Price and Judy Priest outline the processes followed at Oxford Brookes University in raising equal opportunities issues and embedding a commitment to diversity as a key institutional value. They argue that individuals with little formal role power can mobilize change in universities, largely because power is more diverse and dispersed than in private sector companies, and therefore more available to activists. The chapter provides specific examples of the achievements made by activists, and also demarcates the limitations of an activist approach.

Jane Kettle analyses a series of interviews with 'successful' academic women. The focus is on the apparent contradictions between the language and intent of policies intended to achieve equality of opportunity in universities. Particular attention is given to the organizational cultures of universities and how this impinges on equality strategies.

Ruth-Elaine Gibson brings together the experiences of deaf women academics relating to their entry and progression in the profession. She compares and contrasts the educational environments for young women in school education and the conditions of their participation in higher education. She argues that school education, because of its segregative nature, does not prepare deaf people for higher education. Equally, the academy is slow to adapt to meet the needs of deaf students.

Pat Hornby and Sue Shaw present their experiences as management educators and raise questions about how gender issues and the subject of women in management are approached in management course curricula. They express their disappointment at the optional status of the women and management module on their Diploma in Management Studies, and the failure of management courses in general to include explicit and substantive reference to gender issues in their curricula. Catharine Ross explores black women's struggles for inclusion in professional and management programmes in higher education. Drawing upon research into part-time personnel management education, she focuses on the barriers perceived by black women who have sought inclusion in such programmes, and the strategies they have adopted to overcome them. Maggie Humm examines institutional and management values and the new organizational cultures currently being promoted in British universities. She argues that these new strategies will greatly alter higher education towards the millennium and that they are indifferent to issues of equal opportunities. Analysing a key blueprint strategy, *Promoting People*, the chapter concludes with some recommendations for a new equality ethics of higher education.

Breda Gray and Louise Ryan address the many levels of absence and invisibility of Irish women in higher education in England. Their chapter is structured around some of their experiences as Irish women, teaching, researching and seeking funding in England. While highlighting the exclusion of Irish women from course content, they indicate how 'inclusion' may merely result in tokenism or a denial of difference. They explore possible strategies for theorizing the relative absence and invisibility of issues relating to Irishness and, in particular, Irish women. Their central aim is to illustrate the relevance of Irish women's experiences to all levels of higher education in England.

Louise Morley critically examines developments in feminist research and raises questions about the problematic relationship between gender, power,

method and epistemology. As assertions of 'knowledge' frequently both produce and guarantee domination and power, there is a problem as to how
feminism can legitimately claim to be a site of knowledge about women's
oppression without reproducing the power relations it questions. Exploring
the problematics of feminist engagement with methods and methodologies
such as ethnography, action research and grounded theory, and the binary
oppositional location of qualitative and quantitative research, she also draws
attention to the micropolitics of feminist research processes.

Elizabeth Bird provides a narrative of how the interdisciplinary MSc in
Gender and Social Policy was introduced at the University of Bristol in 1989.
She indicates how six years later the problems of owning and resourcing the
programme remain unresolved because it does not fit the institutional framework. The chapter discusses barriers to interdisciplinary work, the problems
of recognition for both students and staff, the experience of students, the
financial and budgetary constraints and the impact of quality assurance measures on teaching standards and research productivity.

Máiréad Dunne considers the theoretical and methodological tensions of
being a feminist researcher in higher education studying social justice issues.
Through an exploration of the theoretical contradictions produced by the use
of established statistical categories alongside reconceptualized notions of
class, 'race' and gender relations, she discusses the contribution of quantitative
data to equal opportunities research and the complementarity of quantitative
and qualitative methods.

Alessandra Iantaffi reports the findings of her literature search on the
subject of women and disability in higher education. She argues that the
experiences of disabled women are more complex than a simple addition of
disadvantages. She also discusses the issue of visibility of disabled women's
bodies, and how this affects their authority.

Val Walsh advocates a holistic perspective, an epistemology of connection instead of separation, in relation to women's contradictory and productive
presence in the academy. Her chapter suggests that the hybridity and multiplicity of pedagogy's roots and praxis – its liminal location – constitute subversion of the dominant and sexualized polarities produced within Western
epistemologies, such as therapy and politics.

Miriam David, Jackie Davies, Rosalind Edwards, Diane Reay and Kay
Standing write as a group of feminist academics, all mothers, researching and
writing about families, family structures and forms such as lone-mother families, and in relation to bringing up children and their education. Their chapter
explores research evidence from their studies of mothers and education, and
reflects on their methodology from their particular vantage point as feminist
academics and mothers. They consider how mothering discourses affect them
and the mothers they study, making it difficult to step outside the discourses
and not make judgments. They also consider the ways in which these dilemmas
influence both the research process and their writing together about their

research in a competitive higher education context. They introduce the notion of structural and moral constraints as a way of classifying the different ways in which choices are influenced by varying contexts.

References

BARNETT, R. (1993) 'Knowledge, Higher Education and Society: A Postmodern Problem', *Oxford Review of Education*, 19, 1, pp. 33–46.

BECHER, T. (1989) *Academic Tribes and Territories*, Milton Keynes, SHRE/ Open University Press.

CURRIE, D. and KAZI, H. (1987) 'Academic Feminism and the Process of Deradicalization: Re-examining the Issues', *Feminist Review*, 25, pp. 77– 98.

MORLEY, L. (1992) 'Women's Studies, Difference, and Internalised Oppression', *Women's Studies International Forum*, 15, 4, pp. 517–25.

Section I

Diversity, Equity and Change

Chapter 1

Women and Careers in Higher Education: What is the Problem?

Christine Heward

Introduction: Careers

In this chapter I review a series of research projects that I have undertaken and bring insights gained from them to bear on the problem of women's careers in higher education. The notion of career developed in the nineteenth century with the abolition of patronage and the reform of the professions, government service, grammar and public schools. Examinations were introduced to select those entering the expanding and increasingly hierarchical government organizations and professions. It is one of the central features of Weber's notion of bureaucracy (Weber, 1968). Young men entered the Civil Service or the Indian Army seeing their futures as a progression up a ladder. In 1988 I published *Making a Man of Him: Parents and their Sons' Education at an English Public School 1929–1950*. When I started that study of 2,000 letters from parents to the headmaster of a minor public school I saw it as a study of careers. Only gradually did I realize that careers are one aspect of masculinities, which became the central focus of the book. Sons' careers were the fulcrum of family ideologies about social class and masculinities. They were the realization of families' aspirations for status maintenance and upward mobility. Fathers planned and directed their sons' educational and subsequent careers as an integrated enterprise requiring a family strategy. Examining the question of what the problem is with women and careers in higher education depends on an understanding of 'career'. The concept of career connotes individual life histories and their relation to family, education and work. They concern individuals within families and their gender and class relations.

Careers in Higher Education

Careers in higher education in the UK became much more institutionalized and hierarchical from the 1970s as institutions expanded. The academic profession became more differentiated and hierarchical as management became an increasingly separate function. These developments were recognized and further institutionalized in a series of reforms such as the Houghton pay settlement in the late 1970s and the implementation of the Jarratt Report in the mid 1980s (CVCP, 1985). From the 1960s onwards single-sex institutions in secondary and tertiary education have become mixed and small institutions closed, amalgamated or merged into large ones. This has had profound effects on gender and power relations and consequently women's promotion prospects in all sectors of secondary and tertiary education.

As a number of historians and sociologists have shown, women were admitted to universities in the UK reluctantly at the end of the nineteenth century after a bitter battle (Burstyn, 1980; Dyhouse, 1984, 1995; Delamont, 1989). As Dyhouse (1995) and Moore (1991) show, they were marginalized, only being admitted to graduation at Cambridge, arguably the most élitist institution, in 1947. Apart from a small number in the medical faculties, most women read Arts and became teachers.

The statistical evidence shows that women have steadily increased their presence as undergraduates. The numbers of women among the staff rose only slowly until 1980; since then it has risen to above 20 per cent. The data in Table 1.1 demonstrate that the continuing increase in the proportion of women among the undergraduate population has consistently failed to yield any change in the proportion of women above the lecturer grade. Any assumption that the increase in the numbers at the bottom will automatically yield a greater number at the top in due time is fallacious. The fruit of nearly two decades of anti-discrimination legislation would appear to be an increasing number of women in the lowest echelons of higher education without any significant change at the top. The universities excluded women for six hundred years, institutionalizing hegemonic masculinities in a hierarchy of value within and among institutions. An attempt to examine the problem of women and careers in higher education must focus on the gender and power relations underlying the stubborn resistance of senior positions to change.

Table 1.1 Women in Universities

	Total staff	% women staff	% all women in senior posts	% women students on degree courses
1912–13	3,135	5.1	5.9	not known
1921–2	4,037	9.7	6.9	27.6
1930–1	5,196	9.9	10.9	28.6
1951	10,861	12.2	11.4	23.7
1972	33,868	10.9	12.0	32.4
1979	39,987	13.7	10.4	37.8
1980	43,017	13.9	11.8	39.8
1990	49,377	21.0	10.7	45.0

Sources: Rendel, 1980, 1984; USR, 1994.

Successful Women Managers in Tertiary Education

My second research project was an investigation of the history of changing gender relations in initial teacher education. I was anxious to explain the decimation in the number of women in senior posts that has been relentless in the thirty years since I began my career in the 1960s. The gradual transformation of the gender composition of universities during the last century contrasts markedly with that in initial teacher education, which has a very different history. From its inception in the nineteenth century, teacher training was the most popular form of post-secondary education for women. Indeed the history of gender and power relations in this sector of tertiary education is unique for it was dominated by women, who held the majority of senior positions for half a century. Uncovering this aspect of women's history and attempting to explain its intriguing gender power relations proved one of the most satisfying intellectual tasks I have ever undertaken (Heward, 1993). In the nineteenth century residential teacher education was provided by the religious denominations, Church of England colleges being the most numerous. The 1902 Education Act set up the Board of Education. The Board provided most of the colleges' funding. To increase the control of this fledgling department and reduce the power of the Church of England clergy in teacher training, a regulation was passed in 1910 that all the principals of women's training colleges should be women. This singular and unknown instance of positive discrimination was highly effective until 1960, when there were 158 colleges of education, 98 of which had women principals. The expansion of teacher train-ing, the coming of the 3-year course in 1960, the change from single-sex to mixed-sex colleges and the opening of a recognizable and attractive career ladder drew in an increasing number of men from the late 1950s (Taylor, 1969). The equally speedy reduction of teacher training places and the amalgamation and merger of institutions in the 1970s, 1980s and 1990s reduced the numbers of institutions of initial teacher education outside the 'old' universities to 58 by 1990, only four of which had women principals.

It is important to note that the period when women's position in the management of teacher education was eroded coincided with that of growing participation by women in the labour market and the introduction of anti-discrimination legislation. The present legislation in the UK is extremely feeble. Unlike that in the USA, where class actions can be brought by groups, that in the UK only enables individuals to bring cases against their employers. It was powerless to prevent the decimation of women among the senior ranks of teacher educators. Significantly, the abolition of women's training colleges was accompanied by such institutions being stigmatized as narrow cultural backwaters with autocratic women principals (Taylor, 1969). Once institutions of teacher education were absorbed into the mainstream of higher education, the institutionalization of hegemonic masculinities ensured that, as large mixed-sex institutions, their management was deemed to require abilities defined in masculine terms, and men were appointed. Despite this essentialist view of the gendered character of the way women and men manage, women like Joan Browne at Coventry College of Education and Kathleen Jones at Avery Hill College managed large colleges very successfully after they became mixed, reforming, expanding and restructuring in response to the often bewildering changes that have convulsed teacher education in the UK. A further indication of institutionalization of hegemonic masculinities in higher education is that the decimation of women in senior positions in teacher education has been completely unremarked. The appointment of men to succeed a generation of women principals was seen as part of the natural order of things. It was not noticed, let alone questioned or protested, in marked contrast to the fuss about such issues as all-women shortlists in the Labour Party.

The investigation of women in senior positions in teacher education suggests that women are able and capable managers of institutions of higher education. However, only the very strongest anti-discrimination measures, namely reserving posts for women, are effective in enabling them to enter senior management in significant numbers. Measures such as these, i.e. positive discrimination, were rendered illegal in the UK by the 1975 Sex Discrimination Act. It is indicative of the strength of hegemonic masculinities in higher education that the history of the achievements of the women who successfully managed institutions of initial teacher education has been stigmatized and ignored (Heward, 1993).

The Glass Ceiling or the Stone Floor?

My third research project was undertaken with a colleague in an attempt to understand gender power relations in higher education within the context of recent anti-discrimination legislation and the introduction of equal opportunities policies (Heward and Taylor, 1992, 1993). Since the 1980s the academic profession in the UK is being restructured as new funding and governance arrangements are introduced. With the abolition of the binary division, a more complex hierarchy of institutions is emerging.

Institutions of higher education resemble the labour market generally. As we have already noted, their work-forces are strongly gender-segmented horizontally and vertically. As with other large employment organizations, women are found in a narrow range of low-paid 'feminine', caring and personal service areas while men are in a wider range of posts. The academic profession manifests features of vertical and horizontal gender segmentation only too clearly. It is organized into subject communities all of which are strongly hierarchical (Becher, 1989). The rainbow of subjects comprising the academic profession is marked by horizontal gender segmentation. Men are found in the physical sciences and technologies; women in the arts, social sciences and medical sciences. Senior positions in all subject areas, even those like modern foreign languages and biology, where a majority of undergraduate entrants are female, are overwhelmingly occupied by men. There are more senior posts in the male-dominated physical sciences and engineering than in the arts and social sciences. In the medical sciences women are found in certain 'feminized' areas – geriatrics, anaesthesia, haematology, psychiatry, paediatrics – and are also found in the lower echelons, especially contract research.

This feature of the continuing exclusion of women from senior positions has attracted considerable attention. The Hansard Society Commission, investigating the poor representation of women in the House of Commons seventy years after women were enfranchised, examined the professions of MPs before they enter the House of Commons. They were particularly critical of the universities, whom they saw as encouraging women to enter universities to solve the problem of falling birth rates. This enthusiasm did not extend to the promotion of women in the academic profession. They found barriers in all routes to parliament and popularized the North American concept of the Glass Ceiling to characterize the structural barrier they saw preventing able women from entering the most senior and powerful positions.

The fastest expanding sector of employment is short-term contract researchers and teachers among whom are a growing proportion of women (Aziz, 1990). While their numbers are increasing in all of the lower grades of the academic profession, the increase among professors and vice-chancellors is glacial. Mason and Jewson (1992) have argued that the gendered labour market may be characterized more aptly as a stone floor of low-paid menial positions to which women are held down rather than their rise being prevented by a so-called glass ceiling. Such a conception conveys the stereotyping and low value of women demonstrated by these data on divisions within the academic profession (see table 1.2).

Under pressure from such sources as the Hansard Commission Report on Women at the Top (1990), equal opportunities policies have been introduced by many institutions of higher education. Many are the product of reluctant

Table 1.2 Full-time academic staff in universities by grade and gender 1993–4

	Wholly university financed (including all tenured appointments)		Not wholly university financed (including short-term research contracts)	
	men (%)	women (%)	men (%)	women (%)
Professors	94.6	5.4	93.7	6.3
Readers, SLs	89.4	10.6	77.0	23.0
Lecturers	76.3	23.7	68.8	31.2
Other	49.6	50.4	58.4	41.6
Total N = 53,809				

Source: USR, 1994.

managements, who have policy statements and formalize procedures, rarely embarking on programmes of action (Williams *et al.*, 1989). They do not address the institutionalization of hegemonic masculinities in genderized assumptions about, for example, merit. It is assumed that the concepts, such as merit, underlying staff selection and promotion procedures, are universal and objective. Women's problems with promotion, it is thought, are associated with their domestic responsibilities, which are ameliorated with career breaks and creches. Despite equal opportunities policies, women in universities remain 'crowded' into low-status, poorly paid 'feminine' jobs.

The evidence suggests that the problem of women and careers in higher education may be more accurately conceptualized as a 'stone floor' keeping them at the bottom rather than a 'glass ceiling' preventing them getting to the top. A further indication of the institutionalization of hegemonic masculinities in higher education is the feeble nature of equal opportunities policies. All too often they are statements of policy ideals, which fail to address gender power relations and rarely provoke actions or change.

Gender-Differentiated Lived Experience within Structures

Encouraged by this work, I began to tap into the work of other women on their position in academe. Finding an adequate understanding and explanation of my own life history became a necessary next step towards a broader conceptual framework (Plummer, 1984). There is increasing interest among researchers in women in the academic profession. Recent studies by Sutherland (1985), Bagilhole (1993) and Morley (1994) have focused exclusively on women, seeking to illuminate women's experience from their own perspective. Sutherland interviewed women in Finland, Germany and the UK. She pointed to the importance of women's domestic and childcare responsibilities for their careers. Bagilhole interviewed women in one university, interpreting her findings within the framework of institutional discrimination. She argued that women were excluded from the male networks which dominate academic institutions. Morley examined the consequences for the self-concepts and consciousness of women academics of discrimination and the strategies they employ to avoid damaging negative effects. Research on careers in general and academic careers in particular have developed further in North America than in the UK (Aisenberg and Harrington, 1988). There, a body of work from a variety of perspectives suggests that the unitary concept of career as an upward progress is simplistic and concepts which can do justice to diverse work histories are required for further understandings and explanations in this field (Gallos, 1989). Research in the UK on women in the labour market, including the professions, is growing steadily. It shows that women may have very different career patterns from men, characterized by diversity and flexibility, with periods out of the labour market, part-time, temporary or occasional 'supply' work as in teaching (Hochschild, 1978; Ward and Silverstone, 1980; Dex, 1984; Martin and Roberts, 1984; Sutherland, 1985; Evetts, 1990). Gallos' conclusion that 'linear occupational advancement is too limiting a perspective for understanding women's careers' is now inescapable (Gallos, 1989, p. 124).

Following Denise Riley's incisive analysis, I see 'woman', 'femininity' and 'feminism' as problematic pluralist constructs, negotiated and often contested (Riley, 1989). I see women and men making individual choices, constructing their own identities and biographies. Structures are the ideological and material constraints within which we actively undertake gendered actions and processes among which careers are highly significant projects.

The starting point for this work was my own life history as a woman academic, which included a desperate struggle to be promoted above the lecturer grade and participation in my own very male-dominated institution in campaigns for action on equal opportunities issues. Theoretically, I drew on my previous work on the construction of masculine identities, on feminist work on life history and autobiography, on Bob Connell's pluralist theory of gender and power (Connell, 1991) and Pierre Bourdieu's study of the academic profession in the Paris universities, *Homo Academicus* (1988). He defines academic power as the ability of senior academics to control the careers of aspirants by evaluating their intellectual output, theses, papers, books and research applications. I concluded that any understanding of women in the academic profession had to examine the interaction of structure and process (Heward, 1993). There is no single barrier or 'glass ceiling' that can be shattered. Rather the deeply institutionalized values of the hegemonic masculinities dominant in higher education accumulate in the careers of women and men to increasingly privilege men and disadvantage women.

Seeing Yourself and Being Seen as Academically Able

To investigate the mechanisms differentiating the careers of men and women in the academic profession, I collaborated with colleagues from the Centre for Research in Ethnic Relations in a small-scale study of the career histories of men and women professors in law and biology (Heward *et al.*, forthcoming). We chose these subjects because half of the undergraduates in them are women. While biology is the most popular science in schools among girls, only 2 per cent of professors of biology are women. Women entered the academic study of biology early, largely as botanists. While they entered the study of law later than they did biology, they are now 5 per cent of professors in law. We interviewed sixteen professors, eight men and eight women. We found all the women except one by snowballing.

The evidence from these respondents suggests that self-confidence, a positive evaluation of their own academic ability from the outset of their career, is a crucial basis for a successful academic career. A number of the respondents talked about the importance of having confidence, especially seeing themselves as academically able. One professor commented:

> when you look around you see people who get on aren't intrinsically very clever. I am not . . . I got a 2.2 degree, so I have no pretensions to being a brilliant academic. I see around me . . . very clever people who don't have confidence and their careers don't move.

This self-confidence may or may not be confirmed by mentors in the academic profession. Other investigations of women and members of minority ethnic groups who succeed have shown that the process by which respondents identified themselves as academically able, the confirmation of these views and encouragement they received from others in the early stages of academic careers were of the greatest significance for their later success (Burton, 1993). For many respondents in this study the basis of their career success was getting a good degree or PhD and being encouraged by their tutors or supervisors to pursue an academic career.

The relation between self-confidence, perceived ability and subject is problematic for women. Thomas' investigation into the experiences of men and women undergraduates in physics and English at 'new' and 'old' universities showed that self-evaluation of academic ability, self-confidence and career plans differed widely between men and women. In physics, strongly identified as a masculine subject, women were in the minority, struggling to maintain a feminine identity in a masculine world. The male students built an identity through commitment to becoming a scientist and pursuing a scientific career. Men 'saw themselves climbing the ladder of success, women were only too aware of having to make a choice between following a career and raising a family: being a physicist or being a woman' (Thomas, 1990, p. 138). In English, where women were in the majority, the men were more self-confident. Individuality and opinion were highly valued and the men envisaged their futures as successful writers, for example. The women were much more tentative in their career plans. Like the women in physics they saw a conflict between femininity and 'selfish' career women who behave like men (Thomas, 1990: 169–71).

In the academic profession the importance of self-confidence and seeing yourself as potentially able and being seen as such continues to the level of chair. Indeed sponsorship may become more salient at the most senior levels. One man described the way he 'was being encouraged to think of myself as a potential professor. I was invited to apply for the chair at – . . . when the VC rang'.

This study provided further evidence of the 'double bind' for women in making themselves more visible and attempting to compete on equal terms with men for preferment. Behaviour such as assertiveness, self-confidence and self-advertisement, which is praised in men, may be criticized as unfeminine and risk alienation from women colleagues. One of the women respondents was dubbed 'over ambitious' by her women colleagues at the same time as she was being encouraged by senior men.

The evidence in this study is tantalizing, raising many issues of the nature and effects of stereotyping and of recipients' responses to it. The effect on women's self-confidence of pedagogies dominated by competitive male values in higher education is now on the feminist research agenda. Spurling (1990), Thomas (1990) and Lewis (1993) have begun the process of explicating their import for women students and staff. How far women seek promotion or eliminate themselves from competition for the 'glittering prizes' of the academic profession, and for what reasons, are intriguing questions. More research is needed on such processes in higher education and how they affect academic careers, especially in their early stages. This pilot investigation supports the conclusion that seeing oneself and being seen as academically able are very important at the outset of academic careers. The significance of gender stereotypes in the formation of self-evaluations of ability needs further research.

Making a Reputation

In the academic profession, 'The main currency ... is reputation' (Becher, 1989, p. 52). Peer evaluation of intellectual work, theses, publications, conference papers and research applications is the basis of academic careers. Respondents varied widely in the kinds of reputations they claimed and the extent to which they saw 'making a reputation' as a conscious active process of self-advertisement. The processes of gaining a reputation also depend on the structure of the subject and its specialisms. The judgments of senior 'eminent' members of a subject are highly significant. They act as 'gatekeepers', admitting or excluding aspirants to the academic profession (Becher, 1989; Bourdieu, 1988).

Subjects also vary in the 'rigour' of their referencing procedures and the prestige hierarchy of their methods of communication within the community (Becher, 1990). For some respondents making and managing an academic reputation by publishing in prestigious journals and meeting the 'right people' involved self-advertisement. The professors of biology were more forthcoming than those in law about their own proactive role in their accounts of their careers and reputations. The processes are more clearly institutionalized in science than in law, with fierce competition for research funding, a large and hierarchical literature of journals and a huge circuit of national and international conferences (Becher, 1990).

Self-advertisement may be encouraged in the socialization of certain gender and ethnic groups more than others. Given the particular nature of subject cultures, certain groups may find it easier than others to adopt the culture and establish themselves in the networks of their subject. These very limited data suggest that women face a series of dilemmas and 'double binds' in constructing an academic career. Making a reputation is about self-advertisement, which poses serious problems for dominant understandings of femininities and female sexualities.

Mentors and Networks

Networks of contacts within the academic community become increasingly important in the middle and later stages of academic careers. Patrons and informal networks are crucial in determining who is invited to apply for posts and who is successful. It is through the informal networks of subject communities that the values by which members of the academic profession are recruited and promoted are sustained. Previous research on the academic profession suggests that the values of 'gatekeepers' are conservative (Bourdieu, 1988; Exum, 1983; Smelser and Content, 1980). How far they also act as mentors, advising and supporting the careers of men like themselves, initiating them and recommending them to the 'brotherhood', as Lorber found in the medical profession in the USA (Lorber, 1984), is not clear. One professor of law described the process of contacts and recommendations which led to his being promoted to a readership. A senior member of the profession, whom he had known at Oxbridge, had a grant for a series of colloquia. Its members were all professors. The respondent was initially invited to a meeting on his particular specialism on which he had written a book. He then became a member of the group:

> One of the professors who was in the group had seen my book and heard me talk and said to somebody else, 'This chap should have been promoted some time ago'. That person then fed it through to the Dean of – Law School who did something about it.

The women seemed to have benefited less from networks of contacts as their careers developed than the men. One said she had been actively discriminated against when a major publishing opportunity was given to a man in another university on the retirement of a senior colleague. Another recent investigation also suggests that women academics find themselves excluded from male networks (Bagilhole, 1993). If opportunities for promotion are not available in a respondent's institution then a move to another is usually the way to progress and the majority of the respondents had moved for promotion. Geographical mobility was more common among the men than the women.

The evidence points to the conclusion that mentoring and networking are all important in the subject communities of the academic profession. The men in this investigation had benefited more than women from such activities, being invited to apply for posts and to edit journals and books, whereas women had to seek out such opportunities.

Conclusions

Women have been able and capable managers of institutions of higher education in the past. Rather than a single structural barrier or 'glass ceiling' ensuring that women remain in the lower echelons of the academic profession, structure and process interact throughout the life cycle. Institutions of higher education are gendered. They are hierarchized in terms of strongly institutionalized hegemonic masculinities. The most prestigious have excluded women for six hundred years. Their hegemonic masculinities, which determine the position of any single institution in the hierarchy, privilege men and undervalue women. The processes of being identified as intellectually able, making a reputation, mentoring and networking tend to provide cumulative advantages to men and disadvantage women. The continuous privileging of men and hegemonic masculinities and devaluation of women and femininities have cumulative effects on the careers of individual men and women, causing increasing divergence most visible among the older age groups. Men are promoted, so that by middle age a number have reached the highest echelons and a significant number have been promoted above the lowest grade, while all but a few token women languish on the lowest grade throughout their careers. Processes of change are complex, uncertain and confused. Equal opportunities policies, based on a deficit model of women's careers, have proved ineffectual. It remains to be seen how far such forms of positive action as targets for the promotion of women in the academic profession can weaken deeply institutionalized values to change the position of women as a group.

References

AISENBERG, A. and HARRINGTON, M. (1988) *Women of Academe: Outsiders in the Sacred Grove*, Amhurst, University of Massachusetts Press.

AZIZ, A. (1990) 'Women in UK Universities: The Road to Casualisation', in STIVER LIE, S. and O'LEARY, V. E. (Eds) *Storming the Tower: Women in the Academic World*, London, Kogan Page, pp. 33–46.

BAGILHOLE, B. (1993) 'How to Keep a Good Woman Down: An Investigation of the Role of Institutional Factors in the Process of Discrimination against Women Academics', *British Journal of the Sociology of Education*, 14, 3, pp. 261–74.

BECHER, A. (1989) *Academic Tribes and Territories*, Milton Keynes, SHRE/Open University Press.

BOURDIEU, P. (1988) *Homo Academicus*, Oxford, Polity.

BURSTYN, J. (1980) *Victorian Education and the Ideal of Womanhood*, London, Croom Helm.

BURTON, L. (1993) 'Management, "Race" and Gender: An Unlikely Alliance', *British Educational Research Journal*, 19, 3, pp. 275–90.

COMMITTEE OF VICE CHANCELLORS AND PRINCIPALS (CVCP) (1985) *Report of the Standing Committee on Efficiency Studies in Universities* (Jarratt Report), London, CVCP.

CONNELL, R. W. (1991) 'Live Fast and Die Young: The Construction of Masculinity among Young Working-Class Men on the Margin of the Labour Market', *Australian and New Zealand Journal of Sociology*, 27, 2, pp. 141–71.

DELAMONT, S. (1989) *Knowledgeable Women: Structuralism and the Reproduction of Elites*, London, Routledge.

DEX, S. (1984) *Women's Work Histories: An Analysis of the Women and Employment Survey*, Research Paper 46, London, Department of Employment.

DYHOUSE, C. (1984) 'Storming the Citadel or Storm in a Teacup? The Entry of Women into Higher Education 1860–1920', in ACKER, S. and WARREN PIPER, D. (Eds) *Is Higher Education Fair to Women?* Buckingham, Open University Press, pp. 51–64.

DYHOUSE, C. (1995) *No Distinction of Sex? Women in British Universities 1870–1939*, London, UCL Press.

EVETTS, J. (1990) *Women in Primary Teaching: Career Contexts and Strategies*, London, Unwin Hyman.

EXUM, W. H. (1983) 'Climbing the Crystal Stair: Values, Affirmative Action and Minority Faculty', *Social Problems*, 30, 4, pp. 383–9.

GALLOS, J. (1989) 'Exploring Women's Development: Implications for Career Theory, Practice, and Research', in ARTHUR, M. B. *et al.* (Eds) *Handbook of Career Theory*, Cambridge, Cambridge University Press, pp. 110–32.

HANSARD SOCIETY COMMISSION (1990) *The Report of the Hansard Society Commission on Women at the Top*, London, Hansard Society for Parliamentary Government.

HEWARD, C. (1988) *Making a Man of Him: Parents and their Sons' Education at an English Public School 1929–1950*, London, Routledge.

HEWARD, C. (1993) 'Men and Women and the Rise of Professional Society: The Intriguing History of Teacher Educators', *History of Education*, 22, 1, pp. 11–32.

HEWARD, C. (1994) 'Academic Snakes and Merit Ladders: Reconceptualising the Glass Ceiling', *Gender and Education*, 6, 4, pp. 249–62.

HEWARD, C. and TAYLOR, P. (1992) 'Women at the Top in Higher Education: Equal Opportunities Policies in Action?', *Policy and Politics*, 20, 1, pp. 111–21.

HEWARD, C. and TAYLOR, P. (1993) 'Effective and Ineffective Equal Opportunities Policies in Higher Education', *Critical Social Policy*, 37, pp. 75–94.

HEWARD, C., TAYLOR, P. and VICKERS, R. (1995) 'What IS behind Saturn's Rings? Methodological Problems in the Investigation of Gender and Race in the Academic Profession', *British Educational Research Journal*, 21, 2, pp. 149–63.

HEWARD, C., TAYLOR, P. and VICKERS, R. (forthcoming) 'Gender, Race and Career Success in the Academic Profession', unpublished mimeo.

HOCHSCHILD, A. (1978) 'Inside the Clockwork of the Male Career', in HOWE,

F. (Ed.) *Women and the Power to Change*, New York, McGraw Hill, pp. 47–80.

LEWIS, M. G. (1993) *Without a Word: Teaching beyond Women's Silence*, London, Routledge.

LORBER, J. (1984) *Women in Medicine*, London, Tavistock.

MARTIN, J. and ROBERTS, C. (1984) *Women and Employment: A Lifetime Perspective*, London, HMSO.

MASON, D. and JEWSON, N. (1992) ' "Race", Equal Opportunities Policies and Employment Practice: Reflections on the 80s, Prospects for the 90s', *New Community*, 19, 1, pp. 91–112.

MOORE, L. (1991) *Bajanellas and Semilinas: Aberdeen University and the Education of Women 1860–1920*, Aberdeen, Aberdeen University Press.

MORLEY, L. (1994) 'Glass Ceiling or Iron Cage? Women in UK Academia', *Gender, Work and Organisation*, 1, 4, pp. 194–204.

PIPER, D. and ACKER, S. (Eds) *Is Higher Education Fair to Women?*, Guildford, SRHE.

PLUMMER, B. (1984) *Documents of Life*, London, Hyman.

POWNEY, J. and WEINER, G. (1992) *'Outside the Norm': Equity and Management in Education Institutions*, London, South Bank University.

RENDEL, M. (1980) 'How Many Women Academics?', in DEEM, R. (Ed.) *Schooling for Women's Work*, London, Routledge, pp. 142–61.

RENDEL, M. (1984) 'Women Academics in the Seventies', in ACKER, S. and WARREN PIPER, D. (Eds) *Is Higher Education Fair to Women?*, Buckingham, Open University Press, pp. 163–79.

RILEY, D. (1989) *Am I that Name? Feminism and the Category of 'Women' in History*, Basingstoke, Macmillan.

SMELSER, N. and CONTENT, R. (1980) *The Changing Academic Market and a Berkeley Case Study*, Berkeley, CA, University of California Press.

SPURLING, A. (1990) *Report of the Women in Higher Education Research Project*, Cambridge, King's College Research Centre.

SUTHERLAND, M. (1985) *Women who Teach in Universities*, Stoke on Trent, Trentham.

TAYLOR, W. (1969) *Society and the Education of Teachers*, London, Faber.

THOMAS, K. (1990) *Gender and Subject in Higher Education*, Milton Keynes, Open University Press.

UNIVERSITY STATISTICAL RECORD (USR) (1968–••), Cheltenham, University Grants Committee and Committee of Vice Chancellors and Principals.

WARD, A. and SILVERSTONE, R. (1980) *Careers of Professional Women*, London, Croom Helm.

WEBER, M. (1968) *Economy and Society*, New York, Bedminster.

WILLIAMS, J., COCKING, J. and DAVIES, L. (1989) *Words or Deeds? A Review of Equal Opportunities Policies in Higher Education*, London, Committee for Racial Equality.

ZUCKERMANN, H. (1988) 'The Sociology of Science', in SMELSER, N. (Ed.) *Handbook of Sociology*, Beverley Hills, Sage, pp. 511–74.

Chapter 2

In the Prime of Their Lives?
Older Women in Higher Education

Meg Maguire

The Invisibility of Older Women

The briefest review of television advertising and women's magazines will reveal the powerful concern in contemporary society with youth and the prolonging of a youthful experience/face/body. The media celebration and fascination with particular women such as Joan Collins, Cher and Joanna Lumley is bound up with their defiance of the ageing process. Age (which becomes unmentionable) and the resistance of ageing (which becomes increasingly commodified through creams, gels, pills and surgery) are set alongside the need to keep slim and healthy while incidentally propping up a multi-million-dollar industry. In Western societies, which are now ever more typified by ageing demographic profiles, there is a concern with attempts to control and reconstruct the body in an age-defying manner (Shilling, 1993). The reason for all this attention on youth/beauty, which centres on women, rests in part on valuing women in relation to their heterosexual attractiveness, while men are valued in relation to their employment status (Itzin, 1990). In this way, a woman's value is sexualized regardless of occupation. For this reason there is a pressure to conform to the tyranny of youth through cosmetic surgery, dieting, clothing, hair-dyes and make-up. Overall then, there is a powerful 'culture of youth' which sits alongside a 'contempt for age' (Gutman, 1987).

Ageing and ageism have consequences for men and women. However, there are very clear messages about older women spoken through 'the wicked old women of fairy stories' (Marshall, 1990, p. 32). Furthermore, the discourses of ageing which relate to women are spoken through pejorative labels like 'old dear,' 'old bag', 'hag' and 'mutton dressed as lamb'. There are no equivalent descriptions for older men. So the experiences of women as they get older are more likely to be negatively constructed. While men undoubtedly suffer from ageism, the experience of the older woman is compounded by ageism/sexism in an analytically and materially different manner. Yet until recently in the UK, age factors have been neglected and absent from much feminist analysis.

A strong critique of the silence within feminist work on women and ageing has been produced by Macdonald and Rich (1984). Barbara Macdonald writes: 'All my life in a man's world, I was a problem because I was a woman; now I'm a problem in a woman's world because I'm a sixty-five year old woman' (Macdonald and Rich, 1984, p. 30). She explains the current invisibility of older women in relation to second-wave feminism, which 'rose out of a different time in patriarchal history – it rose out of a time of a patriarchally supported white middle class youth culture' (Macdonald and Rich, 1984, p. 37). Recently, Arber and Ginn (1991) have suggested that the failure to consider the marginalization of older women in the 1970s and the early 1980s may have had something to do with the way in which many feminist researchers (white, middle-class, younger academics) focused on their personal experiences. They cite Ann Oakley's work on housework and maternity (1974 and 1980) as examples of this.

But Arber and Ginn add that some younger women may have felt that older women 'sold them out'. Particularly in relation to work in the academy, younger women may well believe that older women have 'complacently joined male-dominated academic hierarchies' (Arber and Ginn, 1991, p. 29). Younger women attempting to 'storm the tower' of higher education may well have to settle for part-time work, short-term contracts and insecure futures. Older women in full-time established posts just might seem to them to be as 'other' as senior males in the academy. Alternatively, some younger women may believe that older women in the academy have bequeathed them a legacy of difficulty – 'this old lady is hard to get along with' (Hammond, 1947, in Konek *et al.*, 1980, p. 17). 'I cannot in faith hold a brief for these women, they constitute a major cause of the difficulty of the younger, more ambitious, more capable women' (*ibid.*).

In a recent study of one college of higher education, one of the women tutors recognized the androcentrism which shaped the institution (Maguire, 1993). Liz said:

Women are 'emotional'. They are seen as unreliable. They are liable to go off and have a family, liable to be affected by the menopause. That is a large element of why people who have power to appoint actually do appoint males rather than females. . . . And I do have to say that there are several examples in our institution which let us down in that picture. People (women) who are emotionally driven who then spoil the image for other people (women) so that others coming behind who may be promoted one day, are on a sticky wicket for a start.

Long (1979, p. 14) believes that older women have often felt 'not wanted' or at best 'just about tolerated' in the women's movement, 'victims of young women's ageist assumptions and values'. This perspective is changing,[1] although the contemporary focus is still on the experiences of women over 60 (Neild and Pearson, 1992; Bernard and Meade, 1993). What does not seem yet to have been addressed is the manner in which ageism affects women at every point throughout their (working) lives.

Ageism 'surrounds us, but it passes largely unnoticed and unchallenged' and in this way becomes 'naturalised' (Scrutton, 1990, p. 25).

> Ageism creates and fosters prejudices about the nature and experi-ence of old age. These usually project unpleasant images of older people which subtly undermine their personal value and worth. Commonly held ideas restrict the social role and status of older people, structure their expectations of themselves, prevent them achieving their potential and deny them equal opportunities. (Scrutton, 1990, p. 13)

Until recently the literature on older women and men and ageism has been largely concerned with those over the statutory working age and with the medical and psycho-social aspects of ageing. Most of the research has been undertaken in the field of gerontology where gender has just started to be considered (Bernard and Meade, 1993; but see Arber and Ginn, 1995). Thus the literature has been dominated by perspectives which regarded ageism as having two strands: either 'patronizing' older people by excluding them from making decisions because of their age, or the neglect of older people who no longer contribute to production and are viewed as a drain on resources. This all begs questions such as when does a person become 'older' and when does ageism start? Are 'old' people a homogenous group? More importantly for this chapter, when does a woman become an 'older' woman? Is it over 30, 35, 40 – or is it post-menopause? Is being 'older' differently defined and differ-ently valued in different occupations? (Here it is instructive to read the job advertisements in the free handouts at stations where receptionist and office appointments for women frequently specifiy cut-off age points in the late 20s or early 30s). Is ageing equated with being undesirable (where 'desirability' and 'attractiveness' are heterosexualized constructions with large sections of the patriarchal capitalist economy devoted to their maintenance) or with being wise? Does age have a different impact on women than on men in their working lives and professional/work experiences?

Women and (Paid) Work

The desire/need to participate in paid labour outside the home as well as capital's 'requirement' for cheap part-time labour have sculpted the employ-ment patterns of women this century. During the second world war, women's labour was needed in a variety of non-traditional settings and after this expe-rience many women were not prepared to return to a life of closed domesticity. The 1950s and 1960s were periods of growth in the UK, with low unemploy-ment and greater access for more women to higher education, as well as a time when second-wave feminism came on stream. Women's aspirations and expectations accelerated in this expansionist period although their successes were frequently limited to traditional and feminized areas of labour – paths where men did not want to tread. However, these seemingly prosperous decades were quickly followed by a series of economic crises, captured in the moments of 1970s oil embargo and the mid-1980s 'boom and bust' phenomenon of Thatcher/Lawson economics and the inevitable recession which ensued.

Briefly, the result of neo-liberal economics in the UK has been realized in an enduring period of high unemployment since the mid 1970s matched with the loss of job security for those in employment, set alongside discourses of higher productivity, efficiency and downsizing, or 'right-sizing' as it is sometimes called. 'There are now more than 5 million people working part-time, of whom over 80 per cent are women' (Hutton, 1996, p. 106). At the same time, the powers and rights of trades unions have been severely curtailed. 'Employment on fixed-term contracts increasingly defines many middle-class jobs – from university lecturers to television journalists' (Hutton, 1996, p. 107). The impact of these economic and employment 'reforms' have mostly been differentially experienced by men and women. When employers are looking to reduce costs and hike up profits, labour costs are generally the first area for cutting. Men, on average, still earn more than women, so they are frequently the first to be made redundant. Restructuring for a 'flexible' work-force generally means employing part-time workers (frequently women); this saves overhead costs as well as basic salary costs, while maintaining productivity levels. In a time of economic crisis women, it seems, are more employable than men, but the work they do is poorly paid and women tend to occupy part-time, subordinate positions (Hutton, 1996).

A variety of explanations has been generated to account for the persistence of female subordination in the workplace, from patriarchal relations in capitalism to the gendered nature of work itself. One manifestation of this is vertical and horizontal occupational segregation, where women doing similar work to men are more likely to be classified as doing unskilled work and where men in the same occupation are more likely to be managers. Another outcome is the positioning of women as a 'reserve army' able to move in and out of employment as the economic need arises. In occupations which are traditionally feminized areas of labour, such as education, discourses of maternity (as well as passivity) are employed to constrain and regulate the work of women. While there are a variety of factors which are utilized, sometimes in isolation and sometimes in tandem with other oppressions, to ensure the subordination of women (at work and elsewhere), there is an additional need to focus on the issue of ageism and age in relation to unequal relations for women and between women in paid employment. This is my focus of concern here. More specifically I want to examine this in relation to a particular group of women, a relatively privileged occupational group – women in higher education.

Women who work in higher education are concentrated in subordinate positions within an occupation which is organized and managed by dominant male workers from the same occupational class and educational background. For example, in 1989 in the UK university sector as a whole there were 3852 male professors and 113 female professors (UFC, 1990). Aziz (1990, p. 36), drawing on statistics gathered for the Association of University Teachers (AUT) makes the point that 'the proportion of women promoted is consistently smaller than the proportion of women in the pool . . . from which the promotions are made'. She is concerned that women who aspire to work in higher education are increasingly subjected to forms of 'casualization':

> The number of university staff – mainly researchers, but increasingly, teaching and other staff – now on short term contracts exceeds one quarter. No other profession in this country is in that position. And since more than 60 per cent of the total intake of women were recruited onto short term contracts in both 1986 and 1987, it is clear that women are bearing the brunt of this pressure. (Aziz, 1990, p. 38)

Here it is important to make two major points. Firstly, women themselves are not a homogenous group. Issues of difference such as disability, class, sexuality and 'race' as well as age need greater consideration than is possible here. Secondly, it will be useful to dispel the myth that women in the academy make slower progress than men because of domestic commitments. Toren (1993, p. 439) has shown clearly that women who are married with or without children publish as much or slightly more than single/childless women. Women, however, take longer to progress through the occupational structures and spend much longer in each grade. Thus, it may well be that they are not in the appropriate grade/position to be considered for promotion until they are 'too old'. Toren demonstrates convincingly that women's progress through the academy is restricted in other ways:

> Women's performance (e.g. publications) is evaluated as less worthy and they are given fewer resources and opportunities to influence others and prove their competence (e.g. research grants, graduate students, and appointment to decision-making committees). Accordingly, they are expected, and should expect, lower rewards than men. (Toren, 1993, p. 442)

There is a growing literature on women as teachers in higher education (Stiver Lie and O'Leary 1990; Kelly and Slaughter, 1991; Stiver Lie *et al.*, 1994). There is also an appreciation of the contradictions involved: women who teach in the academy are generally qualified to postgraduate level and are relatively privileged – there are relative degrees of comfort and power which are available to these women (Bannerji *et al.*, 1991). At the same time, these women take longer to progress in the academy when compared to male colleagues of similar standing and the 'minority at lower levels becomes a still smaller minority at higher levels' (Sutherland, 1994, p. 176). However, there are other groups of women 'in' higher education who are sometimes over-looked and whose experiences are frequently rendered invisible in the re-search on women in the academy. These are the secretaries and administrators as well as women students. 'We need to recognise that this is a racist, classist and heterosexist society and that the university is structured to perpetuate those relations' (Bannerji *et al.*, 1991, p. 8). Therefore these power relations will have repercussions for all women wherever they experience or are posi-tioned in the academy.

Older Women in Higher Education

For some time I have been aware of the discriminating effects of ageism for women in education. Older women students and experienced older colleagues, administrators and secretaries, as well as other teachers, were voicing similar concerns. They articulated a concern that their age/sex would limit their op-portunities in their chosen career in education. They were concerned that their chances of promotion decreased as they reached their 50s. They were con-cerned that they were no longer regarded as 'young and bright'. One university lecturer over 50 simply said 'I know I am just invisible now'. I became in-trigued and disturbed by these experiences and comments, as well as by the paucity of space and attention given to these issues and concerns (Maguire, 1995).

There is a need to deal with the differences which obtain in relation to women, as well as their various roles in the academy, and particularly to their disciplines where appropriate. Some subjects are traditionally more 'feminized' than others and many of these settings (health and education) commonly recruit from experienced practitioners as a requirement. For this reason new entrants in these areas may well be older than women who are new entrants in other disciplines. Male managers may be more reluctant to pro-mote these older tutors – they will give less time in service and thus could be regarded as giving less value for money.

However, the main purpose of this chapter is to ensure that age is in-cluded and not ignored in the complexity of social relations of power which marginalize women and position women as 'other'. In order to start to illus-trate the manner in which ageism 'works' in higher education, I have chosen to consider two categories of women: those who work as teachers; and 'mature' women students, who are 'normalized' through the nomenclature of 'non-traditional'.

'Mature' Women Students

Janet[2] is 48 years of age. She is a well-qualified middle-class woman with two teenage children. Recently she decided to move into school teaching. After successfully completing the school-teaching element of a Post-Graduate Certificate in Education (PGCE) she started to apply for jobs. She applied for one post and after the deadline had passed, the head of department got in touch.

> He said I want to tell you something but if you repeat it I will deny I ever said it. Yes he definitely said that. He thought he was being fair just telling me. He probably feels at my age it is unreasonable to go for a first appointment. . . . He said that he thought he should help me and I was not going to be offered an interview because he was not going to take that trouble because I was too old. And in fact he did mention that I was never going to get a job because I was too old.

Janet felt 'terrible' and 'crushed'. Moving into higher education was a risky business financially and emotionally. She had sometimes found it difficult in seminar groups. 'You know, being older. I mean some of them could be my children, but they think I go on too much.' Janet frequently felt silenced by the youth of other students and a certain degree of contempt for her age.

When asked if she ever thought this would happen to her she said that she was aware of ageism in her previous situation but she had taken steps to ensure this would not be a problem in school teaching.

> No, because in fact when I was coming into teaching because I had seen what happened in science, that you have to be careful about your age, I asked. You know, I asked about age – its function in teaching. And I was told 'No problem at all'. It was a career advice place that I went specially to ask because you know at that time I didn't know anybody [in education]. And when I was told, 'No, teaching, it doesn't matter' I thought, well that's it.

As a consequence of the insertion of market forces in the UK school system (devolved funding combined with reduced funding) and the need for so-called cost-effectiveness, it might be that older teachers are less attractive to (male-dominated) selection panels. Additionally, it might be that ageist formations render older women even less attractive to future employers because they might be regarded as less able/less resilient than older males. Of course the converse could equally be true: an older woman might be seen as more reliable and unlikely to take maternity leave. A woman over 50 with lengthy service may also be more expendable; there is the possibility that she will be eligible for early retirement in a relatively short period of time.

Janet was aware of these tensions about age, experience and salary and had considered these factors. She had thought that she would be made an offer which would be quite low, but 'I would accept it anyway'. But she believes the money is a red herring and that being an older woman was the critical part of the equation: 'You know they probably think that it is too difficult for an older woman to take orders or do as they're told. They [older women] make too many suggestions.'

Janet found the experience of being a 'mature' student stressful at times. She found it difficult to establish relationships with other students, many of whom were younger than her. She found the attitudes of some of the 'boys' in her seminar group particularly offensive as they sidelined her 'off time experiences'.

> They start to talk quietly to one another if I try to say anything. If I ever mention I have teenagers at home and know what they are like, their friends and things, they start to switch off. They don't say anything, they just sort of stop. I wonder what they are like to their mothers?

If being an older woman in higher education was difficult for Janet, who had obtained a PhD much earlier in life and was the best qualified student in her group – a fact she kept hidden as much as possible – yet still felt 'out of place' and believed she had to keep quiet, how must it be for 'non-traditional' mature entrants?

Higher education has been characterized by a move from an élite towards a mass system as well as by conflicts over control and funding (Pratt and Hillier, 1991). Many more people now aspire to some form of higher education, a fact which has been recognized by all governments. But this additional provision has to be financially rationalized. Thus institutions are involved in cost-bidding for funds which interrelate with competition for recruitment of new students. There is only ever a limited number (which is decreasing) of 18-year-old school leavers with 'A' levels with their sights on higher education. As more institutions have been empowered to offer degree-level awards, competition for students has increased and new markets have been courted. Thus governments and higher educational institutions became interested in recruiting mature women to courses. The expansion and development of new courses was sometimes a contradictory process. For example, senior managers were keen to put on high-recruiting popular programmes which were relatively cheap to run, such as women's studies – while individual tutors worked to design courses which empowered women as part of their feminist praxis (cf. Morley, 1993).

Rosalind Edwards (1993, p. 86) points out the harsh realities which face the 'non-traditional' older woman student.

> The ethos of the institution overall combined with a realization that particular sets of experiences that formed an important part of their identity were not really admissable, reinforced the sense the women had of being deviants within a system with the norms of the white middle-class bachelor boy student.

The older women were concerned that they had to guard against '"dominating" seminar discussions just because age meant women had more experience to draw upon' (Edwards, 1993, p. 86). They frequently were asked why they had gone to be students, 'at your age – isn't it a bit late?' (p. 145). And unfortunately, in spite of all their efforts to attain a first degree, some of the mature women finally settled for employment which they regarded as non-commensurate with their degrees. They noted the irony of it all: 'Well, there's supposed to be a shortage of women isn't there? They want the older woman back, but I can't see it happening' (p. 148). Others moved into the traditional postgraduate training routes of social work or teacher training, like Janet. Older women were and are 'wanted' in the academy by the institution but, once in, the cost is emotionally high and the occupational and economic gains for individual women may well be few and far between.

Women who Teach in Higher Education

In an earlier piece of work I examined the situation of women who teach teachers (Maguire, 1993). Many of the women had held senior posts in schools and were established experienced managers. Yet when they moved into higher education, generally later than their less experienced, less well qualified and younger male colleagues, they were expected to start all over again. The opportunities for promotion were limited because of their age at entry and they were regarded as educationalists, not academics. They had reduced access to participation in academic matters – conferences, research or writing for publication. Indeed, they acted as 'mothers and providers of space' for their younger male colleagues. Their age had limited their opportunities and had constructed their emotional role. Jill, an ex-headteacher in her early 50s, said:

> When I was in school I felt valued, you know, I had a place. But here I'm just some 'old biddy'. I mean, all the other departments see us like this and so does [the management]. I'm too old for promotion so I'm just here to do all the donkey work. I mean, look at [two younger men]. The minute they do something they get remission and stuff. All I ever get is more teaching, that's all I'm good for. And when I can't do enough of that then they'll put me out to grass.

Chris has worked for many years in social work as a practitioner and as a consultant. She gained her PhD when she was 45 and moved to full-time employment as a research officer on a three-year research project which has since ended. She was 'head-hunted' for a post which was shortly going to be advertised. The specification matched her expertise. It was a full-time lecturing post in a well-established university faculty. As her self-employed partner was finding it increasingly hard to obtain commissions and as they have two school-aged children, Chris was keen to find full-time employment in her field.

She had been signing on as unemployed and was desperate for work. It seemed as if the right post had turned up.

She has since said that she did not interview well, which has to be taken into account, but even so, she was not prepared for what happened. An extremely young and very inexperienced woman was appointed to the post; she had no higher research degree, no research background and very limited practitioner expertise. Chris said:

> I was phoned up and told that a young bright thing had got the job, and do you know, I had never considered that. I had never thought that I was old. It hadn't crossed my mind.

In the interview with me she repeated 'young and bright' a few times. In many ways it seemed as if 'young'n' bright' fitted together as one part of a binary opposition to old and dull. However, an 'interesting' thing happened to Chris soon after her lack of success was known to her ex-colleagues from her research work. She overheard two women in their late 20s discussing her case. Their view was that young women needed and deserved the opportunity to move into higher education and that it did not matter if this occurred at the expense of an older woman. It has to be recognized that there are conflicts and contradictions here in relation to work in higher education, where tactics like 'young blood' first appointments have been instituted in order to break into and displace an ageing staff profile (always seen as a problem). However, Aziz (1990) reports a 'young blood' case which was contested under the Sex Discrimination Act as it was perceived as discrimination against women who have had career breaks. Interestingly, there have never been any major strategies to employ women despite their underrepresentation in the sector. 'That's one way to get permission to oppress – ask the older women, not to be co-equal, but to step aside for the younger woman' (Macdonald and Rich, 1984, p. 40). Barbara Macdonald tells of how one senior woman justified standing down for younger women in the following way: 'established women have the responsibility to boost others. One reason the first wave of feminism died out is that it failed to create new leaders' (Macdonald and Rich, 1984, pp. 40–1). Macdonald adds that this statement 'smacks of maternal self-sacrifice and invisibility' (p. 41).

While Chris did recognize that she had not done well in the interview, the comment in the feedback, 'young and bright', clearly impacted on her and contributed to an awareness of a hitherto unrecognized factor, her age – 'this age thing is becoming an obsession with me' – which has seriously affected her confidence.

> I went to another interview and a young bouncy woman came out of the interview room, she was tremendous – all bouncy and enthusiastic and she said 'They are lovely, you'll love them'. And I thought, I bet she'll get the job. And when I was called in, one male professor

said how unusual that I had got my PhD in the way I had. And I thought how dare he say that. I'm sure my anger came across and I seemed like an older woman who would stand her ground. Needless to say I didn't get the job. But I've lost my confidence, you know.

Chris has finally obtained a university teaching post – she is on a one-year teaching contract.

Conclusion

The discourses of ageism/sexism which make it seem 'natural' to appoint men or (sometimes) younger women, which construct the young white bachelor boy as the normative student, disguise and distort our understanding of gender/age power relations in higher education. In a period of high recession and economic restructurings, discourses which assert the value of youth and the redundancy of age provide additional 'justifications' for selection, rejection and oppression. This chapter has argued that ageist/sexist constructions which are frequently 'normalized' in educational discursive practices need to be revealed if they are to be displaced. Ageism is just one more set of social relations and practices through which academic 'success' and 'failure' can be reproduced. Finally, the intention in this chapter has been to start to provide 'a more meaningful exploration of difference, which will eventually reinforce women's collective efforts to bring about change' (Morley, 1992, p. 524).

Notes

This chapter draws on arguments and data which have been published elsewhere (Maguire, 1995).
1 Much of the pioneering work about and for older women has been undertaken by lesbian writers and researchers such as Macdonald and Rich (1984) and Neild and Pearson (1992) who have fought against ageism compounded by homophobia/homophobia compounded by ageism.
2 Throughout this section I have used pseudonyms.

References

ACKER, S. (Ed.) (1989) *Teachers, Gender and Careers*, Lewes, Falmer Press.
ARBER, S. and GINN, J. (1991) *Gender and Later Life: A Sociological Analysis of Resources and Constraints*, London, Sage Publications.
ARBER, S. and GINN, J. (1995) *Connecting Gender and Ageing: A Sociological Approach*, Buckingham and Philadelphia, Open University Press.

Aziz, A. (1990) 'Women in UK Universities – The Road to Casualization?', in Stiver Lie, S. and O'Leary, V. E. (Eds) *Storming the Tower: Women in the Academic World*, London, Kogan Page, pp. 33–46.

Bannerji, H., Carty, L., Dehli, K., Heald, S. and McKenna, K. (1991) *Unsettling Relations: The University as a Site of Feminist Struggle*, Toronto, Women's Press.

Bernard, M. and Meade, K. (Eds) (1993) *Women Come Of Age*, London, Edward Arnold.

Brown, C. (1984) *White and Black in Britain*, London, Policy Studies Institute.

Edwards, R. (1993) *Mature Women Students: Separating or Connecting Family and Education*, London and Washington, Taylor and Francis.

Featherstone, M. and Hepworth, M. (1990) 'Images of Ageing', in Bond, J., Coleman, P. and Peace, S. (Eds) *Ageing in Society: An Introduction to Social Gerontology*, London, Sage, pp. 304–33.

Gutman, D. (1987) *Reclaimed Powers: Towards a New Psychology of Men and Women in Later Life*, New York, Basic Books.

Hammond, G. (1947) 'And What Of the Young Women?', reprinted in Hammond, G., Kitch, S. L. and Konek, C. W. (1980) *Design for Equity: Women and Leadership in Higher Education*, Project DELTA, Wichita State University, Education Development Center, Newton MA, pp. 16–18.

Hutton, W. (1996) *The State We're In*, 2nd ed., London, Vintage.

Itzin, C. L. (1990) *Age and Sexual Divisions: A Study of Opportunity and Identity in Women*, PhD thesis, University of Kent.

Katz, C. and Monk, J. (Eds) (1993) *Full Circles: Geographies of Women over the Life Course*, London and New York, Routledge.

Kelly, G. P. and Slaughter, S. (Eds) (1991) *Women's Higher Education in Comparative Perspective*, Dordrecht, Boston, and London, Kluver Academic Publishers.

London Strategic Policy Unit (1987) *Danger! Heterosexism at Work*, London, Industry and Employment Branch, GLC.

Long, P. (1979) 'Speaking Out on Age', *Spare Rib*, 82, pp. 14–7.

Lonsdale, S. (1990) *Women and Disability: The Experience of Physical Disability among Women*, London, Macmillan.

Macdonald, B. with Rich, C. (1984) *Look me in the Eye: Old Women, Aging and Ageism*, London, The Women's Press.

Maguire, M. (1993) 'Women who Teach Teachers', *Gender and Education*, 5, 3, pp. 269–81.

Maguire, M. (1995) 'Women, Age, and Education in the United Kingdom', *Women's Studies International Forum*, 18, 5/6, pp. 559–71.

Marshall, M. (1990) 'Proud to Be Old: Attitudes to Age and Ageing', in McEwen, E. (Ed.) *Age: The Unrecognised Discrimination: Views to Provoke a Debate*, Age Concern England, pp. 28–43.

Martin, J. and Roberts, C. (1984) *Women and Employment: A Lifetime Perspective*, London, HMSO.

MORLEY, L. (1992) 'Women's Studies, Difference, and Internalised Oppression', *Women's Studies International Forum*, 15, 4, pp. 517–25.

MORLEY, L. (1993) 'Women's Studies as Empowerment of "Non-Traditional" Learners in Community and Youth Work Training: A Case Study', in KENNEDY, M., LUBELSKA, C. and WALSH, V. A. (Eds) *Making Connections: Women's Studies, Women's Movements, Women's Lives*, London and Washington, Taylor and Francis, pp. 118–29.

NEILD, S. and PEARSON, R. (1992) *Women Like Us*, London, The Women's Press.

OAKLEY, A. (1974) *Housewife*. London, Allen Lane.

OAKLEY, A. (1980) *Women Confined: Towards a Sociology of Childbirth*, Oxford, Martin Robertson.

PRATT, J. and HILLIER, Y. (1991) *Bidding for Funds in the PCFC Sector*, London, CHES, Institute of Education, University of London.

SCRUTTON, S. (1990) 'Ageism: The Foundation of Age Discrimination', in McEWEN, E. (Ed.) *Age: The Unrecognised Discrimination: Views to Provoke a Debate*, Age Concern England, pp. 12–28.

SHILLING, C. (1993) *The Body and Social Theory*, London, Newbury Park, and New Delhi, Sage Publications.

STIVER LIE, S. and O'LEARY, V. E. (Eds) (1990) *Storming the Tower: Women in the Academic World*, London, Kogan Page.

STIVER LIE, S., MALIK, L. and HARRIS, D. (Eds) (1994) *The Gender Gap in Higher Education*, World Yearbook of Education, London and Philadelphia, Kogan Page.

SUTHERLAND, M. B. (1994) 'Two Steps Forward and One Step Back: Women in Higher Education in the United Kingdom', in STIVER LIE, S. MALIK, L. and HARRIS, D. (Eds) *The Gender Gap in Higher Education*, World Yearbook of Education, London and Philadelphia, Kogan Page, pp. 171–81.

TOREN, N. (1993) 'The Temporal Dimension of Gender Inequality in Academia', *Higher Education*, 25, pp. 439–55.

UNIVERSITIES FUNDING COUNCIL (UFC) (1990) *University Statistics 1988–9, Vol. 1: Students and Staff*, Cheltenham, Universities Statistical Records.

Chapter 3

Activists as Change Agents:
Achievements and Limitations

Liz Price and Judy Priest

In the early 1990s equal opportunities was hardly on the agenda at Oxford Brookes. The atmosphere was comfortable and self-affirming. This state of affairs was hardly surprising because there were no difficulties attracting students, no problems recruiting or retaining staff, and no hint of financial difficulties. Furthermore, Oxford Brookes was recognized within the polytechnic sector as a high-quality institution. However, in terms of equal opportunities, all of the classic warning signs of potential discrimination were present. Here was a predominantly white, middle-class, non-disabled place with a preponderance of men in top management positions. The challenge for equal opportunity activists was how to act as change agents when they had little or no role power and when there were no fora for institutional networking. Senior management said they were in favour of equal opportunities but gave no indication that they were keen to change the status quo.

In this chapter, we will outline the process we have followed so far in raising equal opportunities issues at Brookes and embedding a commitment to diversity as a key institutional value. Although it is generally held that top-down management commitment is essential to make progress in developing equal opportunities, we will argue that considerable change can be made with a bottom-up activist approach. We will show how a few individuals (including the authors) have been able to use formal and informal opportunities to influence the forward progress of equal opportunities at Oxford Brookes.

When we talk about activists as change agents we are referring to ourselves and to other committed individuals and groups, including a formal group, the Equal Opportunities Action Group, set up in 1993 to pursue equal opportunities. In describing ourselves as activists we are referring to the roles we play when we take action to exert influence for, and on behalf of, ourselves and others who are disadvantaged or lacking power within our university. Sometimes we have used official channels and at other times we have acted unofficially to exert influence. We recognize that many forms of action are possible, from speaking out or writing (Morley and Walsh, 1995, p. 3), through to acquiring power and shaping the course of future events. For the writers of this chapter, action which enabled us to shape the future direction of Oxford Brookes University was what most interested us. In the process, we both used others' power and gained power ourselves.

Management-Driven Change

In much of the literature from the 1980s concerning the optimum way of achieving equal opportunity outcomes, there is a 'received wisdom' that change originates from the wholehearted commitment of the most senior managers within the organization. A good example of this approach can be found in the research carried out by the Ashridge Management Research Group for Opportunity 2000. The researchers' analysis of companies which had been successful in progressing equal opportunity initiatives and policies led them to the conclusion that four key features generated success (Hammond and Holton, 1990, p. 3). These were:

- **demonstrating commitment**: there has to be a strong and consistent vision from the very top of the organization: equal opportunities change must be led and championed by management as part of overall strategic objectives;

- **changing behaviour**: change requires a strong vision, training and measurement: it must look at and tackle the fundamental structure and behaviour of the organization;

- **building ownership**: led from the top, change is the responsibility of everyone in an organization: getting the message across requires constant and effective communication;

- **making the investment**: to achieve success, adequate and realistic resources must be allocated, in terms of time, people and finance.

Most of the organizations which were studied as models of success for the research, and several others cited by other authors, are large 'blue chip' companies such as Xerox, Digital, IBM, TSB, Littlewoods, Grand Metropolitan and Lucas Industries (Hammond and Holton, 1990; Greenslade, 1991; Dickens, 1994; *Equal Opportunities Review*, 1994). The prescription put forward for achieving change in these organizations has its roots in the 'excellence' literature of the 1980s (Peters and Waterman, 1982; Goldsmith and Clutterbuck, 1984) which called for strategic 'vision', 'champions' for the cause and the building of ownership and shared values. Further, since companies exist primarily to make profits for their shareholders, a strong emphasis is given to the business case for equal opportunities. This involves arguing that equal opportunities initiatives work in the interests of the organization allowing them to:

- compete in the labour market and become an 'employer of choice';

- get closer to the customer by reflecting diversity in target markets with diversity at all levels within the workforce;

- produce cost savings by making a more efficient use of human resources.

(See Hammond and Holton, 1990, and Dickens, 1994 for a fuller exploration of these arguments.)

This argument is packaged as though it is self-evident that everyone has something to gain from the valuing of difference and from progress towards equality of opportunity.

Criticisms of the Model

We have four main difficulties with this model. Firstly, it does not seem to work particularly well, even in those organizations where it was tried. Opportunity 2000's progress report in 1994 showed that there were considerable barriers to taking positive action to achieve equality of opportunity amongst member organizations. Employers were reluctant to set numerical targets, there had been little success in fighting the 'working all hours' culture, and line managers underlined the incompatibility between equal opportunity intentions and the economic drive to reduce staff numbers and increase sales (Lowe, 1994).

Our second difficulty with the model is that implicit in the business case for change is the assumption that 'rational' employers (if only they would see the light) would sign up for an equal opportunities approach. In reality the majority do not. Far from it being good business to change, it suits many employers to exploit numerically flexible (Atkinson, 1984), relatively cheap disadvantaged labour drawn from the secondary labour market (Walby, 1988). This is especially apparent when the working conditions of 'typically' female industries and occupations are reviewed. Consider, for example, retail, hotel and catering, low-level jobs in medical services, hairdressing and so on; in all these cases women's experience of work is generally characterized by low pay, poor career progression and low status. Similarly, women in higher education are concentrated into the lower-level lecturing posts, increasingly casualized part-time work and relatively low-level administrative posts. The costs of making systematic improvements to women's working conditions would be high and unlikely to be welcomed by the majority of employers. Further, it is in the interests of white, male power-holders to protect their favoured position in the labour market. As Dickens (1994) has observed, 'Equal Opportunity is not necessarily the win-win game portrayed in the prescriptive literature' (p. 283). What she is suggesting here is that, far from everyone gaining through successful equal opportunity programmes, in practice, increased opportunities for women and ethnic minorities reduce the chances of the previously dominant group.

Our third problem with the model is that it is mainly derived from experiences in a particular type of organization – large, sophisticated, private sector and hierarchical. The approach cannot simply be transposed onto public sector organizations such as local authorities, which are accountable to their electorates rather than shareholders, or universities, which are accountable to their governors and the wider community. In the case of non-profit-making organizations such as universities, the 'business case' for equal opportunities may have some influence, but concern for social justice and equitable service provision may be even stronger driving forces. Furthermore, within higher education, decision-making is not solely focused on top-down processes as it tends to be in private sector businesses. Rather, it is still the case that 'collegial' systems for decision-making via committee structures, elected posts, academic boards and so on have some influence. That is to say, ordinary members of staff, particularly of academic staff, are still able to find a voice and exert some influence on the direction of their institutions. Recent reforms in funding arrangements for teaching in higher education have caused universities to increase efficiency by increasing student numbers without a commensurate increase in funding. This, together with government pressure to review the management of universities, has led to more streamlined decision-making, the introduction of strategic planning processes, tighter management control through the use of devolved budget and performance indicators, and a requirement to be more responsive to the market (Davies and Holloway, 1995). Whilst this has put some limitations on collegiate autonomy, it is still the case that academics have considerable control over the curriculum which is the main product of universities. It is well-recognized by feminist commentators (see Davies *et al.*, 1994) that the curriculum is central to the process of change in higher education and a top-down approach to reforming it is unlikely to be effective. Thus, hierarchical managerial processes will have an increasing impact in today's universities but they are insufficient on their own. More democratic processes have to be understood and engaged with by those who seek to influence the direction of their institutions. Dispersed decision-making underlines the importance of ensuring that women, ethnic minorities and disabled people do get access to, and the right to speak and be heard in key decision-making committees, as well as access to senior-level posts.

Our fourth objection to the prescribed model for change is that it underestimates the collective power of ordinary members of staff who may exert pressure for change, either through organized trades unions or through looser alliances, such as women's groups, disabled groups, black groups, informal task groups and so on. We acknowledge that the business case for equal opportunities initiatives and the four key areas highlighted by Ashridge Management Research Group are of growing importance as universities adopt more managerial approaches and that we, in our work, could not have succeeded without the support of senior management. However, it is our contention that activists operating from fairly modest positions in the hierarchy can make a difference and mobilize change in today's higher education environment and can probably do this more effectively than in the large 'blue chip' companies studied by Ashridge, largely because power is more diverse and therefore more available to activists.

Power and Influence

To be effective, activists first have to understand the processes through which power is gained and exerted in organizations. We find helpful Morgan's (1986) separation of power into a resource (i.e. something people possess) *and* as a social relationship characterized by the ability to influence someone or something. Several feminist writers (see especially Marshall, 1984) have elaborated on the notion of power as a resource which women need to acquire to have influence in organisations. Marshall (1984, p. 108) builds on French and Raven's (1959) classic typology of five bases of power (reward, coercive, legitimate, referent, expert) to include personal power, power gained through/ with others (e.g. through networking, mentoring relationships, politics) and power gained through structural factors (e.g. centrality to organizational tasks, relative number, visibility). As will be discussed later, change agents need to build their power resources wherever they can, then use them.

In order to have influence within organizations, activists have to use their power in appropriate decision-making fora to shape strategic direction, policy, procedures and action. It is here that struggles over agendas, allocation of resources and conflicts between different interest groups can be seen. This is the notion of power discussed by Dahl (1961) and the one which Morgan (1986) suggests is adopted by most organization theorists. Within higher education, decisions are made both through the bureaucratic management structure which controls the operational and support aspects of the institution, and through professional structures within academic disciplines (Malik and Stiver Lie, 1994). In Oxford Brookes, it has been important for us to understand and act within both.

On a professional level Oxford Brookes has committees to deal with decisions about our main product, i.e. courses and research. Each has designated areas of expertise and defined powers to recommend or direct others. Ideally, committees operate by discussion leading to consensus and are designed to allow views from outside the committee to be heard. Alongside committees there are management structures represented on our organizational chart as a branching hierarchical collection of boxes. At the top is the Vice-Chancellor and three senior managers, each with lines of control to heads of Schools and Departments and, by implication, from the heads to all the staff they manage. The chart shows how power, decisions and resources are intended to move down the organization. Equal opportunities activists (or indeed any activists) need to be comfortable in and have access to both executive and committee-based decision-making in order to push equal opportunities forward. At any given time and for any given decision, one or the other will be the most appropriate forum for managing a particular change.

As we began to gain and use power, we realized we also needed to move beyond our understanding of *overt* influence, to identifying and challenging more subtle limitations to change. This was in line with Lukes' view (1974), where he argues forcibly that power is also exerted in less visible ways when social and political processes are used to limit issues raised. In such cases, mechanisms are deployed to keep items off the agenda and the 'status quo' is used to protect the position of dominant groups. He argues further that power can also be exerted by leaders influencing or shaping the perceived desires of individuals, such that potential conflict is not even recognized. This is what Malik and Stiver Lie (1994) are referring to when they argue that the normative system in higher education, particularly as it is held together by patriarchal values, tends to support the interests of those currently holding power. This kind of analysis is helpful for activists as it underlines the importance of raising consciousness/awareness of inequality and making issues visible. It also shows that conflict and oppression have to be made observable if we are to see differences of interest and tackle inequalities in higher education. As Morley and Walsh (1995) observe, 'Discrimination in the academy can reinforce and restimulate women's wider experience of sexist oppression . . . The creativity comes when one recognizes that this hurt can be transformed into knowledge, action, analysis and energy for change' (p. 2).

All in all, we were facing a robust system and needed a robust model to follow to press for change.

Kanter's Model: The Change Masters

Previous analyses of women in higher education (Davies *et al.*, 1994; Morley and Walsh, 1995; Stiver Lie *et al.*, 1994) have underlined their marginal role and the domination of male values, power and discourse. Although there are considerable difficulties in challenging the prevailing status quo, we remain fairly optimistic about the potential for staff with little or no managerial authority to acquire sufficient power from other sources to act as effective change agents. There are many 'how-to' management books on how to achieve change in organizations, but we have chosen to use Rosabeth Moss Kanter's (1983) exploration of successful change in American corporations to explain how ordinary members of staff can mobilize change in organizations. This book is based on research into forty-seven companies carried out over a period of five years. Although her research, like the Ashridge report, was based on large private sector companies, her recipe for gaining success through innovation and change stresses the contribution of people at *all levels* in organizations. She says of the most innovatory companies that 'there were larger numbers of people at all levels who could grab and use power. And with this power to act came the chance to innovate' (p. 24). She argues that change agents (she calls them 'corporate entrepreneurs', we would call them activists!) can come from any part of the organization, that they can work across boundaries and that they can manoeuvre around the organization in sometimes novel ways. She says that in order to effect change, individuals have to acquire power (derived from information, resources and support) and that whilst change agents may have some power attached to their positions, they have to search for additional power 'capital' elsewhere in the organization. Based on her research findings, she proposes that change agents move through three stages in order to achieve change: first, problem definition; second, coalition building; and third, mobilization (pp. 217–40). In reality, progress through these stages is likely to be messier and more iterative than suggested by the following summary.

Problem Definition

This stage has the dual goal of collecting data about the 'problem' and identifying supporters who may be called upon later to lobby for the proposed change. The nature of the problem is as defined by the change agent, entrepreneur or activist. At this stage the following sorts of information are gathered:

- active listening (to stories or 'information circulating in the neighbourhood');
- taking part in task forces;
- planting seeds ('leaving the kernel of an idea behind and letting it germinate and blossom so that it begins to float around the system from many sources other than the innovator');
- gathering hard technical data;
- collecting political information about the 'existing stakes' in the issue;
- conducting formal surveys;
- shaping up the project for 'selling'.

Coalition Building

This next stage involves pulling in the support and resources to make the project work. This involves:

- finding allies;
- setting up teams of task forces;
- 'clearing the investment', that is to say keeping the appropriate senior manager in the picture (Kanter points out that activists go ahead with their projects anyway at this stage, even where a senior manager expresses disapproval!);
- pre-selling, which involves lining up supporters at higher *and* lower levels in the organization;

- securing 'blessings' from the most senior levels of management;
- formalizing the coalition.

Mobilization

At this stage the prime role of the activists shifts from 'composer' to 'conductor' of the many players on the stage. Activities involved at this stage are:

- handling the opposition/blocking interference; this includes
  - waiting it out
  - wearing them down (repeating the arguments)
  - appealing to larger principles (for example, by tying the innovation to an unassailable value)
  - inviting them in (finding a way that opponents could share in the 'spoils' of the innovation)
  - sending emissaries to smooth the way and plead the case
  - displaying support (asking sponsors for a visible demonstration of backing)
  - reducing the stakes
  - warning the critics (for example by letting them know they will be challenged by top management);
- maintaining momentum (keeping the team charged up);
- secondary re-design of systems and structures to keep the project going (this involves breaking, bending or changing rules to get resources and keep momentum);
- external communication (this involves telling the world what is being achieved, making presentations and managing the press; it also involves delivering on promises).

We have found the Kanter change model extremely helpful in enabling us to use both top-down and bottom-up pressure for change. The model outlines steps we might usefully take next and offers encouragement by showing that difficulties we have encountered are by and large the result of predictable events rather than our own mismanagement. Where difficulties are indeed our own fault, the model helps us learn from our errors. We now go on to use the model to explore our progress through the cycle of change.

The Problem-Definition Stage

In our case, this stage began in 1989 when Oxford Polytechnic, as it was then known, left local authority control. At incorporation, the polytechnic took with it a range of well-developed policies, one on equal opportunities directly, and others on equal-opportunity-related matters such as maternity/paternity leave, job sharing and career break schemes, and sexual harassment. The polytechnic also had a tradition of regularly reviewing and modifying courses which in a few Schools included equal opportunities issues. There were also considerable support structures for students. For example, the needs of students with disabilities were addressed by providing specially adapted accommodation. A disabled users' group met regularly around that time, and a specialist adviser was appointed. Similar support was in place for international and mature students. Further, there was a nursery in place for children of both staff and students. All these measures were seen as relatively progressive for the time.

Despite the widely held view that equality of opportunity was not a problem, some staff and students felt otherwise and sought to define the case for equal opportunities over the next four years. They established interest groups and made their views known in public meetings. A women's forum began to meet and raise issues, a task force was formed to consider methods of widening participation in higher education of underrepresented groups, and a series of lunchtime seminars was held where equal opportunities issues were raised. When they were not resolved within the remit of the series, enthusiasts continued to meet and plan further action. People were identified who were interested in, and willing to speak about, equal opportunities issues; where they were sufficiently senior, these spokespeople sounded out support for equal opportunities at senior level. One deputy head of a School wrote a report comparing equal opportunity initiatives at Oxford Polytechnic with those taken in other higher education institutions, which resulted in the vice-chancellor taking personal responsibility for equal opportunities and requiring Schools to report on equal opportunities progress in their annual operating plans. By late 1992, around twelve different groups, papers or fora had made comments about and recommendations concerning equal opportunities. Many of the recommendations received support in committees and at Academic Board, but it was not clear how they should be taken forward. It was obvious to many activists that a new tack was needed.

In Kanter's terms, all of the activities described so far began the process of 'planting seeds'. In addition, aside from action generated by activists, some executive/management decisions were also made which spread the message. For example, it became mandatory for all those involved in recruitment to attend training which included an equal opportunities session. This made approximately 300 people aware of the legislation on sex and race discrimination. Rudimentary statistics were available for the first time from the personnel department about recruitment and an attempt was made to carry out an employee audit of ethnic origin, gender and disability. Both were very incomplete but nonetheless pointed to profiles which indicated that there was a difference between saying we were an equal opportunities institution and actually being one.

We then reached a critical stage. Kanter says that the next move must be political. Successful change agents need to gather information about the political climate of the organization and identify elements that are likely to be enhanced by the desired change. This we did by tapping into strategic changes being made to the direction of the university. In 1992, Oxford Polytechnic became Oxford Brookes University and the then deputy vice-chancellor launched an ambitious project to review our mission and to establish the kind of university Oxford Brookes would seek to become. He called this project Agenda for Brookes and set up a steering group to drive the discussions forward which met for ten months and produced a 108-page document listing all the areas to be reviewed. The group also organized a residential conference for sixty-five of the senior management to discuss the document. The university was buzzing with discussion, argument and expectations.

At about the same time as the Agenda for Brookes initiative began, a small ad hoc group of equal opportunities activists commissioned a study by the University of Central Lancashire to review equal opportunities at Brookes. Unlike the previous papers, the Lancashire report was written by outsiders and was backed by more systematic information-gathering than had hitherto been undertaken. It argued for a new and vigorous approach to equal opportunities, basing its recommendations on values such as equity and fairness. At about the same time, the Agenda for Brookes group was arguing for change based on a business case – they argued that Brookes needed to carve out a more diverse market share in the newly enlarged higher education sector thereby guaranteeing our funding. The best way to do this, they argued, was to be recognized as an institution where diversity, wider access and clear links with the community were valued.

The vice-chancellor then suggested that governors should have equal opportunities on the agenda of one of their 'strategy days', and as a result they decided to set up a ten-member group with a budget of £150,000 to take action on equal opportunities over a period of two years. In effect, the governors were saying that they recognized that Brookes was no longer amongst the most progressive institutions for equal opportunities and that it made business sense to move towards being so. This was the moment when we, as activists, moved from defining the problem and getting others to listen, to the next stage where we were building a coalition of activists and those with managerial power that would push for change.

The Coalition-Building Stage

As a way of marking the institution's move from talk to action, the vice-chancellor proposed the appointment of Joanna Foster, ex Chair of the Equal Opportunities Commission, as a governor, and then hosted a public lecture by her in which she addressed equal opportunities as her central theme. He invited city and county public figures and many Brookes staff, and about a hundred people attended. Soon afterwards, the vice-chancellor announced that Helena Kennedy would become the Chancellor, and the personnel department appointed an officer whose job title reflected her responsibility for equal opportunities. Amidst this surge of support and interest, the newly-formed Equal Opportunities Action Group (EOAG) began to meet.

Kanter suggests that at this stage in the change process, finding allies is a priority. The EOAG took a different tack, choosing instead to backtrack and seek once again to define the problem. This was probably unavoidable because we, as members of the group, did not have access to all the information we needed to plan ahead and because we had not all been involved in earlier efforts. However, not seeking allies at this stage did cause difficulties. Groups who had in the past championed equal opportunities felt marginalized and ignored. This was especially true of the trades unions, the personnel department, and (to a lesser extent) individual enthusiasts. However, over time, we were able to meet with the Women's Forum, the trades unions for academic and for support staff, the group for disabled students, the personnel department, and the newly-formed Ethnic Minorities Forum.

We were also busy allocating funds within our terms of reference for pump-priming and research projects. The largest sum was set aside to implement a job evaluation scheme. Interestingly, what we did to push for a job evaluation scheme re-ran the steps we had taken so far in Kanter's change cycle. For this particular issue, we had once again to define the problem via a research document and plant seeds in support of the idea by taking with us as many staff as possible. We then had to test the political viability of a job evaluation scheme by consulting several other higher education institutions either doing it or contemplating going down this road. Once we felt reasonably sure it was an idea with a future, we sought allies, and secured support from a variety of groups and individuals. Thus, the Kanter model is helpful not only in describing the whole equal opportunities strategy, it is equally relevant for any sub-issue as well.

We are now towards the end of the coalition-building stage and, as Kanter suggests, we are busy 'securing blessings' from management. The vice-chancellor remains publicly supportive, as do the governors and the chancellor. We have visited all Schools and Departments to address a meeting of their staff and have received open support from many heads. We have run mandatory awareness training for all managers and course leaders and were allocated a session at the senior management annual residential conference in early 1995. As a result, senior managers have a clear understanding of the main issues around equal opportunities and the large majority have expressed support for our programme of action. Concurrent with the officially sanctioned action for equal opportunities, we continued to raise new issues from the bottom up; for example, we began exploring equal opportunities in the curriculum and launched an ambitious survey on harassment and bullying.

The Mobilization Stage

At this stage, Moss Kanter advises us as activists to wait out opposition or wear them down. So far, we have been able to do this successfully in the case of job evaluation. Whereas in the past 'it's far too expensive' had brought all movement on this issue to a halt, the cost has not, as yet, stopped consideration of the case. We have also been successful in waiting out or wearing down our critics who have stated throughout our first year, 'You're doing nothing'. Our first annual report listed at least twenty key achievements alongside more minor ones to offer the critics, as well as the reminder that to expect us to turn Brookes into a comprehensive equal opportunity institution in one or two years was unrealistic. Our second annual report continued to cite areas of considerable achievement.

The model predicts that objections will continue and offers strategies for dealing with them. For example, to the comment that becoming more diverse will both cost too much to achieve and require too many resources to maintain, we have appealed to larger principles such as fairness, the need to generate increased student applications or strategic business planning. To the reminder that equal opportunities is only one of many values embraced by the university, we have noted the centrality of diversity in the university's mission statement. We need to continue to foster smoother relationships with Personnel and the unions, inviting them in and gaining emissaries who will speak on our behalf. In time, we need to ask senior management to develop consequences for non-compliance, then warn those who do not comply about their behaviour. Fairly regularly, we will need displays of open support from management for what they have espoused and though this is a top-down requirement, it is likely to need a bottom-up push to ensure their continued interest. In other words, we will return to the beginning of the cycle, starting again but starting at a different place in the institution's development of equal opportunities.

Moss Kanter (1983) talks of the need to maintain momentum at this stage of the change process. The EOAG as originally constituted only had a two-year mandate but this has now been extended by a further year. We are currently concentrating on embedding equal opportunities in all decision-making processes at Brookes. This involves building a more action-oriented approach to equal opportunities into the strategic and operational planning process, ensuring that guidelines for the operation of our recently overhauled committee structure facilitate equal opportunities outcomes and further developing equal opportunities checklists and approaches in our quality assurance processes. We are also researching and investigating new areas of work; for example, the employment opportunities of lower-paid support staff, issues relating to gay, lesbian and bisexual staff and students, and the further development of equal opportunities in the curriculum.

Achievements and Limitations

We have clearly made progress as activists and Oxford Brookes has made progress towards equal opportunity. Contrary to the Ashridge model for success, we have initiated change from the bottom of the organization which has resulted in major steps forward for equal opportunities. We have managed to build commitment and vision about equal opportunities into the publicly stated core values of the organization. We have won considerable resources for equal opportunities, including the establishment of a half-time seconded Head of Equal Opportunities, at a time of some financial constraint. The most senior management are now expressing commitment to making Oxford Brookes into an equal opportunities institution and asking for our help in doing so. It is too early in the development of longitudinal monitoring statistics for us to quantify our progress, but we do judge that the university has come a long way over the past two years. It is no longer only activists and the EOAG who have contributed to improved practices; many other individuals and groups across the university have challenged previously accepted approaches and made changes to what they do designed to extend equality of opportunity to both students and staff. Just some of the developments include changes to the curriculum in many different subject areas to make it more 'inclusive', plans to build on Access and Passport schemes, improved support for staff and students with childcare needs, the establishment of some School-level equal opportunity committees/groups and a positive engagement with equal opportunities issues when the university launches an 'Information Technology Term' later in 1996.

However, there are limitations. Short-term funding of the EOAG makes our future uncertain and it is difficult to plan very far ahead. Further, short-term secondment of members, some of whom have little prior experience of 'activism', means that a good deal of time is taken up helping new members acquire the skills to be effective. In addition, we are finding it a challenge to judge the most effective 'voice' in which to influence decisions. One day, we find ourselves facilitating support groups or helping individuals understand the equal opportunities issues in the day-to-day work environment. Another day, we are presenting closely argued documents to senior management about strategic policy issues. Whilst these skills make us effective change agents in Kanter's terms, they also make us weary. In fact, one of the authors of this chapter is now taking a rest from equal opportunities activism to concentrate on new professional areas of work. The other has become the seconded Head of Equal Opportunities which has delivered different power resources and the need to adapt her role; the style which she now has to adopt as a senior member of the university is not quite the same one as was appropriate when she was an activist with no managerial authority!

At this stage, the main challenge for Oxford Brookes University is to keep our momentum going, to keep our team charged up and to spread responsibility for equal opportunities further into Schools and Departments where, we hope, other activists will arise to trigger future change.

References

ATKINSON, J. (1984) 'Manpower Strategies for Flexible Organisations', *Personnel Management*, August, pp. 28–31.

DAHL, R. (1961) *Who governs? Democracy and Power in an American City*, New Haven and London, Yale University Press.

DAVIES, C. and HOLLOWAY, C. (1995) 'Troubling Transformations: Gender Regimes and Organizational Culture in the Academy', in MORLEY, L. and WALSH, V. A. (Eds) *Feminist Academics*, London, Taylor and Francis, pp. 7–21.

DAVIES, S., LUBELSKA, C. and QUINN, J. (Eds) (1994) *Changing the Subject: Women in Higher Education*, London, Taylor and Francis.

DICKENS, L. (1994) 'Wasted Resources: Equal Opportunities in Employment', in SISSON, K. (Ed.) *Personnel Management*, Oxford, Blackwell, pp. 253–96.

EQUAL OPPORTUNITIES REVIEW (1994) 'Profile on Kate Corfield', *Equal Opportunities Review*, 54 (March/April), pp. 17–18.

FRENCH, J. and RAVEN, B. (1959) 'The Bases of Social Power', in CARTWRIGHT, D. (Ed.) *Studies in Social Power*, Michigan, The Institute for Social Research, pp. 150–67.

GOLDSMITH, W. and CLUTTERBUCK, D. (1984) *The Winning Streak*, Harmondsworth, Penguin.

GREENSLADE, M. (1991) 'Managing Diversity: Lessons from the United States', *Personnel Management*, December, pp. 28–33.

HAMMOND, V. and HOLTON, V. (1990) *A Balanced Workforce?*, Berkhamsted, Ashridge Management Research Group.

KANTER, R. M. (1983) *The Change Masters*, London, Unwin Hyman.

LOWE, K. (1994) 'Campaign Sizes Up Equality', *Personnel Today*, 8 November, p. 10.

LUKES, S. (1974) *Power, A Radical View*, London and Basingstoke, Macmillan.

MALIK, L. and STIVER LIE, S. (1994) 'The Gender Gap in Higher Education: A Conceptual Framework', in STIVER LIE, S., MALIK, L. and HARRIS, D. (Eds) *The Gender Gap in Higher Education*, World Yearbook of Education, London and Philadelphia, Kogan Page, pp. 3–10.

MARSHALL, J. (1984) *Women Managers, Travellers in a Male World*, Chichester, John Wiley and Sons.

MORGAN, G. (1986) *Images of Organisation*, Toronto, Sage.

MORLEY, L. and WALSH, V. A. (Eds) (1995) *Feminist Academics, Creative Agents for Change*, London, Taylor and Francis.

PETERS, T. and WATERMAN, R. (1982) *In Search of Excellence*, New York, Harper and Row.

STIVER LIE, S., MALIK, L. and HARRIS, D. (Eds) (1994) *The Gender Gap in Higher Education*, World Yearbook of Education, London and Philadelphia, Kogan Page.

WALBY, S. (1988) 'Segregation in Employment in Social and Economic Theory', in WALBY, S. (Ed.) *Gender Segregation at Work*, Milton Keynes, Open University Press, pp. 14–28.

Chapter 4

Good Practices, Bad Attitudes:
An Examination of the Factors Influencing
Women's Academic Careers

Jane Kettle

This chapter is an analysis of the experiences of a sample group of women academics in English universities. They were interviewed for a piece of research, the central task of which was to identify factors inhibiting the academic careers of women in universities. The perceptions and explanations of individual women who, in terms of rank and status, were successful, were used as case studies. The purpose was to hear and compare individual women's perceptions of their own experiences, identifying those factors which most influenced or affected them and to relate these to policies designed to enhance equality of opportunity. Findings indicate that while, for the most part, practices and procedures in universities do not actively discriminate against women, the acceptance and currency of particular values and beliefs makes it difficult for women to succeed, despite the existence of formal policies to redress inequalities. It is likely that the dominant culture of universities has been 'important in both differentiating men and women and providing men with more credentials. The forms of closure against women are usually more subtle because of the explicit discourse of meritous achievement' (Walby, 1989, p. 227).

Equal Opportunities Policies in Universities:
Rationales and Realities

There is considerable historical and contemporary evidence that women are underrepresented within the upper echelons of the academic and managerial hierarchies of universities and are clustered in low-status, part-time or temporary posts (Rendel, 1984; Jackson, 1990; EOC, 1990; CUCO, 1994). For those women who have ostensibly been successful, and attained professorships, there is still disadvantage in the form of pay differential (AUT, 1992). Numerically, women have gradually increased their presence in academia; yet in 1994 they represented only 23.8 per cent of total full-time academic staff in the 'new' universities, and 15.9 per cent in the 'old' universities. As we progress through the last decade of the twentieth century, women hold only 12 per cent of all principal lectureships and just 5 per cent of professorships (CUCO, 1994). Women academics have not increased their presence in the same proportions as female students.

At the centre of all commentaries on perceived or invisible barriers to women's progress in academia, there are references to the need for appropriate equal opportunities policies. Such policies are associated with strategies to improve the position (usually in the labour market) of disadvantaged groups, including women. Disadvantage within the liberal tradition (which informs anti-discrimination legislation) is taken to mean an unintended but considerable consequence of outdated practices and procedures. This is problematic, for such strategies 'deny women's difference, since the goal is to become equal with the normative male value' (Franzway *et al.*, 1989, p. 96). There is also a danger that the presence of formal procedures generates a sense of complacency. Their existence reinforces the notion that current processes and practices are fair and efficient. Equal opportunities policies inevitably focus on the primacy of individual merit being acknowledged, yet the question of individual merit is particularly fraught. Williams *et al.* (1989) carried out a review of equal opportunities policies in higher education in the late 1980s. Various aspects of inequality were examined, including gender issues. They considered that equal opportunities was a problematic concept for many higher education staff, who held as unassailable those taken-for-granted liberal assumptions about the fairness of their institution's structure and practices. The researchers concluded that they were observing a 'lack of understanding of progress to date. A tone of moral superiority plus ignorance of the issues and available evidence was pervasive. Individual merit was seen as a neutral and non-negotiable attribute, and discrimination or bias as unacceptable but not likely to occur' (Williams *et al.*, 1989, p. 24). This was reinforced by the evidence presented to the Hansard Society Commission (Hansard Society Commission, 1990), and examined with concern by the Committee of Vice-Chancellors and Principals (CVCP, 1991). The Commission on University Career Opportunity (CUCO, 1994) identified a series of structures operating as obstacles to the development of equal opportunities policies in general. These are resources, working arrangements, training, recruitment and selection, targets, and attitudes and culture.

University Culture: Patriarchy or Meritocracy?

The focus of the case studies and analysis in this chapter is a consideration of 'attitude' and 'culture'. A definition of organizational culture is not easy to encapsulate: however, emphasis can be placed on the sharing of values and social realities, including beliefs, traditions and practices which are, to an extent, shared and transmitted from one generation of employees to the next (Bate, 1994). Certainly there may be unstated but powerful mechanisms which reinforce the culture of any organization, and these can include the way rewards and status are allocated, as well as managerial role modelling and coaching. This expression of culture rests less on the presence or absence of equal opportunities policies, and more on the forms of decision-making and how power and authority are accumulated, legitimated and maintained.

In the arena of higher education, the right to speak, or legitimacy, is granted to those possessing cultural capital, that is, recognized resources and values (Bourdieu, 1988). For example, Jackson (1991) suggests that a male style of working places less value on 'caring' and more on those qualities traditionally identified as male, so that women either have to choose to assimilate male values or attempt the difficult task of changing those values. The acceptance and currency of a particular range of attitudes and beliefs indicates a notion of a cultural sense of self for men which validates a masculine model of academic professionalism. Academic women then 'experience daily the tension between their subordinate role in the sexual hierarchy and the ideology of equal opportunity which extends to women the promise of equality' (Crompton and Mann, 1986, p. 126).

Clearly, the wider operational system of values and beliefs affects both the implementation and perception of institutional strategies for equality of opportunity (Baker, 1987).

The Case Studies

Eight women from different universities were approached for interview. The criterion for their selection was that they had 'succeeded'; that is, they had reached positions of seniority (necessary to be able to provide an account of any visible or unseen barriers to reaching this status), or they were prominent (particularly in terms of publications) within academia. Complete confidentiality was maintained. Geographical locations and the subject areas of the respondents are not revealed, to protect their anonymity.

The purpose of each open-ended interview was to pursue the actual and perceived experiences of successful academics, considering institutional features, including management style, apparent criteria for promotion and existence of equal opportunities policies. Each respondent also offered comments on her own personal experience, with specific reference to potential barriers she may have faced during the course of her career. The subsequent analysis followed from their views, rather than squeezing them into some predetermined mould. Although the responses indicate a use of particular terms and concepts without a full articulation of meaning, certain features or themes were highlighted prior to the interviews to indicate an identification of what Walby (1989) theorizes as a patriarchal culture. These include male hierarchies and a belief in equitable practices without systematic reviews: marginalizing and ignoring senior women, criteria for promotion emphasizing attributes that men are more likely to possess; unfriendly working practices and informal networks based on patronage. Whilst the first seven case studies described here illustrate aspects of patriarchal practice, the final case study reveals a situation where many of these issues appear to have been addressed successfully.

Personal Narratives

Respondent 1

This respondent was aware, on taking up her first post in this university, that she was entering a male-dominated department and would face stress as a result of this. She described the predominant managerial style of the university as 'fairly aggressive, macho, competitive and top-down'. She saw the power structure being set by what was described as a team, but was really a group of competing individual men. In her experience,

> it is a real problem that there's a very narrow conception of who a good senior manager is . . . there is a tendency to undervalue what I would call the soft management skills of listening and noticing if staff have got problems beyond the institution which could impinge on their performance . . . financial management and systems planning are more valued . . . this goes over and above research and teaching performance as criteria for promotion.

This woman was aware of the stated policies on equal opportunities, but added: 'senior management think they're great, but they don't understand the implications of how they're worked through in practice. It's rhetoric.' Her clear perception was that 'everything is framed in such a way that women have to change their behaviour to do better in the organization, when it should be looking critically at its own practices'. As a senior woman in the institution she 'sometimes sees [herself] not as successful but as surviving day to day' and is strained, overloaded and despairing. She has found the overall institutional culture of the university unhelpful. More generally, she identified factors which bar women's progress in academia:

> Style prevents women from being promoted in the first place because they don't display the qualities which are seen to be valued, and it also prevents women from wanting to be involved in that, because they see it as antithetical to their own ideologies and it makes women feel marginalized. . . . Women are less willing to play the careerist games that men do, they are much more critical of their own performance. Women are more used to rationalizing non-success and non-achievement . . . also they can see the isolation and vulnerablilty of the women who do make it.

Recognizing this, her analysis is that most of the barriers to women in academia are attitudinal; this can be insidious because 'you can say there are equal opportunities for women in structural terms but in real terms there aren't'.

Respondent 2

This woman identifies her university's distinct managerial style:

> Yes, it's Thatcherite. The dominant managerial style at the top of the university is a financial and accounting type approach following re-structuring, with a very managerialist thrust and ethos.

There were conflicting pressures leading to criteria for being worthy of promotion: 'the three key ones are administration, teaching and research. [She's] not sure which is the key to success . . . bringing money in is an important feature.' She feels 'the university is skirting round the equal opportunities issue, there's some awareness but not a lot of positive feelings'. She thinks that she has been successful partly because she is good at her job, in terms of knowledge of her subject 'and also putting work first'. There is a lower than average representation of women at all levels in this university:

> It hit me what a male organization it was when I started. There are lots of older men who have been here for years and years and women who are well-qualified but have moved around come here and are faced with an organization that appears to reward (with promotion and status) its long-serving men and it's difficult for women to fit in.

The message has come across to this respondent that she has to queue up behind the senior men for promotion. This is a silent but explicit indication from those whom she referred to as male gatekeepers. This raised clear fears

> that there has been a tradition of women doing a lot of unseen work for years and years and getting no reward. I explicitly said that I am not the Marge Proops of [subject area]. On the other hand I take my job seriously and work very hard and pull more than my weight, being continually concerned that there will be no reward (in terms of promotion or acknowledgment).

Finally she argued that though there are barriers facing all women in being successful in an academic career, these were most evident close to the top of university hierarchies:

It's a gentleman's club, academic life, because there's so much that's unwritten, intangible . . . men occupy most of the senior positions, they are gatekeepers and the rules of the game aren't clear . . . to get anywhere, women have to be eliciting the support of the male gatekeepers. Women get appointed on merit, it does count, but more at the lower levels. The problems occur at the higher levels, it's within the organization.

Respondent 3

Respondent 3 saw that the management style of the university was in a state of change. There has been a shift away from democracy to the decision-making process being contained within the directorate who

make decisions in meetings every Monday morning; the main power is within the directorate, so much so that they don't fully understand that there is widespread disillusionment with them, especially around the process of restructuring.

An indicator of fitness for promotion is academic productivity in the form of publications, judging from the allocation of professorships, although innovation and academic leadership are gaining prominence. Equal opportunities policies are not stated clearly enough. As a senior woman in the university, she feels as though she is used as a token and 'wheeled out on every public occasion'. Her position means she gets asked to sit on a lot of interview panels, and she feels that decisions made over appointments reflect an attitude to women:

They can't recognize that women can lead from behind, not pushing forward, nurturing rather than aggressive and this is less valued. This is becoming part of the ethos of the institution and is bad news for women; either you flatter or cajole or boost egos and this is a subordinate and subjugating thing.

Generally, she feels that there are barriers to women in pursuing an academic career: 'You'd think more would get through than do'. She thinks a lot of it is to do with the 'cloning principle' at recruitment where there is a narrow, male definition of a good management style without sufficient regard to 'track records . . . and insensitivity to personal interaction'.

Respondent 4

This academic had witnessed a concerted effort within her department to be non-hierarchical and there is a lot of emphasis on discussion. However, the university was run

by long-established men . . . the senate has a notion of being democratic but distant . . . the departments are autonomous except for
budgets . . . the faculty boards are all-powerful; committees mediate
between the departments and the hierarchy.

Administration, teaching and research were the criteria for promotion
but the passage to senior lecturer

is a threshold that most women don't cross . . . administration is seen
as less important than research or having got money for research (as
opposed to publications).

Respondent 4 found life in this university alienating and was beginning to
feel embittered because she

doesn't feel part of it, it's like a men's club and – may be worse than
most because of its science base. Any general meeting you go to is
full of elderly, boring-looking men; this is a problem.

Altogether, she was 'not surprised at where women are'. She knows a lot
of women she admires who have just decided that they've had enough and
they haven't really 'slotted in' to the career structure. Her assessment is that
'women are more interested in staying put and avoiding promotion with all the
associated administrative tasks'. Her belief was that women did more pastoral
work than men and this was not recognized as valuable. She thought barriers
to women are largely attitudinal and that the university was

dominated by men, it's staffed and run by men, most of the courses
are disciplines that men have traditionally dominated. There is a very
low representation of women in some departments and gender issues
just don't come into the curriculum.

Respondent 5

This academic worked within an identifiable managerial style which is

hierarchical, white-male-dominated . . . the advert for the new [sen-
ior management role] says they want an authoritative, decisive,
forceful team leader. It's a sort of contradiction of equal opportunities because since incorporation the sector has moved into a top-
down managerial style.

Policy, power and decision-making were centralized. There appeared to be
definite criteria for promotion. One was 'having research but if women have

research records I don't think it helps them – it's useful for men'. She sees this as part of the general discounting and decompetencing of women. The other factor is being on committees; the allocation of course leaderships is 'all done by who you know . . . the idea is beginning to grow of progression planning but as a rationalization of current practice'. There is a clear statement of intent for equal opportunities and other codes are being developed. Her view was that all senior women in the university were in the support or 'soft' areas. She felt she had no formal power and was often ignored or misrepresented. In her experience, she has met considerable hindrances during her academic career; including 'long-term periods of not being recognized, validated or supported'. As the only woman at this level in the university this respondent argued:

> it's a very hostile environment for things like mixing with senior management – women are invisible – like other women in the university I find a conspiracy of silence.

In general, her perception was that women fail to proceed with academic careers because of

> an interplay of factors. We've all got the idea that what we do is fair . . . it's threatening to some people to suggest they need to examine their own practices . . . there's also complacency.

Her strong belief was that the greatest barriers to women in academia are attitudinal: to do with self-guilt (thinking one should have been able to do it better), marginalization, getting ideas stolen or hijacked and being ignored.

Respondent 6

Respondent 6 felt that there was more than one style and culture operating in the university, but that it was very much the professoriat that held the power. Until recently there were two women professors, now there were four out of a total of over seventy. Research and publications were the most important criteria for promotion; that is

> clear and unequivocal, it overrides everything else including managerial knowledge. Networks certainly operate across the institution . . . the crucial thing is whether or not you feel comfortable operating in that set-up.

The statement of equal opportunities extended to four lines contained within the statutes which were changed recently: the focus was on merit, although they 'never specify what merit is, but say that nothing irrelevant should count'. She felt that the reasons for her success were her track record of research and the 'grounding' she has had in other universities. However, she considered herself as still very much an outsider, both within her department and within the institution. Quite explicitly, this respondent argues that the key to women's underrepresentation in academia generally can be ascribed to

> discrimination – overt and covert . . . if you want to track it back, track it back to the discrimination in the recruitment of students pre 1975 . . . there were fewer women coming through. Having said that, there's discrimination all through the system, which although it's shifted a bit is still there along with all the standard difficulties women have in relation to their lives.

Taking the analysis further, from her perception it was possible to identify barriers to women's progression, both practical and attitudinal. The hours of work are too long and exclude women with children:

> You won't get along if you've got caring responsibilities . . . there's also a closure around networking and patronage which excludes women from the exchange. It's the informal feature of networking that's an inherent feature of academic life that's such a problem.

There were a few male academics in the university who thought that having so few women around was a problem, but the majority thought they were so meritocratic that it was not an issue for concern. The respondent considered that the university

> has a dominant group which disproportionately represents a male view of the world, and that is central to the personnel and the hierarchy. Also, as an intellectual institution, it represents the intellectual ideas of men which are therefore overemphasized.

Respondent 7

Respondent 7 identified a clear and explicit management style and institutional culture which focused on the concept of 'quality'. Ultimately, the director had the last say and his personal preference defined the culture. While she described the director as 'reasonably accommodating, kindly and pragmatic', the four male assistant directors were 'more strongly masculine' and operated a hierarchy of access which leads to 'an all-male culture'. The respondent identified a 'Thatcherite' power culture focusing on budgetary control which was permeating the institution via devolution. Academic productivity (publications) and managerial style both acted as criteria for promotion but 'they're not harmonious'. She described being rejected at interview on grounds that were not featured in the person specification (one reason was that she had not been there long enough). Since then she has had a few articles published and said that 'it's been huge for me, the cost benefit has been out of all proportion from the outlay'. There was no equal opportunities policy at that time, but one was in preparation. This was significant for her, because such issues

> were not on the agenda three years ago but are becoming clearer . . . my background has given me a lot of skills to correlate with the current management style and climate, so I can do things in the same way.

Respondent 7 was very aware, however, of being a woman. This awareness was 'prompted by the behaviour of others such as older traditional men'. Her feeling was that she has been 'outspoken, innovative, successful' within her department but states that getting noticed was purely a matter of chance. Her unequivocal assertion was that women

> have to adopt a style to get on . . . I feel strongly about what's not valued such as caring roles, and this is the choice of the male management structure . . . it's fitting in with male-defined ways of working and ditching natural tendencies, fitting in and going the cost-effective route . . . it's not the way I would choose it but I hope I can influence change.

Generally she feels so few woman get through

> because they don't know how to go about it in that they are not motivated to aspire to seniority . . . are lacking in the skills to negotiate the system and don't have that element of time of be committed.

She was adamant that she was not being presumptuous; rather it was the male definitions of what is valid that women do not know about and cannot gain access to.

> Overt discrimination is manifested by one-off comments . . . the definitions of criteria by men exclude women's strengths . . . it's about being tough and not displaying emotion, and women are socialized into thinking it's OK to display emotions. You can take each aspect of a woman's work here and find areas where she's hampered by male structures.

Respondent 8

This professor considered that the managerial style of her university had changed in the last few years. The atmosphere was of a 'large business'. It was not that people had become unfriendly, but that the working day now extended from 7.00 a.m. to 7.00 p.m. The committee structure was very hierarchical and it was the deans who had the power. The culture was hierarchical, though not macho. Although research, publications and administrative ability had traditionally been criteria for promotion, teaching ability was gaining in prominence and teaching professorships had now been established. There was an equal opportunities committee and the policies were very well-stated.

> There's a great deal of awareness, the provost (and the last one) keep in mind the proportion of men and women at lecturer grade and try to keep that higher up and whenever possible, improve. If only men are shortlisted, they are asked to go back and review all the applications from women, to ensure rejection can be justified.

Respondent 8 felt that the university is a 'very woman-friendly place'. While she believed that part of her success had been down to luck (suggesting a tendency to undervalue her achievements), 'also the Provost . . . is good at recognizing good points and ignoring weak ones and this boosted my confidence a great deal'. It was accepted that the university had a 'great pride in being non-denominational and whoever you are, you can make your way up'. This attracted her and made joining a very positive choice. Women have a reasonable profile with about 25 per cent of professors being female. For herself, she 'was unambitious for a long time, but if you don't fight for yourself no-one else will'. She has been hindered by one or two uncooperative male colleagues, and she was interested to learn why women fall behind generally and has done some research within her discipline, in which 75 per cent of undergraduates are women. Her observation was that

> It is at the post-graduate stage that women drop out . . . they change jobs following partners . . . they tend to do more inside the department, allowing little time for university-wide recognition . . . it is important to release them to take on college or university jobs. Women are less concerned with status, and value different qualities and men heads of department take advantage of women, where there are things to organize involving complicated negotiations with people as their skills are better.

It was her firm belief that the barriers to women are largely attitudinal and that even if there was commitment from the top, there could be problems.

> This is what women colleagues say. Men go drinking in the common room after 5.30 p.m. This excludes women with caring responsibilities, but a lot of women say they feel excluded from that type of life and it's not decisions being taken but people get to know each other and think, oh this is a good chap. Women don't get a look in.

Overall she felt somewhat cushioned as her department and faculty had a lot of women spread through the ranks, but she acknowledged that younger women may have a very different perspective. It was a better experience for her in this university than in others she is familiar with.

Explanations and Observations

The experiences and perceptions of these women suggest that barriers to women academics are shaped more by cultural factors than by practical constraints. It is significant that five out of eight of the respondents have no childcare responsibilities. For while it is acknowledged that women with family commitments still carry a double burden of responsibility, the fact that women who are free of this practical constraint are still disadvantaged would speak against operational and structural explanations in favour of cultural indicators. There is a common theme whereby each respondent considers her university to be deeply hierarchical; where criteria for promotion are weighted in favour of men; where aggressive management promotes unfriendly working practices, where informal networking goes hand in hand with a devaluation of what are considered to be feminine attributes. The unquestioning emphasis on merit, and failure to reflect and review existing working patterns, leads respondents to consider that equal opportunities polices by themselves are tokenistic and shallow.

The universities described appear to display and reflect a series of attitudes and cultures which, when taken as a whole, act as invisible but stalwart barriers to the career progression of women academics. The respondents supplement Bagilhole's (1994) research in a single institution, where evidence suggests that senior women academics are less confident in their abilities and experience greater social isolation, feeling that their scholarship is more likely to be trivialized and discredited.

While it is relatively straightforward for a woman to embark on an academic career, the case studies provide details of the way in which gender is a significant organizing principle in universities, and the ways in which women give meaning to their experiences. These women feel uncomfortable or ill at ease with the values and behaviours surrounding them. Although Edwards (1994) suggests that many women academics may not see themselves as wanting to challenge prevailing ideas, and may need to be alerted to the fact that they are working in male-dominated institutions, the respondents described in this chapter show no evidence of the 'Queen Bee' syndrome (those strongly individual women who deny the existence of disadvantage). Rather, they show a level of reflexivity and ambivalence, acknowledging that participating more fully involves engaging with the existing unwritten rules and procedures, and all that this implies (Gray, 1994).

The culture of individual institutions is crucial to the success or failure of initiatives to enhance women's progress. While it might be claimed that ultimately it is merely insensitivity, or even business-like behaviour, the results of current common practices and behaviours are to exclude, marginalize and undervalue women. Many equal opportunities policies operate quite comfortably in those organizations which reflect the male way of operation as standard and deny rewards to those groups whose behaviour or characteristics do not conform. The very subtlety of the operation of attitudes and cultures inhibits the power of most policies to redress inequalities. There can be, however, facility for change within existing structures. The experience of Respondent 8 reflects this. This university has been singled out for praise for its efforts to enhance women's progress and this is borne out not only by the location of women in the overall hierarchy (women's representation at all levels is significantly greater than the national average), but also by the perceptions that there is commitment at the most senior level to breaking down historical and structural patterns of gender inequality.

Conclusion

It has been suggested that equality of opportunity at work remains a myth in the university sector (Hilton, 1991). I would assert that those elements of equal opportunities policies focusing on gender have been concerned to try and increase women's representation within existing hierarchies without questioning or changing those hierarchies. Changing structures and cultures which give authority to a very particular type of person are not likely to be impacted upon by merit-based equal opportunities strategies, where seniority may in fact only give the illusion of power. A genuine desire to enable women to progress requires a thorough review of professional practices. As Franzway *et al.* insist,

> Reform is not just a matter of changing personnel at the top. It is a matter of unpicking a complex texture of institutional arrangements which intersect with the construction of masculinity and femininity. (Franzway *et al.*, 1989, p. 31)

Equal opportunities policies must shift their focus from procedures and processes to culture and attitudes before barriers can be thoroughly challenged. Fine words are not enough, even when put in place with a formalized equal opportunities statement and structure. Deeply embedded ideologies in management, combined with casual interchange and spurious judgmental value positions, still serve to undermine women who seek to move to the top in higher education. That reform or change is possible and achievable has been illustrated by Respondent 8: the prevailing culture of her institution has been undermined and weakened by practical commitment from senior management. Likewise, evidence from this case study suggests that senior women are aware of the key issues identified by Willcocks (1994): personal, structural and particularly cultural, whereby an antithetical, patriarchal organizational ethos may be faced and challenged.

References

ASSOCIATION OF UNIVERSITY TEACHERS (AUT) (1992) *Sex Discrimination in Universities: Report of an Academic Pay Audit Carried Out by the AUT Research Department*, London, Association of University Teachers.

BAGILHOLE, B. (1994) 'Being Different is a Very Difficult Row to Hoe: Survival Strategies of Women Academics', in DAVIES, S., LUBELSKA, C. and QUINN, J. (Eds) *Changing the Subject: Women in Higher Education*, London, Taylor and Francis, pp. 15–28.

BAKER, J. (1987) *Arguing for Equality*, London, Verso.

BATE, P. (1994) *Strategies for Cultural Change*, London, Butterworth Heinemann.

BOURDIEU, P. (1988) *Homo Academicus*, Cambridge, Polity Press.

COMMISSION ON UNIVERSITY CAREER OPPORTUNITY (CUCO) (1994) *A Report on Universities Policies and Practices on Equal Opportunities in Employment*, London, CUCO.

COMMITTEE OF VICE-CHANCELLORS AND PRINCIPALS (CVCP) (1991) *Guidance on Equal Opportunities in Employment in Universities*, London, CVCP.

CROMPTON, R. and MANN, M. (1986) *Gender and Stratification*, Cambridge, Polity Press.

EDWARDS, M. (1994) 'Women Breaking the Glass Ceiling, Are We Prepared to Count the Cost?', presentation at WHEN conference, Preston, November.

EQUAL OPPORTUNITIES COMMISSION (EOC) (1990) *Women and Men in Britain*, London, HMSO.

FRANZWAY, S., COURT, D. and CONNELL, R. W. (1989) *Staking a Claim: Feminism, Bureaucracy and the State*, Cambridge, Polity Press.

GRAY, B. (1994) 'Women in Higher Education: What Are We Doing to Ourselves?', in DAVIES, S., LUBELSKA, C. and QUINN, J. (Eds) (1994) *Changing the Subject: Women in Higher Education*, London, Taylor and Francis, pp. 75–88.

HANSARD SOCIETY COMMISSION (1990) *The Report of the Hansard Society Commission on Women at the Top*, London, Hansard Society for Parliamentary Government.

HILTON, I. (1991) 'Unfinished Business', *Independent on Sunday*, 29 December, p. 11.

JACKSON, D. F. (1990) 'Women Working in Higher Education: A Review of the Position of Women in Higher Education and Policy Developments', *Higher Education Quarterly*, 44, 4 (Autumn), pp. 297–323.

JACKSON, G. (1991) 'He Goes to Mum', *Times Higher Education Supplement*, 21 June, p. 14.

RENDEL, M. (1984) 'Women Academics in the Seventies', in ACKER, S. and WARREN PIPER, D. (Eds) *Is Higher Education Fair to Women?*, London, Nelson, pp. 163–79.

WALBY, S. (1989) 'Theorising Patriarchy', *Sociology*, 23, 2, pp. 213–34.

WILLCOCKS, D. (1994) 'True Confessions of a Woman Manager', presentation at WHEN conference, Preston, November.

WILLIAMS, J., COCKING, J. and DAVIES, L. (1989) *Words or Deeds? A Review of Equal Opportunity Policies in Higher Education*, London, CRE.

Chapter 5

Deaf Women Academics in Higher Education

Ruth-Elaine Gibson

When invited to submit a paper on issues concerning deafness in higher education, I pondered over the undertaking. Originally, I had considered discussing issues concerning my experiences as a deaf woman student in higher education which is worthy of a paper in its own right. As I have recently taken the tentative steps of realizing my ambition to be a lecturer, my (hearing) academic colleagues, quite amazed at my madness, seem to have difficulty understanding my teaching enthusiasm. The aim of this paper is firstly to offer an insight into the rationale behind this ambition, and secondly, to share the experiences of four other deaf women academics employed in universities across the UK. They are either full/part-time lecturers or researchers.

I Can Hear When I Want To

I have never liked being deaf and in May, 1995 I was fortunate to have a cochlea implant. Since having surgery I now feel that I have such an advantage. I can simply 'switch off' when noise becomes horrible and stressful, unlike hearing people, who unfortunately have to cope and bear its burden – unless you are able to purchase ear plugs! The aim of having surgery was to provide a mechanism which would 'improve the quality of my life', which I suppose means that it brings me closer to being like hearing people. The issue of 'quality of life' is interesting and implies the acceptance by the hearing community that deaf people have had a raw deal in their world, and although this is certainly the case, it is necessary to stress that in my view there is nothing 'wrong' in being deaf.

Deafness as 'wrong' occurs through placing a burden upon deaf people generally of what hearing people have perceived to be *their fear* of being without hearing. What are the grounds for these fears? Hearing is more than just hearing sounds, it also involves the interpretation of smell, vibrations and sight. This fear concept has been generated over hundreds of years, by the power and influence of the hearing majority, such as the medical, teaching and social professions who have been wrapped together in a constricting ribbon of politics, adamant to create a society based on their ideas of normality. Matthews (1994) and Oliver (1990) support this and the view that the exclusion of disabled people from society has reinforced the oppression experienced by disabled people and has been the main cause for the negative segregative stigma that has been attached to disability. It is in this sense that disabled people have been viewed as 'patients, special needs, and clients' 'cared for' by bodies of professionals who have taken away, or through the process of 'special' education have eliminated the disabled individual's personal and natural ability to make decisions (good and bad) for themselves, live independently, be accepted by and have access to the same provision of 'public services' available to non-disabled people: 'The failure of . . . , all other professions to involve disabled people in a meaningful way . . . has not just trapped professionals within the medical approach but has had oppressive consequences for disabled people' (Oliver, 1990, p. 5).

For the reader, it is important to be clear about the use of terminology. The image of the word 'deaf' itself raises the ugly adage 'deaf, dumb and stupid,' which of course is not true. This paper will not dwell on the stereotypical models of deafness and deaf women. Their personal experiences and anecdotes that are related throughout this document seem to reverse the adage. It is hearing people that are generally 'deaf, dumb and stupid' on deaf matters. This is a bold statement that by no means implies insult or disrespect on any individual. However, deaf people's lives have been blighted by stigma at this belief.

For this discussion, it is important to define and understand how the word 'deaf' has been used. There are vast differences in the levels of deafness, which can occur at any time in life through accident, illness or simply through genetic profile. It is commonly assumed that usually deafness can be corrected by the wearing of a hearing aid – or indeed (in the deaf community) by a cochlea implant. This is a complete myth. Nonetheless, more recently there has been an increasing awareness that deaf people belong to a minority group, as it has its own language, culture and society:

> There is a growing awareness of Deaf people as a linguistic minority group. A discrete cultural group who use sign language and identify themselves as members of the Deaf Community. It is increasingly common to use an upper case 'D' to indicate those Deaf people who identify themselves in this way. (Padden and Humphries, 1988)

Deaf Women Don't Need Equal Rights!

Despite the impact of the feminist movement of the 1960s and 1970s for equal rights to education, employment and public services, deaf women who were hidden from the eyes of society at the time were 'naturally' excluded in this drive for full recognition. Indeed it has only been in the last decade that there has been a growing movement of groups of disabled people, mainly constructed of disabled men, who have demanded and fought for the same rights that the women's and black movements fought for all those years ago (Matthews, 1994). The strange thing is that it has only been in very recent times that I have not only been accepted as being a deaf person and a member of the public, but also as a deaf *woman* who (surprise surprise) has a gender and experiences all the situations of a hearing person of my sex (yes, deaf women do menstruate, have sex, get married and have children). Being deaf and being a woman shows the double discrimination that deaf women experience and, as Matthews states, the disability movement has failed to identify the extent to which disabled women experience increased discrimination by virtue of their sex, or indeed their ethnic origin.

A Right to Education?

Oliver's suggestion quoted above describes how the failure to include disabled people in the consultation processes – thus generating the medical labelling and the subsequent approach to providing services for disabled people – has created a trap. The education of a deaf child traditionally within a deaf school would therefore be understandably geared towards an approach deemed acceptable by hearing society. My own scholarly life certainly seemed to have been in this direction; towards what I can hear, not what I can do. With one known grammar school specifically for deaf children in the UK, the standard and quality of education varies widely. When I was conducting research for this chapter, some respondents to the questionnaire had attended an 'oral' school which discouraged sign language:

> I attended a special oral day school for the deaf until 13 then went to – Grammar School until 18. First language English and second BSL (British Sign Language) – in the toilets and out of sight of the teachers! (Respondent)

Some respondents educated in this type of environment faced hardship, fear, punishment and extreme stress, as success in subjects was dependent on their ability to lip-read. Others attended a 'total communication' school – that is a school that encouraged learning through both oral methods and sign language. Why was the level of learning different? By the very nature of deafness: vocabulary, reading and mathematics were taught through what may be seen to be a process of 'force-feeding'. Indeed, through my own involvement with deaf people , it seems that very few actually read and enjoy books; most rely heavily on the 'community grapevine' and television for news. It is clear from respondents' comments that education had been based on the social concepts of life. Mathematics, English language and science faded into insignificance as art and craft-based education dominated. Girls seemingly were discouraged to learn and were taught home-based social skills, while boys were encouraged to seek apprenticeships in industrial-based crafts. I have made an attempt to compare the general education pattern of deaf respondents to that which was generally found in mainstream schools. By obtaining school timetables it was clear that children in deaf schools were being taught a seemingly social-based learning structure, aimed to provide a level of education geared towards survival in society (see Table 5.1).

It appears that education in the deaf school, particularly of deaf girls, seemed geared to basic learning and social technical skills, as opposed to the more formalized mainstream school. Indeed, from my own experience of being educated within a deaf school, children approaching leaving age were given very little encouragement to pursue a worthwhile occupation, never mind a career.

Careers!! People Like You Can't Be Like Us

In the 1970s the provision of support for deaf students in higher education was piecemeal and scarce, mainly based on the goodwill of the college to accept deaf students, rather than being seen as a potential market area for development. A statement issued by the British Deaf Association in 1976 brings home the full impact of provision for deaf young people wishing to further their education at that time:

> It would indeed be the kindest way to say that in Britain there is no provision for secondary further education or vocational training for any deaf pupil other than those so gifted or fortunate as be to able to

Table 5.1 Typical generic curriculum in deaf schools and mainstream schools, 1970–1989

Children educated in deaf schools		Hearing children in mainstream schools	
Boys	Girls	Boys	Girls
Art	Art	Art	Art
Drama	Drama	Drama	Cookery/
Woodwork	Needlework	Music	Needlework
Metalwork	Cookery	Woodwork/Metalwork	Games
Technical drawing	Games	Technical drawing	Geography
Games	Mathematics	Geography	History
General science	General science	History	Physics
English language	English language	Physics	Science
Mathematics	Community studies	Science	English language
Community Studies		Languages	Languages
		English language	Mathematics
		Mathematics	Community Studies
		Community Studies	

take part in the normal education provision for the hearing. (BDA, 1976)

Prior to 1990 organised support services for deaf students were only available at one or two institutions. (Daniels and Corlett, 1990)

This implies that as recently as a decade ago respondents had very limited access to further and/or higher education after school. As the occupational status of deaf women links with educational experiences, a number of respondents faced additional barriers to reaching comparable educational levels with their hearing peers. Indeed a comment from one respondent captures this:

Had one day release to attend local technical college for Chemistry and Maths but not given any support. Sit in the front and copy the notes from the person next to you . . . no I do not have any notes for you . . . if you cannot follow you should not be here. Had to give up this course and tried a correspondence course but this took up too much time and I wanted to socialize after five years in residential school. (Respondent)

Because of the restricted formal education, career guidance and further education was therefore limited, as training for employment is very much based on past educational experiences, much to my consternation and that of many respondents. One said:

As a school girl, I wanted to be a teacher for the deaf but was told you can't because you are deaf and it was like the blind leading the blind. (Respondent)

For me, the careers that were deemed appropriate for deaf young women at that time were in the areas of clerical and administration work, catering, hairdressing and nursery nursing. As such, career advice was based on repressing deaf people, women in particular, to a level that was acceptable to the hearing world. When asked about which career they would have liked to pursue, the majority of respondents had wanted to become teachers or teachers of the deaf; however, career advisors and admission policies in the majority of HE institutions barred the way to realizing these ambitions.

I'm Deaf Not Stupid

My experiences in higher education were very different from further education. Basically the level of support in further education college was equivalent to that in school. This was perhaps due to the very close contacts each college had with school. In my experience, many of the tutors were paid to provide additional one-to-one tutorials in the evening – hence the dissemination and cascade of information about the education of deaf students to other lecturers and staff within the colleges. Also, as the majority of deaf students resided at the deaf school, education support was there in terms of staff and fellow peers. In higher education, however, experiences were very different. Gone was the level of communication and professional support, there was no peer help either. Academic achievement of deaf students depended on personal support levels, and their ability to understand language on a higher scale. As I was the only deaf student at this institution, tutors and lecturers met me with a mixed reaction, i.e. that they would help me as much as possible – *but* if I couldn't keep up with the others then I would be asked to leave. Other lecturers viewed me with quiet reservation and seemed to keep a wide berth, to the extent of clearly avoiding me, preventing any discussions, and being very reluctant to part with any of their notes. So, not only did deaf women have personal difficulties in being accepted and integrated in mainstream higher educational life; tutors themselves were not trained, informed or equipped to work with deaf students, as found from respondents:

> There was usually no time for tutorials so we were promised one later. Then the module tutor would be travelling all over the country. Unfortunately I didn't have a single tutorial so after a week with the group had heavy discussions, then I felt isolated when I went back home because there was no follow-up and twice I didn't hand in my work before the deadline because my motivation wore off. Also at university I was given too much allowance by the tutor saying I could hand in my work months after the deadline – this happened twice! (Respondent)

It is remarks like this that indicate that educational standards were difficult to achieve because they were simply not accessible – physically and psychologically. Schooling did not prepare deaf young people for life amongst hearing people.

> I indicated to the university that no support was necessary. After four terrible weeks at the start of my course, I knew this was wrong. I could not understand many of the lectures and was unable to cope with group work. It took several months to organise the appropriate help for me. (Nottingham Trent University, 1995)

The very culture and traditions held by universities render them as being completely different from further education. In school, deaf children are taught by teachers who have received additional teacher training specific for deaf children, the arm of this level of teaching reaching as far as further education. Lecturers in higher education had not received such formal training or basic information on working with deaf students. Indeed the appointment of many lecturers to the academic profession today may generally be based on their higher-level qualifications and technical knowledge, having received very little or no formal training in basic teaching practices. It may be argued that the techniques of good presentation styles and classroom protocol are lacking in the higher education environment. From my own experiences, many eminent and respected academics can become their own worst enemies when delivering lectures. The way in which they have been allowed to teach over the years may neither have changed nor have been challenged. A lecturer may react strongly when confronted with a profoundly deaf student who simply asks her/him to, for example, stand still. This request may have deep psychological effects on their well-being, if such pacing of the classroom floor is habitual. It may even result in downright hostility. My past work with deaf women academics showed that one of the essential skills a deaf student must have is good lip-reading abilities. It is, however, not possible to lip-read and take notes at the same time, from behind an overhead projector, in a darkened room or from film narration. Indeed, lip-reading skills were voted by respondents to be more important than the use of sign language interpreters. It was found that although we (including respondents) had some access to sign language interpreters, this was fraught with difficulties. The very nature and specialism of the course meant that interpreters themselves had no knowledge of the subject, so sign language was monotonous. As high-level language was spoken, very often this was not contained within the concept of sign language and the interpreter had no alternative but to resort to finger spelling. Meanings underlying connotations in the spoken word, and expressions, were lost in the race for the interpreter to keep track with the lecturer. If you consider that in the UK support services to deaf and hearing-impaired students in many universities and higher education establishments are generally less than five years old, it may be appreciated that the barriers faced not only encompass individual support services but also surround issues of community integration and acceptance by hearing peers. In my experience, my hearing peers often found themselves unwitting, and sometimes unwilling, key players in providing support in the form of photocopying their notes or simply by using carbon copy paper. Indeed being able to speak well and not hear was very difficult for my peers to understand, and help was very often refused in the light of comments such as 'you only hear when you want to':

> I didn't get on with other hearing students very well because they could not understand why I could speak properly yet not hear. But that did not matter because as a mature student I had very good relations with tutors. My group had become very competitive, working hard to achieve the best marks. I liked that as I love a good challenge, we really were high achievers. I managed to get one-to-one tuition from my course tutor, who asked if I knew *why* my group was so competitive. He explained very sensitively that it was because

I was in the group that they wanted to prove to themselves and others that they were not the lowest group of the course. (Respondent)

The late 1970s saw the development of communication services for deaf students in further education, the late 1980s and 1990s for higher education. A combination of assistance is now available for deaf students in higher education – if only limited. The problem does not only lie with the provision of trained sign language interpreters, but with the skill of such assistance in the higher education environment. Generally, interpreters have no knowledge of specialist subjects, and sign language does not readily contain high-level technical/academic jargon. This emphasizes the view that in order to be successful, fluent levels of speech and communication are essential. However, this offers a perception that sign language itself is inferior. Despite the fact that for some respondents sign language is their first language within the deaf community, a spoken language becomes their first language at university/work. This presents a dual problem of recognition and belonging. Good speech and lip-reading has been seen to be sufficient reason to be excluded from the deaf community, yet being deaf means exclusion from the hearing world.

Can You Pay for Support?

Despite recent changes to the student grant systems, in 1990 the Disabled Students Allowance (DSA) was introduced, which provided additional financial support to disabled students. Students eligible for a mandatory grant are able to apply to their local authority for the allowance. Because of its limited amount, it may be true that the level of service available depends on the student's ability to pay. However, a growing number of universities are developing their own support service. Research undertaken by the Nottingham Trent University (1995), provides brief details: 'Durham, Derby, Bristol, Wolverhampton and Central Lancashire, were generally the only institutions with the flexibility to offer support to those students not in receipt of DSA.'

For our respondents, support mainly came from two sources: from classroom colleagues, and the ability to obtain additional support from individual tutorials. All respondents had difficulty utilizing interpreting support, due to lack of high-level language in sign language, and because generally interpreters had no basic understanding of the subjects.

Realizing the Dream

So what has driven deaf women academics to realize their ambition? Luck and coincidence? Recognition by very rare hearing professionals that we can do more than just type letters and peel potatoes? The fact that by tradition, hearing professionals have attempted to control and determine the pattern of our lives has provided the burning fuel 'to prove them wrong', to break out of the stereotypical and medical models of the simple, placid, home-based deaf woman? The driving force has been individual ability, strength and motivation – perhaps generated by experiences of past discrimination – to realize our ambitions. Although all respondents stressed that support and encouragement mainly came from families and partners, it is clear that respondents who pursued higher education did so knowing the barriers to expect. What is clear is that deaf women academics have had an inner drive to work with both hearing students and staff on combating negative images of deaf matters. The impetus has been in developing and improving understanding, attitudes and behaviour of staff and students through their own specialist fields – particularly since many students will become future managers and specialist professionals. As role models for both hearing and deaf communities, respondents have a very crucial function as catalysts for change.

References

BRITISH DEAF ASSOCIATION (1976) Interim Draft Report on the Results of Investigation Made by a Working Party Appointed by the BDA to Make Recommendations as to the Future Policy with Regards to the Employment of Deaf School Leavers, in *The Price of Deafness: Disability Alliance*, pp. 19–20.

DANIELS, S. and CORLETT, S. (1990) *Deaf Students in Higher Education*, RNID Report No. 9, London, RNID, in *Nottingham Trent University Report: Access and Communication/Support for Deaf and Hearing Impaired Students*, p. 1.

MATTHEWS, J. (1994) 'Empowering Disabled Women in Higher Education', in DAVIES, S., LUBELSKA, C. and QUINN, J. (Eds) *Changing the Subject: Women in Higher Education*, London, Taylor and Francis, pp. 138–45.

NOTTINGHAM TRENT UNIVERSITY (1995) *Access and Communication Support for Deaf and Hearing Impaired Students in Higher Education*, Student Care Services, Nottingham Trent University.

OLIVER, M. (1990) *The Importance of Disablement*, Basingstoke, Macmillan.

PADDEN, C. and HUMPHRIES, T. (1988) *Deaf in America: Voices from a Culture*, Cambridge, MA and London, Harvard University Press, p. 44.

Appendix

This chapter has made reference to a number of different support services which are clarified below:

Interpreters

Interpreters translate what is said by the lecturer or other students into British Sign Language (BSL) or Sign Supported English (SSE), and will provide a voice-over for the deaf students' contributions when required. BSL is a language in its own right, with its own grammar, idioms and characteristics. SSE is a form of signed English Language using the signs of BSL.

Registered interpreters are highly trained professionals, who undertake registered professional training courses validated by the Council for the Advancement of Communication with Deaf People (CACDP).

Communication Support Workers

As there is a shortage of trained professional sign language interpreters, particularly in the higher education sector, this has partly resulted in the development of Communication Support Workers. These professionals are expected to facilitate communication between deaf students and others in a number of ways:

- sign language

- lipspeaking

- notetaking

- video transcriptions

- liaison with lecturers regarding notes and handouts

- advice to lecturers regarding issues such as good communications practices.

Notetakers

Because it is not possible to lip-read/follow an interpreter and take notes at the same time, professional notetakers will attempt to record as detailed as possible a synopsis of the lecture – being more detailed and accurate than the average student's notes.

Lipspeakers

A lipspeaker simply repeats the words of the speaker without using any voice.

English Language Tutorials

Some deaf students will require additional support in the reading, preparation and presentation of assignment, work and dissertations, particularly understanding new vocabulary and concepts.

Technical Tutorials

The technical tutor provides a one-to-one tutorial which aims to reinforce the student's understanding of technical/professional areas/fields. This is particularly useful where individual project work, assignments and dissertations are required.

Note

Information has been derived from the 1995 report, *Access and Communication Support for Deaf and Hearing Impaired Students in Higher Education*, by the Student Care Services of Nottingham Trent University.

Chapter 6

Women in Management Education: The Token Topic?

Pat Hornby and Sue Shaw

As practitioners with the primary responsibility for the coordination of human activity in organizations it can be argued that managers' most significant contribution ought to be their ability to inform and be informed by multiple perspectives and to employ that information to guide appropriate action. As management educators we are constantly reminded of the need to facilitate managers' development of the skills necessary to deal strategically with highly complex 'soft' organizational problems. At the heart of this perspective of management education is a recognition that organizations are, and deal with, environments that are made up of multiple stakeholders with a variety of needs, values and expectations. Systems and contingency models of organization have long since moved management education from prescriptive, one-best-way approaches to organization. We encourage managers to reflect on the ramifications their decisions have beyond their immediate concerns and to adopt a systemic approach to decision-making, taking account of environments beyond and sub-systems within the organization. It is surprising then that the curricula associated with management courses fail, by and large, to address explicitly a major source of difference between the management population and the populations with which it interacts, i.e. gender. Indeed, as we have experienced the treatment of women in management as a topic on a management education programme, we have been struck by the similarities between the treatment of the topic and the experiences associated with women working in management positions in organizations. One of the ways in which this similarity between the topic and its subject-matter manifests itself is via the process of marginalization. Our perception is that as an option the topic is too easily consigned to the margins and is further prone to be treated in this way via its association with a marginalized group.

Marginalizing Women in Management

The marginalization of the topic, women in management, in management education, has an obvious parallel in organizations themselves. The use of male norms and the identification of managerial sex-typing (Schein, 1973,

1975) has not only contributed to the marginalization of women, but by definition rendered women inferior. Recent research by Schein (1994) suggests that despite women's increasing representation in management, managerial sex-typing continues, at least amongst men, and constitutes a major barrier to women's progression into senior management. It is here that marginalization is most in evidence. As Handley (1994) says, 'For women reaching the top in organizations or entering the (traditionally male) professions, marginality is a key issue.' Hearn and Parkin (1988) have described women's marginality in organizational leadership in spatial terms. They argue that 'Leadership roles can be conceptualised as part of the centre or core of organizational activity while other roles can be seen as part of the periphery as boundary roles' (Hearn and Parkin, 1988, p. 19). They go on to suggest that this spatial distance between the centre and the periphery tends to run along gender lines with women relegated to the boundary roles.

Marshall's (1995a) account of the experiences of sixteen female middle and senior managers reinforces the view that women are still not widely accepted as equals when they reach senior positions. She recounts the tensions for women seeking to legitimize their position and suggests that recognizing, appreciating and living with marginality can be an alternative to embracing male patterns of management. We believe we have experienced these same tensions in relation to the teaching of the topic of women in management. In a recent review of gender research (Marshall, 1995b) it is observed that many mainstream management and organizational theorists (e.g. in areas such as leadership and culture) appear to conduct and report their work in a gender-free vacuum, seemingly unaware of the gender-related critiques of their areas. Although referring specifically to research, we recognize corresponding weaknesses in the teaching of these mainstream topics, i.e. the lack of reference to gender-related critiques. The absence of gender critique in the core modules forces examination (if it is to take place at all) to take place in isolation from core modules and therefore from mainstream topics, thus ensuring the continued marginalization of the subject-matter. Teachers delivering mainstream modules can effectively wash their hands of any attempt to provide a gender-related critique of their subject-matter, on the grounds that it is dealt with elsewhere on the course.

Marshall's (1984) re-interpretation of Kanter's (1977) analysis of relative number[1] provides a useful framework for examining how our experience of one women in management option is perceived and delivered. The option, in a sense, represents the token woman in Kanter's skewed group. It is perceived by some staff and students as being different from the other options. Its novelty value was particularly evident in the early years of its delivery. What is more, it has been suggested that it is a soft option compared to others; not a 'real' option like marketing or small business. Recent informal canvassing by the authors of the opinions of students not selecting the option revealed some students' suspicions that the option is neither 'business-like' (i.e. considering issues of importance for organizational effectiveness and efficiency) nor academic (i.e. addressing an academic literature) in its approach but is, rather, process-oriented and a forum for women to 'bemoan their lot'. Though these notions of business and academicism are themselves part of the problem in the sense that they are often used in management education as uncontested terms when they are in fact open to a great deal of interpretation, we would argue that students find the topic at least as 'business-like' and 'academic' as others on the course. In fact we feel that, in practice, we have conformed almost too rigidly to a formal, content-oriented approach to the teaching of women in management. We suspect that our primary motivation for doing so stems from our suspicion that a topic that is different on one major dimension (i.e. with respect to its content) cannot perhaps afford to be different on too many other dimensions (e.g. delivery and assessment) – rather like female managers power-dressing, perhaps. Marshall (1984) has described the way token women are perceived by the dominant group members in terms of visibility, polarization and assimilation. Tokens stand out and have a high degree of visibility because they are rare. Whilst there are positive aspects to this, Kanter's research has suggested that negative aspects and secondary considerations receive the most attention. She reports that a common reaction in this situation by women is both to overachieve and to attempt to limit visibility by avoiding public events.

The parallels are striking. In the early years of the women in management option both the institution at large and the department's management were keen to promote 'the product' and the developer of 'the product' externally and within. Encouragement was given to present the development not only as innovative and exciting but also as evidence of commitment to equal opportunity issues in the curriculum. Colleagues were curious about the early progress and success of the module. How would it 'go down' with students? Would it be academically rigorous and of sufficiently high quality to meet the standards set by the rest of the course? Certainly the terms 'quality' and 'rigour' are value-laden and we have surprised ourselves at our own willingness to accept and indeed embrace, on occasions, the terms as defined by the dominant group. Martin (1994) describes the way in which black and white female managers in her study succeeded in transcending the 'taken-for-granted' interpretations of the dominant group by drawing attention to and engaging in discourse with those very interpretations. By focusing on and questioning the partiality of the regime of truth (Foucault, 1980) subscribed to by the dominant group, black and white female managers were able to assert the legitimacy of their own interpretations. One feminist perspective of power in organization emphazises the agency to stand up for alternative values and interpretations (Konek 1994). This is a power 'to' rather than a power 'over' which can be used to reinforce or to change the status quo. Like women managers, we have felt great pressure to conform to the dominant view in our teaching; to beat them at their own game rather than to question the rules. Another response has been to downplay the module and even dismiss it at times within our own portfolio of teaching. We are conscious of the extent to which we manipulate the priority and centrality of the area in relation to our other 'academic' concerns depending on the context. Contextual factors which seem to effect our own willingness to fully 'own' 'women in management' include the audience, the forum and our own current feelings of security and status. It would seem that we constantly feel the need to re-evaluate our relationship with the subject, at times distancing, at times embracing, and experience discomfort at constantly feeling the need to do so.

The existence of a token woman has the effect of encouraging dominant members to exaggerate the differences between the two social types, leading to polarization. Anecdotal evidence from the students suggests that certainly in some years and amongst some of the groups, people who take the option are perceived to be 'unusual'. We are aware in at least one case that pressure was put on an individual to elect something more creditable and she swapped options. Linked to this is the fact that the module tends to be seen as one which is taught *by* women and *for* women. Marshall makes the point that the process of polarization and the process by which dominant members exaggerate difference, rather than moderating the dominant group's culture, actually strengthens it by making the majority more aware of their commonalties. In this way, the perpetuation of the programme in its existing format, with gender marginalized and optional, is ensured. It legitimates the subject being left as a marginal subject. Interestingly enough, and consistent with the idea that the token woman may be under considerably more pressure to identify with the dominant norms, is the suggestion made by other members of the course team that perhaps the time is now ripe to widen the option out to 'managing diversity' or 'gender and management'.

One final point on the issue of marginality. The tone so far suggests that to be marginalized is disadvantageous. In some respects, we have fallen into the trap of approaching this from a male perspective, seeing women as the problem. Several writers have argued for the value of marginality when it is chosen to designate difference or to signify resistance as opposed to being that which is imposed by oppressive structures (hooks, 1990; Feral, 1985; Stenstead, 1988). Konek (1994) suggests that,

> when the analysis becomes woman centred, rather than organization centred . . . the possibility arises that career women may experience empowerment incidentally, relationally, and expressively, as functions of their own self-definition. They may experience empowerment holistically, in ways that transcend career specific or organizationally defined limitations. (Konek, 1994, p. 221)

Linda Martin describes this process of empowerment in the black and white women managers in her study. She points out that empowered women have derived a 'sense of self' from 'consciously constructed positive identities', the outcome of which were more 'innovative, enabling, collaborative and accountable managers' (Martin, 1994, p. 114). Having a different interpretation or perspective can be a positive experience as long as it is expressed and developed.

Curriculum Decisions in Relation to Women in Management and Gender

A detailed consideration of the content of the curriculum on postgraduate business and management programmes is beyond the scope of this chapter. However, what is relevant here is the specific question of the place of gender issues. Foreman and Leeming (1994) in their study of top women managers, found that 81 per cent of their respondents felt that management should contain courses on gender issues for women and men together: women-only courses were not advocated. The issue of what women want is part of the wider question of just how relevant management education is for women. Leeming (1994) suggests that the education providers share some of the responsibility for failing to attract an increasing number of women onto the MBA programmes. She argues that the key issues are not around image, scheduling or fees, but rather more deep-seated factors of management education, such as content and style. She questions whether this will actually change until there are more academics willing and able to directly address the relevance of management education for women.

At a formal level the need for change in management education has been recognized, and, more specifically, concerns about the representation of women on courses and of gender issues on curricula have been identified. The recent higher education charter includes a declaration that higher education providers should outline and take steps to improve numbers of underrepresented groups on appropriate courses. In Australia, a recent industry task force on leadership and management skills identified a need for improvements in university management courses (Smith and Hutchinson, 1994). Of the six core curriculum units they commissioned at MBA level, one was 'Effective Organizations: Gender Issues in Management'. However, Still (1993) argues that in Australia the topic of women in management, despite being an academic research field in its own right, has failed to infiltrate the mainstream. 'As a result, the legacy of the traditional male managerial model has meant that gender issues are rarely acknowledged as a core element in management reading and electives on the topic are usually avoided by men' (Still, 1993, p. 30). She reports that those academics who are willing to confront gender issues in their research frequently face overt and/or covert hostility from peers and students since the topic is rarely seen as a strategic business issue. It is clear that academic institutions have a vital role to play in ensuring that women in management is placed high on their own academic and business agenda. Such support must be seen to come from the very top of institutions if it is to be afforded any credibility at the level of the student. Our experience in this country reflects that described by

Still. Despite some formal attempts at change, the status quo in management education persists.

Central themes in the discussion of the process of arriving at a management curriculum are the questions of what constitutes a valid, discrete topic in management education, which criteria are employed to arrive at that decision and who is involved and how. Clearly there are a number of levels of classification of topics. Here we acknowledge the level of course module (i.e. a set of interconnected sub-topics delivered over a number of sessions, for the duration of a term or more) and the level of module sub-topic which would form the basis for one or two sessions in a module. We also refer to the degree of centrality and student discretion to select (i.e. a topic may be 'core' and an essential requirement of the course or optional/elective). The 'module' classification indicates size and status of topic and could be seen as a way of organizing interrelated topics in a simplified cognitive framework. It also says something about the relative importance attached to the subject by the designers of the programme. In our experience the inclusion of women in management or indeed gender at the level of sub-topic and especially at the level of module is rare. Rarer still is the placing of these topics at the core of management programmes, thereby ensuring that all management students consider the issues they raise. This outcome enables managers and management educators effectively to ignore gender issues if they so choose. Only those who already express a concern for gender issues in relation to management need ever be troubled by such inquiry. Those who are not interested (and therefore, we would argue, who are in most need) may never be exposed to views on the subject contrary to their own.

A clearer understanding of how this state of affairs has developed may emerge if we consider the process via which we currently arrive at a course design consisting of a set of optional and core module topics and sub-topics. What criteria are applied and how has the tradition of management education been established? By a process of induction one could produce a 'rational' model of the criteria for selection of management topics which may include:

- practical relevance to the general population of managers

- potential effect on the 'bottom line' of organizational performance

- reflection of some major functional or project management domain within organization

- contributing to either 'content' issues or 'process' issues

- reflection of academic interest as evidenced via the academic literature.

Most topics could not meet all of these criteria, but all would have to meet some. A typical, and indeed topical, example is the area of organizational strategy. It could be argued that this topic observes both the academic and a number of the more practical criteria outlined in the list above. Strategy is a highly fertile area of academic interest with prestigious journals dedicated to the topic and with an apparent consensus among management students and managers in general of the importance of adopting a strategic approach to the problems of organization. However, it is not associated with a traditional, functional, area of organization (unlike, for instance, marketing or finance). There is also an element of 'fashion' in the selection of topics. For instance, total quality management (TQM), stress and innovation are sub-topics within the broad remit of organization and behaviour, which have all had their moment and may reappear in various 'guises' in curricula and managerial practice. However, despite the changing nature of the priority accorded them, in their heyday there was little debate about their importance and centrality to course design.

So what of women in management? Certainly there is a good deal of literature and recent years have seen the introduction of a number of academic journals dedicated, in some respects at least, to the study of gender issues in the organizational context (e.g. *Gender, Work and Organization*, *Women in Management Review*, *Sex Roles*, and *Gender and Education*). We would also argue that, based on our own experience of teaching it, the topic is an ideal vehicle for the introduction of a more critical approach to management theories and practices. It can facilitate students' critical inquiry into the more traditional topics found elsewhere on the course. It can provide a means of focusing critical thought as well as a link between seemingly unrelated, discrete traditional topics, thereby encouraging students to see relationships and disparities otherwise hidden from them. From a practical perspective, the topic instils an orientation to reflect and question, skills associated with a strategic approach to organizational decision-making. Despite the academic interest evidenced by the publications mentioned above, and the educational and practical strengths outlined here, we are disappointed to have to echo Leonie Still's (1993) concerns based on the Australian system (see above). We can only conclude that the supposedly 'rational' framework proposed here (and indeed any other similarly rational framework) cannot be used to justify the exclusion of women in management from management curricula. It is an inadequate framework for justifying inclusion and exclusion of topics on management programmes.

We argue that one must resort to a more 'irrational' and social model of the process to explain the exclusion. We would also point out that a crucial factor appears to be the support proffered the topic by 'powerful' academics and practitioners. Such support, we argue, is derived not on the basis of explicit, objective criteria, but via a social and cultural process which allocates meaning and priority to management concepts. It allows the most dominant group members to establish a code of understanding which dictates subjective and implicit criteria and effectively ignores all other meanings. A number of authors in the area of strategic decision-making have proposed that the sharing of cognition is central to the decision-making process and that that process is a social one (e.g. Daniels *et al.*, 1994; Dunn and Ginsberg, 1986; Reger and

Huff, 1993; Thomas and Venkatraman, 1988). '[M]anagerial cognitions are influenced by the social and cultural environment of managers' (Daniels *et al.*, 1994, p. S22). They argue that this can result in shared beliefs, assumptions or paradigms within a function, organization or even industry. Similarly, Hutchins (1991) has proposed a model of distributed cognition in which he describes the social processes via which individuals engage to arrive at a shared understanding of problem situations. He explores some of the potential sources of error in such processes and concludes that one of the major problems is the locking out of diversity of view. As individuals struggle to arrive at common views and understandings the process is at once assisted, as simplification and shared views (sometimes referred to as heuristics or stereotypes) facilitate efficient (though not necessarily effective) action, and hindered, as diversity of perspective is increasingly reduced. Hornby and Lewis (1994) have recently attempted to synthesize these writings with the work of Ibarra (1992) and others who are concerned with analysing the social networks of people in organizations, to arrive at a model for understanding the relationship between social networks, management decision-making and gender. They propose that the exclusion of women from the most dominant (and male) coalitions in organizations places a virtually insurmountable cognitive barrier between women in organization and the dominant coalition. This analysis suggests that the process via which shared understanding of what constitutes management education is arrived at and practised may, for the sake of efficiency, undermine alternative interpretations, regardless of their validity. Apart, of course, from the cognitive constraints on the decision-making process one must also consider the power relations involved. When the most senior representatives in the decision process are also members of the most closely linked network and form a homogeneous gender grouping, then the decision outcomes produced are likely to be subject to very little alternative scrutiny. Challenging such decisions is likely to prove difficult and dangerous. We are concerned that the formulation of management curricula falls into the category of decision process and outcome described here.

Although there is always the possibility that a less powerful group will be allowed to inform the decision-making process in specific instances (e.g. to address criticism of the course made by an enlightened stakeholder group), unless the dominant cognition is properly challenged, what is likely to occur is a very partial and temporary recognition of a marginal view. We may draw an analogy with Piagetian concepts in the area of children's cognitive development. From this perspective children move from assimilation, in which new concepts and knowledge are simply 'tagged on' to their current schemas for understanding the world. Errors in children's performance may still occur as they operate outdated schemata. However, the contradiction becomes clearer to the child in relation to the assimilated knowledge. Eventually children will move to accommodation in which the new knowledge is fully integrated with their perceptual schema and is allowed to affect their understanding, such that they are prepared to redefine the perceptual schema they currently operate

(Piaget, 1952). A real change in the traditional approach to management education, allowing gender issues to inform all other aspects of the area rather than simply be bolted on, can only occur when the dominant perspective recognizes the contradiction between itself and feminist perspectives and moves to accommodate them, bringing about a transformation of the 'traditional' approach. The real issue for women in management is how we move from assimilation to accommodation: an accommodation which leads to a redefinition of the current, dominant and traditional view of management education and *not* simply a distortion of the alternative to enable it to live alongside the traditional without changing it.

Conclusion

We have argued that the position of the topic of women in management as it relates to traditional management course curricula is analogous to that of women managers in organizations. Both are subject to marginalization and tokenism. We propose that the process via which decision-makers arrive at shared cognitions and the power relations in the decision process serve to thwart attempts to move gender considerations to a more central position on management course curricula. For women in management to become a core subject would necessitate a fundamental change in the nature of management education. As long as it refuses to allow women in management to inform it and change it the topic is confined to a 'bolt-on' status at the periphery of the curriculum.

The story so far may sound rather depressing. We believe, however, that our analysis contains its own way forward. By examining some of the ideas associated with women's strategies for survival in management one is able to identify some means of progressing the topic of women in management. Deborah Sheppard has identified two broad coping strategies used by female managers for dealing with the 'profound ambivalence' they encounter in feeling at once successful and accomplished at having 'arrived in a world of male status and power' and at the same time uncomfortable and cautious about the prospect of having to constantly 'perform', of not having arrived because of one's own ability and of not having a safety net in case of adversity (Sheppard, 1989). 'Blending in' is a strategy characterized as conforming to the prevailing expectations of male co-workers. By blending in the female manager is, in our terms, coping with her 'assimilated' status. The second strategy identified by Sheppard is referred to as 'taking a rightful place'. In taking a rightful place, the female manager accepts organizational goals 'but with an articulated critique of the male dominance'. Here it could be argued that the female manager is making moves to be properly accommodated in the mainstream management role (i.e. forcing change in the nature of the role in general via an articulated critique). Of course, some women elect to fulfil their career goals outside the mainstream and could be said to have adopted a third strategy; perhaps 'taking a different place' would be a good way of character-izing it.

With respect to the topic of women in management we suggest that for full accommodation to occur a strategy akin to 'taking a rightful place' must be adopted. In particular, we are advocating the need for articulated critique. The relationship between women in management and the topic is a complex one. Like the proverbial chicken and egg it is hard to see which comes first, change in management practice or change in management education. However, the analysis we offer places a great deal of responsibility on educators. As part of the remit of education *is* critique, it follows that management educators *should* be critiquing as a matter of duty. Similarly, research in the area of women in management must be able and willing to critique the mainstream academic management literature. As teachers and researchers we must confess to disap-pointment with regard to some of the literature in the area of women in management. Here we would concur with Martin (1994) that the notions of 'women's management style' and 'male organizational culture' as they are discussed in essentialist theories of gender and organization are limited with regard to their usefulness in considering agency and change in organization. They can lead women only to assimilation or exclusion (i.e. taking a different place). Indeed their failure to properly critique the mainstream means that the research itself either runs parallel to mainstream ideas neither affecting or being affected, or becomes so much a part of the mainstream that no alterna-tive analysis is offered at all. Women are characterized as either being differ-ent or the same. On the basis of the analysis presented here, it is clear that, as management educators with a concern for gender issues in organization and management, we must be prepared to engage critically with mainstream views. If we want the topic to be central and core, then we must articulate its role with respect to mainstream views of management education. We have to provide a critique that will render the need for change in the mainstream irresistible.

Note

1 Kanter argues that group dynamics and processes are influenced by (amongst other things) the gender composition of the group. Her model identifies four potential group types according to the relative number or proportion of one gender to another: uniform, balanced, tilted and skewed. A skewed group has a preponderance of one gender over the other with the latter being designated 'tokens' (Kanter, 1977).

References

DANIELS, K., JOHNSON, J. and DE CHERNATONY, L. (1994) 'Differences in Mana-gerial Cognitions of Competition', *British Journal of Management*, 5, S21–S29.

DAVIDSON, M. J. and BURKE, R. J. (1994) *Women in Management: Current Research Issues* London, Paul Chapman Publishing.

DUNN, W. N. and GINSBERG, A. (1986) 'A Sociocognitive Network Approach to Organizational Analysis', *Human Relations*, 40, 11, pp. 955–76.

FERAL, J. (1985) 'The Powers of Difference', in EISENSTEIN, H. and JARDINE, A. *The Future of Difference*, New Brunswick, Rutgers University Press, pp. 88–94.

FOREMAN, E. K. and LEEMING, A. M. C. (1984) 'Women Managers' Perspectives on the Quality and Accessibility of Management Education in Business Schools, *BAM 1994 Annual Conference Proceedings*, BAM.

FOUCAULT, M. (1980) *Power/Knowledge: Selected Interviews and other Writings*, trans. C. Gordon, Brighton, Harvester.

HANDLEY, J. (1994) 'Women, Decision Making and Academia: An Unholy Alliance', *Women in Management Review*, 9, 3, pp. 11–16.

HEARN, J. and PARKIN, P. W. (1988) 'Women, Men and Leadership: A Critical Review of Assumptions, Practices, and Change in the Industrialised Nations', in ALDER, N. J. and ISRAELI, D. N. (Eds) *Women in Management World-Wide*, New York, Sharpe, pp. 17–40.

HOOKS, B. (1990) *Yearning: Race, Gender and Cultural Politics*, Boston, South End.

HORNBY, P. and LEWIS, S. (1994) 'Gender, Social Networking and Management Decision Making', *BAM 1994 Annual Conference Proceedings*, BAM.

HUTCHINS, E. (1991) 'The Social Organization of Distributed Cognition', in RESNICK, L. B., LEVINE, J. M. and TEASLEY, S. D. (Eds) *Perspectives on Socially Shared Cognition*, American Psychological Association, pp. 238–307.

IBARRA, H. (1993) 'Personal Networks of Women & Minorities in Management: A Conceptual Framework', *Academy of Management Review*, 18: 56–87.

KANTER, R. M. (1977) *Men and Women of the Corporation*, New York, Basic Books.

KONEK, C. W. (1994) 'Leadership or Empowerment? Reframing Our Questions', in KONEK, C. W. and KITCH, S. L. (Eds) *Women and Careers: Issues and Challenge*, London, Sage, pp. 206–33.

LEEMING, A. (1994) 'Climbing Up the Ladder, Women Developing Management Education', paper presented at BAM.

MARSHALL, J. (1984) *Women Managers: Travellers in a Male World*, Chichester, John Wiley.

MARSHALL, J. (1995a) *Women Managers Moving On: Exploring Career and Life Choices*, London, Routledge.

MARSHALL, J. (1995b) 'Gender and Management: A Critical Review of Research', *British Journal of Management*, 6 (December), pp. 553–62.

MARTIN, L. (1994) 'Power, Continuity and Change: Decoding Black and White Women Managers' Experience in Local Government', in TANTON, M.

(Ed.) *Women in Management: A Developing Presence*, London, Routledge, pp. 110–40.

PIAGET, J. (1952) *The Origins of Intelligence in Children*, New York, International University Press.

REGER, R. K. and HUFF, A. S. (1993) 'Strategic Groups: A Cognitive Perspective', *Strategic Management Journal*, 14, pp. 103–24.

SCHEIN, V. E. (1973) 'The Relationship between Sex Role Stereotypes and Requisite Management Characteristics', *Journal of Applied Psychology*, 57, 2, pp. 95–100.

SCHEIN, V. E. (1975) 'The Relationship between Sex Role Stereotypes and Requisite Management Characteristics among Female Managers', *Journal of Applied Psychology*, 60, 3, pp. 340–4.

SCHEIN, V. E. (1994) 'Managerial Sex Typing: A Persistent and Persuasive Barrier to Women's Opportunities', in DAVIDSON, M. J. and BURKE, R. J. (Eds) *Women in Management: Current Research Issues*, London, Paul Chapman, pp. 41–52.

SHEPPARD, D. L. (1989) 'Organizations and Power: Sexuality: The Image and Self-Image of Women Managers', in HEARN, J., SHEPPARD, D. and TANCRED-SHERIFF, P. (Eds) *The Sexuality of Organization*, London, Sage, pp. 139–57.

SMITH, C. and HUTCHINSON, J. (1994) 'Addressing Gender Issues in Management Education: An Australian Initiative', *Women in Management Review*, 9, 7, pp. 29–33.

STENSTEAD, G. (1988) 'Anarchic Thinking', *Hypatia*, 3, 2, pp. 87–100.

STILL, L. V. (1993) *Women in Management: The Forgotten Theory in Practice, or How Not to Change a Future*, Women in Management Series, Paper No. 18, School of Business, University of Western Sydney, Nepean, New South Wales.

THOMAS, H. and VENKATRAMAN, N. (1988) 'Research on Strategic Groups: Progress and Prognosis', *Journal of Management Studies*, 25, pp. 537–55.

Chapter 7

Struggling for Inclusion: Black Women in Professional and Management Education

Catharine Ross

It is often argued that black women[1] experience a 'dual disadvantage' in relation to education as a result of their position as women in a sexist, male-dominated society and as black people in a racist, white-dominated society (Taylor, 1993, p. 438; Benokraitis and Feagin, 1986, p. 127). This chapter seeks to explore the disadvantaging faced by black women in seeking inclusion in professional and management education, and the strategies which they have adopted to overcome it.[2]

Most people follow professional and management education in order to further their careers in those occupational areas, and this chapter therefore starts by examining the participation of black women in professions and management, and the relationship between inclusion in professional and management education and participation in those occupations. The 1991 Population Census (Office of Population Censuses and Surveys, 1993) reveals the cumulative effects of gender and racio-ethnic origin on participation in professions and management (cf. Cox, 1990, p. 6). While racio-ethnic origin has a clear effect upon the proportions of working people in professional occupations – for example both Indian men and women are more likely to be employed in professional occupations than men and women from any other groups, and African-Caribbean men and women less likely – the proportion of working women in professional work is consistently lower than that of men from the same ethnic group (Office of Population Censuses and Surveys, 1993). Thus 4.5 per cent of Indian women are working as professionals compared with 12.4 per cent of Indian men; 3.6 per cent of Pakistani women compared with 6.6 per cent of Pakistani men; 1.9 per cent of white women compared with 7.1 per cent of white men, and 1.6 per cent of African-Caribbean women compared with 4.7 per cent of African-Caribbean men. It is also noticeable that the proportion of Indian working women who are professionals (the highest proportion for women) is still smaller than that of African-Caribbean working men (the lowest proportion for men). In management occupations, too, women are consistently underrepresented by comparison with men from the same racio-ethnic group. However, this time Indian, Pakistani and African-Caribbean women and men are all underrepresented by comparison with white people of the same gender.

Human capital theorists such as Becker (1975) have argued that education is a crucial determinant of occupational status, differential position in the labour market and differences in income being related to investment in education. Neo-Weberian theorists such as Johnson (1972), Collins (1975), Murphy (1984), Crompton (1987) and Witz (1992) also highlight the importance of educational credentials in effecting social closure and exclusion. However, as Collins argues, that education is not neutral but favours the inclusion of a particular group, that group 'setting up job requirements in its own favour and discriminating against those who do not use its vocabulary' (Collins, 1975, p. 87), while Murphy (1984) argues that 'the market dominated by property classes determines the necessity, value, and nature of the credentials required for positions and in that way structures the very nature of credential groups' (Murphy, 1984, p. 551).

Certainly, entry to many professions is controlled – at least overtly – through the requirement that members possess professional qualifications (Crompton, 1987). According to neo-Weberian approaches to the study of the professions, a profession is not an occupation with particular characteristics, as earlier theorists had argued (see for example Carr-Saunders and Wilson, 1964; Millerson, 1964), but 'a means of controlling an occupation' (Johnson, 1972, p. 45), and credentialization assists this process by limiting access to those who have pursued the professional body's educational programme. Excluding people from professional education, therefore, is one way of excluding them from the profession itself. Witz (1988) describes how, although the 1958 Medical Act did not explicitly exclude women, its requirement that doctors possess a university medical degree or membership of one of the medical corporations resulted in women's exclusion, because women were not admitted to the necessary medical courses. Aspiring female doctors therefore adopted 'an equal rights tactic of credentialism' (Witz, 1988, p. 79), trying to gain access to the professional courses and qualifications in order to gain entry to the profession itself.

The linkage between management education and attainment of managerial status is less clear than that between professional education and professional status. Managerial qualifications are rarely considered essential for recruitment to an organization, although they may be important in allocating promotions. A 1987 report on management education stated that most new managers-to-be would receive no formal training in management, and one-third would still have received no training by the time they were in mid-career (National Economic Development Office *et al.*, 1987). The 1992 Labour Force Survey indicated that only 24.7 per cent of managers and administrators had had any form of higher education; 15.3 per cent had no qualifications of any kind (Employment Department, 1992). Exclusion from or inclusion in management is therefore at the discretion of existing managers, who may or may not choose to use management credentials as the basis for that inclusion.

The distinction between professions and management, however, is not clear-cut. The recent growth of managerialism in many areas of professional activity has resulted in the increasing incorporation of traditionally independent professions, such as the medical profession, into management activities and culture (Harrison and Pollitt, 1994). Moreover, many professions, such as the personnel profession, discussed below, have always operated within other employing organizations, and have never been independent of the management of those organizations. Access to such organizational professions, Crompton (1987) argues, is therefore not only dependent upon the possession of professional credentials but also upon the culture and rules of the employing organization. A woman with professional qualifications may therefore find herself appointed at a lower level than a man, even though they have the same qualifications (*ibid.*).

In fact, professional qualifications are often not necessary for entry to junior positions in many organizational professions, and as a result many people only start to study for them part-time *after* they have obtained their first post. This enables their managers to influence who will possess the professional qualification by awarding and refusing support for part-time education. Greed (1991) reveals that many surveyors are sent to study for further qualifications after, rather than before, they are appointed to professional positions (Greed, 1991, p. 31), indicating that credentialization may be being used to legitimate past appointments, rather than to determine new ones, and Collinson *et al.* (1990) argue that one reason why women are underrepresented in senior positions in the insurance industry is that they are less likely than men to be sent on the in-house training and external professional courses necessary for promotion.

Brown (1992) argues that this absence of clearly defined entry criteria in the form of credentials increases the potential for discrimination, and that this is why the proportion of black people has not grown as strongly in management as in professional occupations (the data Brown draws upon, and also the census data cited above, categorize most organizational professions as management occupations). Although there is evidence that senior members of professions which do have profession-wide entry credentials are still able to discriminate against women and ethnic minority staff (see for example King *et al.*, 1990, a study of solicitors), Brown argues that it is still easier for ethnic minorities to gain inclusion in these professions because access to them is *more* dependent upon individual study and achievement of qualifications than access to other occupations. This might partly explain the higher proportion of Indian and Pakistani women than white women in professional posts and the lower proportion in management positions, outlined above.

Black women, it is therefore suggested, may find it more difficult to gain inclusion in organizational professions and management than in more independent professions because individual managers in the former have greater control over access to posts, both directly, by determining recruitment criteria, and indirectly, by controlling access to valuable education. The following section explores this further, focusing on the example of professional personnel management education and examining the different forms of exclusion perceived by black women, and the ways in which they have fought them.

Exclusion from Professional Personnel Management Education

The personnel management profession is interesting in this context for two reasons. In the first place, it is an organizational profession, operating within other employing organizations and largely subject to their cultures and rules. Although it has a professional association and process of credentialization, the association's own careers literature makes clear that no particular qualifications are necessary to embark on a career in personnel (Institute of Personnel Management, 1993). Armstrong finds that hierarchies within personnel management in industry are 'unrelated to the formal hierarchy of the profession' (Armstrong, 1984, p. 113), and Watson (1977) argues that the most important point of reference for individual personnel practitioners is not the professional association, but the management of the employing organization.

Although there are some full-time programmes leading to professional status, the majority of personnel students study on a part-time basis (Institute of Personnel Management, 1994) and interviews with lecturers as part of this research indicate that most of these part-time programmes are targeted at people already employed in personnel.[3] Initial access to professional personnel education is therefore controlled to a large degree by the student's manager, and to a lesser degree by educational establishments or the professional association itself. The manager also determines at which levels in his or her department, if any, professional qualifications are necessary. Although professional qualifications are not usually necessary for entry to junior personnel positions, managers are becoming increasingly dependent upon them as a way of controlling access to more senior posts (Long, 1984). In order to attain a senior personnel post, therefore, it is usually necessary to have been appointed to a more junior post in a personnel department, and then sent on the professional education scheme – access to both being controlled predominantly by individual managers.

The second aspect of personnel management which makes it interesting in this context is the fact that it is a predominantly female profession. Data for 1994 from the Institute of Personnel Management – one of two professional associations which merged in July 1994 to form the Institute of Personnel and Development – indicated that 63.2 per cent of Institute of Personnel Management members were women, and monitoring of the Institute of Personnel Management's part-time education indicated that 80 per cent of those starting the education programme in 1993 were women (Institute of Personnel Management, 1994). The explanation for this overrepresentation has been traced back to the occupation's origins in industrial welfare work, which was regarded as women's work (Niven, 1967).

Black women, however, are underrepresented in the professional body. The 1993 statistics for the Institute of Personnel Management indicate that only 1.9 per cent of women members were of African-Caribbean origins, and 1.2 per cent of Asian origin. Although figures for the representation of black women on Institute of Personnel Management courses are not available, only 2 per cent of men and women offered places on the courses were of non-European origin (this figure must be treated with caution, due to a low response rate) (Institute of Personnel Management, 1994). Possible reasons for the underrepresentation of black women on these predominantly female courses are explored below.

Research Methodology

In order to identify the barriers perceived by black personnel practitioners, a detailed questionnaire survey of black personnel practitioners was conducted in late 1993 and early 1994. Given the small number of black personnel practitioners, a purposive sampling technique was used to ensure that the personnel practitioners surveyed met the requirements of the survey in terms of racio-ethnic background and industry.[4] In total, forty-one black personnel practitioners were surveyed. Around three-quarters of respondents were female. Of these, almost two-thirds (61.3 per cent) were of African-Caribbean origin; 25.8 per cent of Indian origin; 6.5 per cent of Pakistani origin, and 6.4 per cent of other origins. There were no responses from women of Bangladeshi origin.

The small sample size means that these experiences cannot be taken to be representative of all black female personnel practitioners, but are rather indicators of the range of experiences which black women perceive, the interpretations which they put on them, and how they respond to them. Additionally, it must be noted that the survey is to some degree a survey of the 'winners', as all those surveyed have obtained access to personnel work, and so are some way towards achieving inclusion in their chosen profession.

Research Findings

The questionnaire has identified several barriers which black women perceive as contributing to their exclusion from part-time personnel education. As almost all part-time personnel students are already employed in personnel (see above), underrepresentation in personnel posts was one of the most frequently cited barriers. Some respondents argued that this underrepresentation was partly due to black people's lack of interest in or awareness of personnel work. However, a greater proportion cited discrimination by employers as contributing to the low proportion of black women in personnel work and hence on professional courses. 'Ethnic minorities are underrepresented in most professional areas of work', one black woman commented; 'There are a number of factors including discrimination during recruitment and selection for jobs and training'. Another black woman reported being asked in interview: 'How are you going to get on with white managers? How are you going to get on with white male managers?'. Others reported experiences such as: 'In three instances it was obvious from the secretary's face when she/they directed me from reception that they did not realize I was black. The interviews consequently were short or not informative enough'; 'I felt that I had been discriminated against [in] a post which I had applied for. By far I was the best qualified, most experienced, and had special knowledge. In the end a white person got it – as usual,' and 'At interviews, [I] received clear indication of who they were looking for – preferably white male'.

Another barrier perceived by some was lack of managerial support – both in terms of finance and time – to undertake part-time education. Although some of the black women had funded themselves, the cost was felt to exclude many who are not yet employed in personnel, or not sponsored by their employers. One respondent thus felt that the Institute of Personnel Management (as it was then) should 'provide sponsorship for IPM studies for those who cannot get employer assistance or first job in HR [Human Resources]'. The day release required by many courses was perceived to present additional barriers for students not supported by their manager.

Some black women felt that their employers were reluctant to send them on the professional education scheme, even though they were working in personnel positions. One black woman of Pakistani origin argued that 'I have had to put myself forward for any training. Further education has not been available'. Another woman of African-Caribbean origin reported that when she initially asked to be sent on the professional education scheme she was turned down, and was finally sent when a male colleague (of Pakistani origin) finished the course he was on at the time and also asked to go on the professional education scheme: 'They refused me the first time, which I was aggrieved about, because when – finished his [course] . . . he wanted to do the IPM . . . so they couldn't let him go and not let me go'. These women, however, were in the minority. Most of the respondents felt that exclusion from personnel jobs was the greatest barrier to their inclusion in professional education, and found that once they had obtained personnel positions they were able to gain entry to education with little difficulty. Indeed, one black woman felt that her ethnic origin had helped her to gain access to education programmes, pointing to 'efforts made by senior management to provide opportunities to me as a black manager to train'.

Not all of the perceived exclusion was operated by employers, however. Some respondents perceived that they had been excluded from appropriate taught courses by the professional body's entry requirements. (Clearly, the aim of entry requirements is precisely to exclude people judged by the profession to be inappropriate for the course. The issue here is therefore whether the entry requirements exclude black women who would otherwise be appropriate.) Students who do not have the academic qualifications or length of management experience required for entry to the professional education scheme have to first undertake a certificate programme – an additional year's training. One black woman (of African-Caribbean origin) who had considerable experience in equal opportunities work, but no qualifications beyond 'O' levels, thus found that she 'had to present strong arguments to get onto course [*sic*]. Informed all other students had some years of experience in management and personnel. I was directed towards the Certificate in Personnel Practice.' National Vocational Qualifications in personnel, not available at the time of the research, might help to reduce this form of exclusion.

However, exclusion from participation in the courses was not the only exclusion perceived. Some of the black women surveyed felt that their exclusion continued after enrolment, because the curriculum did not reflect their experiences or values, or because other course members excluded them from discussions and activities.[5] Some felt isolated because they were the only black person in their class; one black woman, who had successfully completed the professional education scheme, had nonetheless 'never attended any local IPM branches, as I feel I wouldn't fit in'. Another was concerned at the attitudes of her fellow students and lecturers towards equal opportunities, finding that they were mainly concerned with the minimum legal requirements, and how those could be avoided.

Struggles for Inclusion

Many of the black women surveyed perceived that they had had to struggle to overcome exclusion, by applying continually for personnel posts; fighting to have entry requirements to professional education waived; paying for personnel management education themselves; doing the course in their own time (perhaps making use of flexi-time arrangements); pressuring employers to send them onto the programme; and becoming involved in the development of curricula. These are strategies of 'inclusionary usurpation', to use Murphy's (1984) classification, in which the women struggled to gain inclusion to professional education, and hence to the profession, on its terms and on an individual basis, rather than by changing the profession ('revolutionary usurpation'). The structures which excluded them therefore continue to exclude other black women.

The continued existence of exclusionary structures, however, should not be taken as evidence that the black women's inclusionary strategies are inadequate. The success of the strategies must be measured against the aims which they were designed to fulfil, and there is no indication that any of the black women surveyed had aimed to radically 'open up' professional education to outsiders; rather, they had aimed to become one of the exclusive group of those on professional courses themselves, and in this they had often been successful. (It must be remembered that the survey included only those

women who had obtained personnel posts, and therefore had already overcome one of the major barriers to inclusion in personnel education.)

The aim against which the success of the black women's strategies *should*
be measured, however, is that of achieving inclusion in more senior personnel
posts. As argued at the start of this chapter, most people follow part-time
professional and management education in order to further their careers, and
the black women personnel professionals surveyed were no different. 'Wanted
the professional qualification to help further my career'; 'Wanted to operate at
a professional level'; and to 'increase my employment marketability', were
some of the reasons the black women gave for undertaking professional personnel management education.

The research indicated, however, that this goal was not always met. Several of the black women had found that personnel education did not further
their careers as they had hoped. One reported that:

> Before I got married and was trying to obtain a post as a person-
> nel officer (to progress from secretary), out of eighty applications I
> received one or two interviews. After marrying, it was not obvious
> what my ethnic origin was, but, whilst I got more interviews, some
> recruiters focused on my not having a degree rather than my experi-
> ence and IPM qualifications.

Another commented that: 'I have my IPM qualifications, yet do not feel
that they are taken into consideration when I apply for posts'. On one occasion
she had been passed over for promotion in favour of a white, junior colleague
– in spite of the fact that she was professionally qualified and the junior
colleague was not. The white colleague was then sponsored to take the professional qualification, reflecting Greed's argument that qualifications may be
used to legitimize positions that have already been achieved (Greed, 1991, p.
31). Like the female surveyors in Greed's study, the black women felt that
'every time they work out and achieve what is required in terms of qualifications or experience, the men move the goal posts and change the rules' (*ibid.*).

A possible explanation for this, and the explanation put forward by
Greed, is that while educational criteria are ostensibly used to exclude those
who do not have the required knowledge, their more important function is to
exclude those who do not 'fit' into the subculture of the profession or occupation. Thus even if black women achieve inclusion in personnel education, they
may be unable to translate that into promotions in the workplace because they
remain different, or are perceived to be different, from that subculture. This
suggests another reason why non-organizational professions, with their profession-wide entry criteria, may be easier for black people to access than organizational professions or management (see discussion of Brown, 1992, above).
Johnson (1972) argues that the single educational routes into the former serve
to socialize entrants into the subculture of the profession, ensuring that they
do 'fit', and it is possible that this reduces the need for further exclusionary

mechanisms. In organizational professions and management, by contrast, the potential for such socialization is limited by multiple entry routes and the part-time format of much of the education, and thus a higher proportion of applicants may not conform.

Achieving inclusion in professional personnel education, therefore, does not necessarily lead to the career progression for which the black women aimed – it merely means that their rejection can no longer be justified on the grounds of their lack of professional qualification. In this organizational profession, professional membership is just one of many criteria which managers may draw upon to select candidates. Long's 1984 survey of personnel workers found that personnel management lacked a 'defined career structure', and had 'a hidden structure of requirements' for career success (Long, 1984, p. 142), and this ambiguity makes it relatively simple for managers to justify the rejection of black women applicants. Sending black women onto professional education schemes may satisfy managers' desire to appear committed to equal opportunities, without actually committing them to any changes in the ethnic and gender composition of senior personnel positions.

Indeed, it is worth noting that while white women comprise the vast majority of professional students and have little difficulty in gaining access to the first few levels of the profession, even they are underrepresented in the top levels. In 1993 only 15 per cent of Companions of the Institute of Personnel Management (the top level in the profession, awarded by invitation only) were women. Moreover, black women's perception that routes into personnel management allow more scope for discrimination than those into some other professions may discourage them from seeking inclusion in personnel work in the first place. As one black personnel manager argued, 'Black people have to be more careful in choosing a career. . . . Personnel is probably perceived to be too vague and therefore too risky'.

Conclusion

The black female personnel staff surveyed perceived that the greatest barriers to inclusion in professional personnel education operated at the level of the employer, and only to a lesser degree at the levels of the professional body and educational establishments.[6] The findings thus support Brown's (1992) argument that black people may be more likely to gain inclusion in those professions to which access is controlled in the first instance by educational establishments, than to posts which rely more upon the support and sponsorship of existing managers, not only because of greater discrimination in the latter, but also the reduced opportunities for socialization, and black people's own assessments of the risk of discrimination.

Managers' control over recruitment and promotion, and their power to impose or waive educational requirements, questions the effectiveness of inclusion in professional and management education as a strategy for inclusion in senior managerial and organizational professional positions. Such a strategy assumes that closure from these positions is based upon educational credentials, which, following Murphy (1984), this chapter suggests is only partially the case. Rather, it suggests that educational credentials are just one of several criteria which can be used to justify the exclusion from senior positions of those who are perceived not to 'fit'. Black women who struggle to gain inclusion in such professional and management education may therefore find that they are still excluded from senior positions because of their double disadvantage: they are women, and they are black.

Notes

1 Throughout the paper, the term 'black' is used to refer to people of South Asian, African and Caribbean racio-ethnic origins (see Cox, 1990, p. 6), who are identifiably different from the ethnic majority (Dadzie, 1993, p. x). The use of this single term is not intended to imply that 'black' people form a homogeneous group, but rather to recognize their shared experience of racism. Additionally, it is acknowledged that not all people who are included in this definition of 'black' would define themselves as black.

2 The chapter is therefore predominantly concerned with external factors affecting inclusion in education (cf. Taylor, 1993) – such as different opportunities and discrimination – rather than internal factors such as level of motivation and career aspirations. However, as will become apparent later in the chapter, the distinction between the two is not always clear-cut: aspirations may be influenced by earlier differential treatment (cf. Mirza, 1992; Taylor, 1993) or by perceptions of probable discrimination.

3 The merger of the Institute of Personnel Management with the Institute of Training and Development in July 1994 (forming the Institute of Personnel and Development), and the ongoing development of National Vocational Qualifications, have increased the range of routes into the professional personnel association since the research described below was undertaken. However, if anything, National Vocational Qualifications are likely to be even more limited to existing personnel staff than the taught educational programmes.

4 The sample was drawn from two sources. In the first place, twenty-seven existing contacts were approached directly. In total, nineteen responses were received from this sample. In order to generate responses from a wider range of personnel staff, and to ascertain whether responses from existing contacts were systematically biased, a semi-structured sample of fifty private companies, local authorities and health authorities in areas with relatively high proportions of black people in the local population was contacted. Personnel managers in these organizations were asked to circulate copies of the questionnaire to black staff within their personnel departments. Twenty-two responses were received from eleven organizations through this

means. Many of the organizations were unable to assist with the survey because there were no black personnel practitioners in the organization.

5 Benokraitis and Feagin note that 'when they move into educational settings, minority women face some real barriers to the achievement of their aspirations' (1986, p. 127) and cite research by Kendall and Feagin (1983) which reveals the expectation that female ethnic minority medical students should adapt to white, male norms.

6 It must be noted that the research was conducted at a time when part-time students were in demand from educational establishments.

References

ARMSTRONG, P. (1984) 'Competition between the Organizational Professions and the Evolution of Management Control Strategies', in THOMPSON, K. (Ed.) *Work, Employment and Unemployment*, Milton Keynes, Open University Press, pp. 97–120.

BECKER, G. (1975) *Human Capital – A Theoretical and Empirical Analysis with Special Reference to Education*, New York, National Bureau of Economic Research.

BENOKRAITIS, N. and FEAGIN, J. (1986) *Modern Sexism: Blatant, Subtle and Covert Discrimination*, Englewood Cliffs, Prentice-Hall.

BROWN, C. (1992) ' "Same Difference" ': The Persistence of Racial Disadvantage in the British Employment Market', in BRAHAM, P., RATTANSI, A. and SKELLINGTON, R. (Eds) *Racism and Antiracism – Inequalities, Opportunities and Policies*, London, Sage, pp. 46–63.

CARR-SAUNDERS, A. and WILSON, P. (1964) *The Professions*, London, Oxford University Press (first published by Frank Cass, 1933).

COLLINS, R. (1975) *Conflict Sociology: Towards an Explanatory Science*, New York, Academic.

COLLINSON, D., KNIGHTS, D. and COLLINSON, M. (1990) *Managing to Discriminate*, London, Routledge.

COX, T. (1990) 'Problems with Research by Organizational Scholars on Issues of Race and Ethnicity', *Journal of Applied Behavioral Science*, 26, pp. 5–23.

CROMPTON, R. (1987) 'Gender, Status and Professionalism', *Sociology*, 21, pp. 413–28.

DADZIE, S. (1993) *Working with Black Adult Learners*, National Institute of Adult Continuing Education.

EMPLOYMENT DEPARTMENT (1992) *Labour Force Survey, Spring 1992*, London, Employment Department.

GREED, C. (1991) *Surveying Sisters – Women in a Traditional Male Profession*, London, Routledge.

HARRISON, S. and POLLITT, C. (1994) *Controlling Health Professionals*, Buckingham, Open University Press.

INSTITUTE OF PERSONNEL MANAGEMENT (1993) *Careers in Personnel Management*, London, Institute of Personnel Management.

INSTITUTE OF PERSONNEL MANAGEMENT (1994) *Membership and Education Survey*, London, Institute of Personnel Management.

JOHNSON, T. (1972) *Professions and Power*, London, Macmillan.

KENDALL, D. and FEAGIN, J. (1983) 'Blatant and subtle patterns of discrimination: Minority women in medical schools', *Journal of Intergroup Relations*, 9, pp. 21–2.

KING, M., ISRAEL, M. and GOULBOURNE, S. (1990) *Ethnic Minorities and Recruitment to the Solicitors' Profession*, London, Law Society.

LONG, P. (1984) *The Personnel Professionals – A Comparative Study of Male and Female Careers*, unpublished paper, Institute of Personnel Management.

MILLERSON, G. (1964) *The Qualifying Associations*, London, Routledge and Kegan Paul.

MIRZA, H. S. (1992) *Young, Female and Black*, London, Routledge.

MURPHY, R. (1984) 'The Structure of Closure: A Critique and Development of the Theories of Weber, Collins and Parkin', *The British Journal of Sociology*, 35, pp. 547–67.

NATIONAL ECONOMIC DEVELOPMENT OFFICE, MANPOWER SERVICES COMMISSION, NATIONAL DEVELOPMENT COUNCIL and BRITISH INSTITUTE OF MANAGEMENT (1987) *The Making of Managers – A Report on Management Education, Training and Development in the USA, West Germany, France, Japan and the UK*, London, National Economic Development Office.

NIVEN, M. (1967) *Personnel Management 1913–1963*, London, Institute of Personnel Management.

OFFICE OF POPULATION CENSUSES AND SURVEYS (1993) *1991 Census – Ethnic Group and Country of Birth, Great Britain, Vol. 2*, London, HMSO.

TAYLOR, P. (1993) 'Minority Ethnic Groups and Gender in Access to Higher Education', *New Community*, 19, pp. 425–40.

WATSON, T. (1977) *The Personnel Managers*, London, Routledge and Kegan Paul.

WITZ, A. (1988) 'Patriarchal Relations and Patterns of Sex Segregation in the Medical Division of Labour', in WALBY, S. (Ed.) *Gender Segregation at Work*, Milton Keynes, Open University Press, pp. 74–90.

WITZ, A. (1992) *Professions and Patriarchy*, London, Routledge.

Chapter 8

Equal Opportunities and Higher Education

Maggie Humm

British universities have been under a great deal of public scrutiny during the last decades. Issues of status and access, combined with funding crises of various kinds, have made dramatic changes both to educational culture and quality. There has been, predictably, little scrutiny of the culture or quality of equal opportunities in higher education. For example, the last Commission for Racial Equality (CRE) report on policy, *Words or Deeds?: A Review of Equal Opportunity Policies in Higher Education*, concluded 'that a tone of moral superiority or complacency plus ignorance of the issues was pervasive' (Williams *et al.*, 1989, p. 24). Nor has there been very much recognition of the special contributions made by women staff, academic and non-academic, since the literature on women in higher education is sparse (Humm, 1991).

If the unequal power relations which clearly underpin all academic practices have not been systematically addressed in gender terms, they are currently the focus of attention by government bodies. There is a high level of institutional interest in a large-scale reorganization of education, signalled by the redesignation of the former polytechnics as (new) universities. Just as school-teaching practices are constantly being challenged by National Curriculum changes on the basis of social productivity, that is, of matching curricula to perceived personnel changes, so, too, university autonomy is a target of assault on the basis of more accurately identifying 'customers and satisfying their needs' (CVCP, 1993, p. 5).

A key player in higher education policy-making is the Committee of Vice Chancellors and Principals of the Universities of the United Kingdom (CVCP), which since 1992 has represented both old and new universities. Currently, the CVCP is involved in extensive educational policy research and this has resulted in the production of a 'blueprint' strategy, *Promoting People*, which expresses the kind of 'core management tasks of universities' needed to revolutionize university organization by the millennium, specifically by reorganizing academic pay and conditions.

In Britain, academic salaries are negotiated nationally (with local differences) in scales appropriate to each different grade (lecturer, senior lecturer, professor etc.) with (small) annual increments. However, unlike America and some European countries, promotion between grades is *not* measured by universal peer standards, but frequently occurs in internal competition in which academics compete against each other for an ever decreasing number of promotions. Not surprisingly, men dominate full-time academic posts, both in number – men are 78 per cent of full-time academics – and in status – women are 73.9 per cent of lecturers and only 5 per cent of professors (Universities Funding Council, 1993).

Promoting People examines this problem of educational stasis and status in British higher education, not in gender terms, but by considering the relationship between overall staffing practices, pay differentials and organizational change. Part of a broad movement called Total Quality Management, *Promoting People* is a fundamentally more radical proposal than others to date, because it deliberately refuses the traditional liberal approach, which concentrates on removing barriers *within* existing frameworks, and argues that all existing salary structures should be replaced. It is important to understand that the CVCP's determination to break with the past is part of a long-term conservative/technocratic political context which has witnessed a wholesale centralization of power in public sector provision. For example, the Further and Higher Education Act (1992) enabled 'the attachment of any condition to the payment of funds to any group of universities by the Government' (CVCP, 1993, p. 28).

Promoting People is an important document because it highlights in microcosm the university scenario of the 1990s and beyond 2000: proactive conservative personnel policies and a resulting reduction of academic professional autonomy. The study takes the form of a brief, very highly selective, examination of international case studies of personnel, pay and organizational structures, with the objective of clarifying what pay systems and institutional structures best encourage staff and institutions to bring about educational changes.

Promoting People attempts to uncover what it perceives to be the underlying issues which shaped higher education in the 1980s and early 1990s and what might be the key to change. There is, the report claims, an indissoluble link between pay structures and the culture of education, which has not been addressed by universities in Britain. Changes in educational culture, the report argues, can be manipulated (or 'encouraged') by differential pay and benefits. The report's researchers looked at public sector initiatives: the Citizens' Charter, the Civil Service 'Next Steps' Agencies and commercial organizations such as British Petroleum and PowerGen, as well as universities in the Netherlands and the USA. The report's overall conclusion is that higher education needs to move away from individual rewards to team awards with a pay structure which can mirror that shift, and introduce a 'single integrated pay structure' (CVCP, 1993, p. 6). Rather than the existing kind of university hierarchic management structures, the report recommends that new departmental teams are to make flexible decisions about, for example, whether staff recruit more students and take a direct pay rise, rather than increasing staffing or have fringe benefits and no pay rise. *Promoting People* proposes that universities introduce a basic (low) salary scale 'X' with additional 'Y' elements to be added to staff salaries, depending on the financial health of institutions. 'Y' elements could be freely chosen by staff teams. Only in this way, the report claims, can there be a real strengthening of 'human resource management' to allow institutions to reach their full capacity.

The report rightly questions the nostalgic, cosy and mythical image of universities as places of quiet reflection and serious research and moves behind this facade to examine the harsher reality. *Promoting People* asks how the academic profession can respond to a period of recession and the need for innovations in the market place. Certainly it is clear that the current hostile economic climate is a major contribution to the report's choice of themes but this cannot obscure the fact that the system of higher education was not equitable nor innovative in the first place. Yet *Promoting People* has many contradictory elements and there are huge and glaring absences in its work. *Promoting People's* pay = culture is, I feel, too superficial and ignores the deeper structural factors that account for the static quality of higher education, as well as offering an inadequate trigger to encourage innovations by both men and women. In addition, the report does not attempt to deal with the key factors which do inhibit change which are discriminations and stereotypical conceptions of race and gender. For example, the report praises any move

from	to
limited competition	more intense competition
standardized work	flexibility
jobs for life	less security

as well as from	to
old culture	open culture
analysis	action
fear of mistakes	calculated risk-taking.
	(CVCP, 1993, p. 10)

The second group of qualities are traditionally associated with masculinity, even if such qualities are not shared by all men (Stanley and Wise, 1983). Women staff will not be empowered by further privileging these qualities, but only by challenging the universality of artificial masculine qualities as criteria for successful educational management.

Yet it is the contradictions in *Promoting People* which are initially more glaring. The first is the conclusion drawn from an analysis of the intensely individualistic academic pay structures of both the Netherlands and the USA, that this world shows 'a movement away from individuals in hierarchies towards teams and collaboration' (p. 15). Similarly, the report argues against a Pay Review Body, because such a body would not be 'appropriate for a diverse group of employees', yet these employees can suddenly, and magically, produce effective teams choosing performance-related 'Y' payments. In addition, non-pay benefits (job title, professional development, support for teaching/research/administration, study leave and so on) are not quantified in the proposed pay *model* which is to be constructed from income derived from admissions/retention rates. Yet most academics would argue that these 'fringe' benefits are not fringe but central to their perception of educational culture.

The key to all these contradictions and absences, I think, lies in a revealingly simple rhetorical shift. Equal opportunities has been supplanted by 'equal value' (p. 16). The economic force of 'value' is not at all the ethic of 'opportunity'. I would argue that it is not the present *pay* structure which inhibits change and equity, but an intransigent culture which will not be altered merely by pay or 'value' differentials.

Promoting People begins from the assumption that culture is quantitative and that it is operational. In general, the report assumes these operations involve adding a bolt of financial inducement here or a door handle of necessary resources there. University culture will resemble a Ford car, a welded object, probably already obsolete and certainly a pollutant. In this way the report seems to believe that a 'functional' university culture can turn out graduates who did not fail and may even one day come to own a Ford car, but who clearly cannot be said to have succeeded.

I believe that educational culture involves understanding and celebrating differences, for example, differences of race and gender, not organizational similarities. This is why a simple functionalist model of higher education, allowing teams to eliminate some inequalities, will not do. For example, it is precisely the illusory team/peer liberalism of higher education that allows gender divisions to be maintained and renewed. Women staff experience the misogyny of management both epistemically (in the sexist discourses of an institution) and procedurally (in its sexist practices). Feminists have demonstrated that the knowledge hierarchies of higher education – its denigration of 'soft' female-identified subjects – favour the concerns and interests of males (Smith, 1992; Spender and Sarah, 1980). In general, feminist approaches of the 1980s were directed towards eradicating sexism through either 'equal opportunity' or 'anti-sexist' initiatives (Burchell and Millman, 1989). Where equal opportunities opts for awareness-raising, for example asking for in-service training, anti-sexist approaches aim to transform the patriarchal and ethnocentric nature of educational work in separate agendas like women's studies. Although vital, equal value clauses leave embedded epistemic structures intact. The equal right to sit on management committees is not often accompanied by the conditions for equal *participation*, so that, not surprisingly, I think that the creation of gender appropriate processes, which I will summarize below, is at least as important as cost-effective pay scales. In any case, such scales attend only to surplus value, without looking at other categories of economic value, for example 'use value'.

Higher education does not actively discriminate against women, rather through its inculcation of particular processes it makes it very difficult for women to succeed (Acker and Warren Piper, 1985). So what are the current strategies which *Promoting People* should have addressed? Higher education has several features.

First, there are the gender dynamics of institutions where women function as two kinds of bodies – the objectification of academic staff and the obsessive body-counting of undergraduate numbers (the majority currently female). Despite some gains in the last decade, women are grossly underrepresented in senior positions. The report suggests that pay-rewarded team work will ameliorate this through a peer appraisal system, but appraisal is a good example of objectification.

For example, a male team member whose previous intellectual highlight was a study of intermediate technology does not constitute a serious appraiser for a woman who specializes in feminist theory and its application to issues of sexual violence. Appraisal here is of very dubious function. To expect that women staff will readily reveal their 'personal objectives' to a male academic, even when told appraisal is in a context of 'equal value', grossly underestimates the sexual politics that structure academic institutions, even though these politics may not be 'actively' visible (De Lyon and Widdowson Migniuolo, 1989).

Second, there is the *institutionalization* of recession planning. Management actually spend *more* on appraisal schemes and validation committees while cutting library budgets. The report makes no mention of this crucial feature and also ignores the *commodification* of education in cheap, standardized units and the relation between this and educational culture.

Third, there is an uneasy but extremely clever balance proposed in the report between *centralization* and apparent *local autonomy*, what Japanese car manufacturers operate as the kanban system. Here the core, or central managers, control resources and more importantly control the *timing* of resources. As Julia Kristeva argues so well in 'Women's Time', 'a psychoanalyst would call this "obsessional time", recognizing in the mastery of time the true structure of the slave' (Kristeva, 1992, p. 217). Managers operate in an 'obsessional' linear time – excessively protracted if it is a case of equal opportunities, and excessively swift if it involves resources, for example, inviting staff to apply for research assistants two days into the Christmas vacation with a one-week deadline. Also, as the editors suggested to me, managers also operate a politics of non-decision-making. Simultaneously staff will be turned into local mini-managers, or peripheral workers, having to spend an increasing amount of time collecting cost-benefit data *for* management rather than, as the report hopes, making local 'flexible decisions'.

Fourth, the report makes no mention of daily university events: sharp attacks on the vulnerable (mainly women): the firing of catering staff, misuse of part-timers, the isolation of senior women faculty, as well as the more obvious examples of sexist 'discourse' – a lack of campus security and routine sexual harassment, all of which are central issues of educational culture, at least for women staff.

Fifth, the report provides no solution for already excessive over-recruitment, even in a period of government capping. For example, I found out on the first day of a new academic year that my first-year women's studies class, usually of twenty-five to thirty, and for which I had prepared handouts/booklets for that number in a room seating only thirty, was now to have eighty-five students.

So what are the alternatives? First, I think we need to understand, when constructing positive alternatives, that the educational cultures these alternatives will address are themselves constructions (Harding, 1992). We also need to understand that staff are living currently not only in houses with negative equity, but in an intellectual atmosphere of negative equity and low morale. *Promoting People* does not address the needs of a gender-appropriate educational environment, which I will outline below. Such a question involves a complex analysis of institutional functions. But the first step would be to assess how women's underrepresentation at management levels reduces women's influence and power over policy initiatives in the first place.

Second, the report makes no mention of pay issues which are important to women academics, for example the problem of the career break. Career development for women does not involve an easy linear progression, and teams are even less likely than benign managers to support 'absence'.

Third, reinforcing a market economy in higher education, increasing competition between institutions for numbers, and encouraging local teams to act as financial managers, does not provide an encouraging environment for women who are traditionally less willing to ask for performance awards/promotion (Acker and Warren Piper, 1985). Many studies show how women's choices and opportunities in educational management include dealing not only with issues of sex-stereotyping and discrimination but also with the perceptions women themselves have about their own development (Kramarae and Spender, 1993).

Promoting People also makes no mention of the symbolic order of higher education, which is a rich source of gender messages, from the timing of meetings late in the day to process-led documentation. The development of management planning in higher education increases the likelihood of an association between organizational roles and masculinity. *Promoting People* is *technicist*, that is to say, the report describes cultural problems of staff relations as technical and open to rational planning. Nor does the report mention the value of working, even briefly, in single-gender or ethnically segregated groups, which provide support and are frequently an effective stimulus for change. Other issues not mentioned include newly qualified staff, disability, and anti-racist and anti-sexist work.

The report's advocacy of a different educational management *seems* close in style to those characteristics typically, if essentialistically, associated with women – notably collaboration and cooperation. However, the translation of this worthwhile ethic into *process* ignores the existing status and power held by men in universities. The report acknowledges the powerful potential of team work, but I am also painfully aware that women's current potentials have yet to be fully realized by institutions.

One key device to introduce would be obligatory training programmes which specifically count as a pay gain. Currently, most training is ad hoc and unsystematic and even when training is acquired in the currently fashionable postgraduate certificates in teaching and learning, this is not recognized in pay differentials. Women's lack of training in *management* skills has a long history and the report needs to address the whole gendered culture that has therefore historically shaped management planning. For example, some women (and some men) are not so interested in 'risk-taking'. The 'new culture of calculated risk-taking' may be unappealing to women, who often prefer to promote a systematic approach to research and development (Turkle and Papert, 1990). The issue here is not that one style is necessarily better than another, but rather that *Promoting People* gives preference only to one, traditionally if artificially characterized as a male-centred approach, putting women staff at a disadvantage. Pay benefits are distant and precisely *not* visible. To encourage those new to management (currently ethnic minorities/women) *significant* and frequent rewards are crucial, not invisible earnings. We do not need perform-ance-related pay, but we do need performance-related affirmative action – what the State University of New York in the 1970s called 'bonus lines' – extra resources for departments hiring more minority staff. We need to carefully differentiate between short-term and long-term goals with clear agendas for each. For example, President Clinton's Secretary of Health and Human Serv-ices, Donna Shalala, when she was appointed Chancellor of the University of Wisconsin-Madison, instituted mandatory ethnic and women's studies, gender and race orientation programmes for all staff and students, and a woman of colour as Vice-Chancellor in charge of affirmative action planning.

Although I have limited my analysis to key and potentially realizable aims of equal opportunities in British higher education, a more fundamental theme must be urgently addressed in any analysis of equal opportunities for the millennium, which is the need for a whole new ethics of higher education. For example, *Promoting People* largely describes new operating values and norms in *process* terms. Ethical issues of *accountability to others*, involving an ethics of affiliation and respect for others over measurable, linear objectives, are not addressed.

Finally, as Evelyn Fox Keller argued long ago about science, if current management practices continue we will see an even deeper educational reces-sion at the end of the 1990s than we do at the beginning (Keller, 1992). We are at a crossroads. The old familiar forms of higher education are being replaced. As women academics and scholars we need to have a say in shaping the future form of any educational culture. Unfortunately, *Promoting People* does not include our voices. Neither does it include equity or justice.

References

ACKER, S. and WARREN PIPER, D. (1985) *Is Higher Education Fair to Women?*, Slough, SRHE and NFER/Nelson.

BURCHELL, H. and MILLMAN, V. (Eds) (1989) *Changing Perspectives on Gender*, Milton Keynes, Open University Press.

COMMITTEE OF VICE-CHANCELLORS AND PRINCIPALS (CVCP) (1993) *Promoting People: A Strategic Framework for the Management and Development of Staff in UK Universities*, London, CVCP.

DE LYON, H. and WIDDOWSON MIGNIUOLO, F. (Eds) (1989) *Women Teachers*, Milton Keynes, Open University Press.

HARDING, S. (1992) 'Epistemological Questions', in HUMM, M. (Ed.) *Feminisms: A Reader*, Hemel Hempstead, Harvester Wheatsheaf, pp. 319–22.

HUMM, M. (1991) '"Thinking of things in themselves": Theory, Experience, Women's Studies', in AARON, J. and WALBY, S. (Eds) *Out of the Margins: Women's Studies in the Nineties*, London, Falmer Press, pp. 49–62.

KELLER, E. F. (1992) 'Feminism and Science', in HUMM, M. (Ed.) *Feminisms: A Reader*, Hemel Hempstead, Harvester Wheatsheaf, pp. 312–17.

KRAMARAE, C. and SPENDER, D. (Eds) (1993) *The Knowledge Explosion*, Hemel Hempstead, Harvester Wheatsheaf.

KRISTEVA, J. (1992) 'Women's Time', in HUMM, M. (Ed.) *Feminisms: A Reader*, Hemel Hempstead, Harvester Wheatsheaf, pp. 216–18.

SMITH, D. (1992) 'Women's Perspective as a Radical Critique of Sociology', in HUMM, M. (Ed.) *Feminisms: A Reader*, Hemel Hempstead, Harvester Wheatsheaf, pp. 306–10.

SPENDER, D. and SARAH, E. (1980) *Learning to Lose*, London, The Women's Press.

STANLEY, L. and WISE, S. (1983) *Breaking Out*, London, Routledge and Kegan Paul.

TURKLE, S. and PAPERT, S. (1990) 'Epistemological Pluralism: Styles and Voices Within the Computer Culture', *Signs*, 16, 1, pp. 128–57.

UNIVERSITIES FUNDING COUNCIL (1993) *Universities Statistics 1991–2: Vol. 1: Students and Staff*, Cheltenham, Universities Statistical Record.

WILLIAMS, J., COCKING, J. and DAVIES, L. (1989) *Words or Deeds?: A Review of Equal Opportunity Policies in HE*, London, CRE.

Section II

Feminism in the Academy

Chapter 9

Irish Women in Higher Education in England: From Invisibility to Recognition

Breda Gray and Louise Ryan

Ireland was one of the English empire's first and nearest colonies; Irish immigrants have settled in England and contributed to English society in a number of ways for over two hundred years; Northern Ireland is directly ruled from Westminster and the possibility of a peaceful future there is a central concern of both the English and Irish governments at present. The colonized in Ireland were largely white and, unlike most colonies, Ireland is located geographically within Western Europe. Irish people are currently the largest ethnic minority group in England. In view of these facts, how can Irish affairs and Irish women's experiences *not* be relevant to understanding Englishness, English affairs and English feminisms?

This chapter addresses the many levels of absence and invisibility of Irish women in higher education in England.[1] Our combined experience of working/ studying in higher education in England amounts to eight years. In addition to our teaching experiences (in three different institutions), we have also been actively involved in English academia through our research, attending conferences and seminars, and giving papers.

We begin the chapter with some examples of our own experiences of Irish women's invisibility within course content. We discuss why it is important that issues relating to Ireland and Irish women in particular need to be integrated within the English higher education system.[2] We explore the possible ways in which Irish women might address their current invisibility and finally, we attempt to theorize the social relations which inhibit the development of Irish women's power/knowledge positions within the higher education system in England.

As an Irish woman in higher education in England one is clearly an outsider, a foreigner, but none the less usually white and English-speaking. This leads to a very difficult dilemma – does one simply shut up and play the game or does one continually remind people one is Irish and call attention to the invisibility of Irish women in higher education in this country? Challenging invisibility can be a lonely and isolating experience. The response is often one of resistance from colleagues and students who question the relevance of Irish women's experiences. In the next section of the chapter, we describe some of our experiences of exclusion, invisibility and homogenization under the term

'Irish'. In order to maintain the personal nature of our different experiences we describe them in the first person, speaking *from* the specificity of our individual experiences rather than attempting to speak *for* the entire social category of Irish women.

Personal Experiences

[I]f critical social theory has taught us anything in the last two decades it is that power relations are tied to the most mundane of everyday performances . . . that discourses of the everyday are the realms in which subordination is exercised and legitimated and that whole social systems are reproduced in the unthinking moments of the quotidian. (Keith, 1991, p. 189)

The difficulties that many Irish people experience in England are most often associated with discrimination in relation to employment, housing, anti-Irish jokes and negative stereotypes (Curtis, 1984). However, within higher education, it is most often the ongoing, persistent and subtle incidents that have the effect of excluding Irish issues or rendering them invisible. Drawing attention to such instances often seems petty, like making a big deal out of something trivial. It is for this reason that we often find ourselves questioning our experiences, noting the more discriminatory behaviour that other groups encounter, and decide against speaking out. Yet it is this process of silencing oneself that adds to the power of these ongoing low-level experiences to define Irishness as absent or present in particular ways.

Our first example relates to a recurring experience we have both had within higher education and in other settings in England. Whenever a conversation turns to our being Irish, invariably women, mainly of other Western nationalities, comment on Ireland as being a particularly oppressive country for women. Such comments always make us feel uneasy. This is because they position us as being a product of a particularly patriarchal and backward society. By doing this the speaker is positioning herself as being from a more liberated and enlightened country. However, our experiences of patriarchal oppression in Ireland and England have been different and not necessarily comparable along a continuum. It is important to acknowledge the diverse workings of patriarchies in different contexts. It is also necessary to recognize the ways in which existing hierarchical conceptions of nationalities and feminisms can be reinforced. A more fruitful focus for discussion may be the relationships between Irish and English patriarchies and feminisms.

Another example relates to one of our experiences of seeking funding for postgraduate research in English universities. Despite having lived and worked in England for seven years at the time of applying to do postgraduate research, it was suggested in one instance that I should seek funding for my research from Ireland. The implication seemed to be that work by any Irish woman on Irish-related issues would be more appropriately funded by an Irish institution. Why is the study of Irish women's identities and migration to England (which is the subject of my research) seen as outside the realm and responsibilities of both funding sources and institutions for higher education in England? I encountered the same response when I sought funding to give a joint paper with a colleague on gender and Irish national identity at an international conference. In this case the conference organizer felt that I should look to Irish funding agencies for support, despite the fact that I am studying at an English university and contributing to research production in England.

In a context of tight financial resources, Irish students studying Irish-related topics are not seen as a totally legitimate part of the responsibilities of the English higher education system. However, successful Irish academics living and working in English institutions of higher education (such as Seamus Heaney[3] or Anthony Clare) are seen as legitimate members of the English academic world.

The following example relates to one of our experiences of teaching which involved an unhelpful incident with a student. During my lecture, which focused on the experiences of women in Ireland, one student appeared uninterested and even resentful of the subject-matter. At the end of the session I challenged this behaviour which I found rude and distracting. The student immediately retaliated by accusing me of having a problem. She accused me of being over-sensitive in relation to all matters to do with Ireland and Irishness.[4] When I mentioned that Irish women were rarely if ever dealt with in course material, she accused me of having 'a chip on my shoulder'. In this way my professional and academic credentials were being cast aside and I was being labelled a 'crank'. The student excused her rude behaviour by projecting the 'problem' on to me. I was Irish and so clearly over-sensitive and obsessed with my subject-matter.

A further example is still painful to recall. At an evening social event for students, one of us made a silly error and approached the buffet table from the wrong end and almost collided with a student. She smiled at me and said 'Oh well, you are Irish'. I was shocked. I was totally unprepared for this 'racist' statement. With one word this student had reduced me to a racial stereotype which denied me any individuality. It also quickly defined me as in some way inferior to her. The assumed power relationship between student and staff was immediately reversed.

In conversations with students and colleagues, even little words like 'we' or 'us' or 'our' can make all the difference. Are they including me in that construction of 'we English' and so denying my different nationality/citizenship/identity? Or are they excluding me in a construction of 'us' and 'them'? Very often I find that students and colleagues tend, at least in the beginning, to include *me personally* in 'us' or 'we English' but tend to exclude Ireland and Irish people more generally from all focus and discussion merely by rendering it and them invisible. These verbal encounters are important because language constructs and reflects our experiences, helping to shape our sense of identity.

Invisibility within Course Content

In this section we point to selected omissions within the curricular areas of feminism/women's studies, sociology, history, race and ethnic studies.

Feminism/Women's Studies

The virtual invisibility of Irish women in feminist theory and women's studies courses in England needs to be understood within the wider context of ethnocentrism. Feminism in England, with a few notable exceptions, has a major difficulty when it comes to addressing Irish women. On the one hand, there is a tendency among all of English academia to co-opt successful Irish people – George Bernard Shaw, Samuel Beckett, Oscar Wilde, etc. – and appropriate them into the English canon. This is equally true of successful Irish women like Eva Gore-Booth and Anna Wheeler, whose Irishness is either not mentioned or who are actually labelled British. In Dale Spender's book *Women of Ideas*, the Irish feminist Anna Wheeler appears under the large bold heading GREAT BRITAIN. Throughout the chapter British women are referred to including Wheeler in that broad category. Only six pages into the chapter are we told that Wheeler actually came from Ireland but thereafter she is still referred to as British (Spender, 1983, p. 390). In another recent book, Valerie Bryson, while discussing the contribution made to early feminism by Anna Wheeler, completely neglects to mention that Wheeler was Irish (Bryson, 1992). On the other hand, there is a tendency to avoid or to ignore more controversial or complex characters, especially when it comes to nationalists. When giving lectures on women's history/suffrage history to women's studies students at both BA and MA levels, I am continually shocked by the numbers who do not know that Irishwoman Countess Markievicz was the first woman elected to Westminster. The fact that she was serving a prison sentence for nationalist activities at the time of her election may have something to do with her invisibility in feminist history in England.

In recent years many feminists from Asia and Africa have written about the ethnocentricity of European feminism (Bhavnani and Coulson, 1994; Brah, 1993). Antoinette Burton (1990) argues that feminism in England must be understood within the context of colonialism. English feminism of the nineteenth century was deeply influenced by the Empire and this is quite clear in feminist attitudes to India and other distant parts of the Empire. In our view, this is equally true of nearer parts of the Empire – perhaps even more so. English feminists have been ambivalent in their attitudes to Irish feminists; either including them as just like 'us', and thus denying differences, or ignoring them completely and thus rendering them invisible. For example, English feminists of the late nineteenth century treated Ireland to some extent as their own backyard and Irish feminists repeatedly complained that British women were insensitive to the realities of life in Ireland (see *Irish Citizen* newspaper 1912–1920). In the *Irish Citizen* of 9 August 1913, Dora Mellone of the Irish Women's Suffrage Federation claimed that she was surprised on coming to London to discover how little English suffragists knew about Ireland and how many misconceptions abounded. This legacy of colonialism continues to influence attitudes to Ireland and to Irish feminists among feminists in England (Hickman and Walter, 1995; Smyth, 1994; Coulter, 1993).

Sociology

Mainstream sociological literature in England rarely mentions Ireland when studying comparisons between Britain and other countries within Europe. Ireland as 'a European country' is rarely addressed. In our experience, students are often very confused about which parts of Ireland are in the UK, and some are unaware that any part of Ireland is independent. They think that it is like Wales or Scotland, or being surrounded by water perhaps of similar status and size to Jersey or the Isle of Man.[5]

A recent research project carried out by an Irish academic, Professor James O'Connell, at Bradford University (reported in the *Guardian* of 21 October 1994) found that 13 per cent of his respondents described Irish people as 'not quite the same as us but not foreigners either', compared with a large majority who felt a closer affinity with Irish people than with continental Europeans or Americans. While acknowledging some of the commonalities between us, these views obscure the many real differences between Irish people and English people. They include Irish people in some sort of union with British people in potential opposition to other 'outsiders'. These issues have begun to be addressed since the mid 1980s following the establishment of Irish Studies Centres in English Universities (Hazelkorn, 1990; Greenslade, 1991; Kells, 1995).

In addition, there is the question about why social structures and relations in Ireland have not featured more widely in sociological studies. One clear reason is that as an English colony Ireland did not fit the picture of a European industrial sovereign nation-state. The roots of sociology are located in a Franco-German tradition which focused on the larger countries in Western Europe – Britain, France, Germany. The main concerns were class conflict, science, rationality, state power, education, social change. All of these were grounded in assumptions about industrial development. Since Ireland was alone in Western Europe in not experiencing an industrial revolution, it was not included in sociological studies. Similarly, Ireland's status as an English colony until 1922 denied it a separate existence. This contributed to it being overlooked in sociological investigations. Nowadays, although Ireland poses a very interesting example of an economy largely dependent on multi-national corporations, and while many important studies have been carried out by Irish sociologists (Bell, 1988, 1993; Clancy *et al.*, 1992; Curtin *et al.*, 1987; Gibbons, 1988; O'Connor and Cronin, 1993; Tovey, 1992; Walsh, 1991, 1993), to our knowledge these are largely absent from most sociology courses within higher education in England.

History

Perhaps more than any other subject, history addresses issues relating to Ireland, but this tends to be solely Anglo/Irish relations focusing on government and armed conflicts. The role of women is usually absent. In Ireland, as in many other countries, women have not featured strongly in history texts until very recently (Ward, 1991). However, the work which has been done by Irish women on Irish women over the last ten to twenty years is rarely available in English university libraries (which raises the issue of resourcing) and so recent input is often absent from English history courses on Ireland.

Race and Ethnic Studies

Race and ethnic studies courses may provide a good opportunity to address the question of Irish people in England. This has been made easier by the publication of a number of reports which supply ample statistics which are useful teaching aids (Hazelkorn, 1990; Greenslade, 1991). In our experience some white students are deeply resistant to the inclusion of the subject of Irishness and Irish experiences within such courses and seem very uncomfortable discussing Irish people as an ethnic minority. There are a number of reasons for this: the input on Irish ethnicity may be small, a token gesture tagged on to the end of a unit. The students read this as a sign of its relative unimportance. Secondly, some white students may find studying a *white ethnicity* challenging to their preconceived ideas about their own ethnicity.

Resourcing

Because Irish women have been invisible for so long in English higher education, there tends to be an absence of any literature on Irish women in libraries. This means that including a section on Irish women in a course unit may mean ordering a significant quantity of books and reports. This involves long-term planning and cannot be done at short notice. The absence of resources is also off-putting to students, so they tend to shy away from pursuing research in this area. In a context of 'issue overload', seemingly endless 'identity politics' and ever increasing expectations of lecturers and students, the issue of Irish women may be seen as just another one to add to an already long list.

Why Should Irishness and Irish Women's Issues Be Addressed within Higher Education in England?

We want to suggest that Irishness and Irish women's issues *are* relevant to teaching practice, staff relations and curriculum development in higher education in England. One of the ways of rendering Irish women marginal in higher education is to construct us as a marginal case without much to offer to mainstream knowledge. While women are already defined in terms of 'special interest', Irishness makes us doubly marginal. During Jesse Jackson's campaign for the Democratic nomination to run for President of the USA, he was considered within the Democratic Party to be 'not genuinely representative because he was the spokesperson of "special interests"' (Radhakrishnan, 1987, p. 215). Radhakrishnan suggests that 'If Jackson's interests are "special interests", the implication is that certain interests are "natural", "general", "representative" and ideologically neutral and value free' (*ibid.*). The same is surely true when it comes to including issues of Irish identity within the English higher education system. Irish women's issues are, like Jesse Jackson's, seen as based on 'race' or nationality. The 'special interests' argument is one of the strongest resistant arguments against hearing what Irish women have to say. As Gayatri Spivak points out, 'the putative centre welcomes selective inhabitants of the margin in order better to exclude the margin' (Spivak, 1987, p. 107).

Irish women's perspectives, experiences and politics have much to contribute to a range of disciplines in English higher education. Their structural positions within Ireland, their experiences of migration to England and life in England as a white ethnic minority may help to illuminate the workings of patriarchal English society. They also have much to contribute to a critique of categories of universalisms such as Western feminisms, capitalism, imperialism, colonization, nationalism, migration, and much more. An engagement with Irish women's perspectives, because Ireland is located within Europe and the so-called 'West', might contribute to feminist efforts to challenge colonial patriarchal academic ideas about knowledge and a unified view of 'the West'.

Dilemmas for Irish Women Lecturers and Students in English Institutions of Higher Education

We do not speak *only and always* as Irish women; we have some choice and agency in relation to our subject positions and responses to social structures and relations. Gayatri Spivak asserts that she will not allow herself 'to occupy the place of the marginal that you would like to see me in, because then that allows you to feel that you have an other to speak to' (1990, p. 122). In this way she defies being positioned and challenges the ways in which difference is already constructed for her to occupy. Yet, when an Irish woman lecturer or student is faced with the options of how she might challenge the stereotypes of Irish women, transgress these or attempt not to occupy the place of the marginal, her options are limited. Whatever behavioural options we might choose, they all fall into some stereotype of Irishness. Whether one is strident, quiet, diplomatic, assertive or easy-going, there are a range of stereotypes that can be applied such as argumentative, temperamental, stroppy, eloquent, warm, friendly, fighting, asexual, moralistic (Catholic) and so on. One option seems to be inverting the stereotypes, emphasizing them and playing with them. This course of action requires a confidence, ingenuity and lots of extra effort which may not be easy to achieve.

Language, accents and humour shape the lived reality of daily experiences in both the class room and the staff room, intentionally or unintentionally operating in powerful ways to marginalize and ridicule. The Irish person who challenges these may be labelled humourless and defensive. A consciousness of our difference, or our difficulty in being understood, may lead to a change in accent, an accommodation to the norms. Phrases, ways of expressing ourselves are lost or forgotten as we cease to use them. Alternatively, we develop a way of talking which is very different from how we behave at home. As bell hooks puts it, I 'talk the right kinda talk' in the academic environment and keep my vernacular for 'private spaces of my life' (hooks, 1991, p. 90). This may lead to feelings that one is taking the 'easy option' and trying to fit in as best one can, and this may lead in turn to a sense of guilt that one is not being true to oneself. On the other hand, one may adopt a different strategy, taking the option of challenging and confronting prejudice and ignorance. To quote bell hooks again:

> There is another more difficult and less acceptable choice, that is to decide to maintain values and traditions . . . while incorporating meaningful knowledge gained in other locations, even in those hierarchical spaces of privilege. This choice makes a lot of people uncomfortable. It makes it hard for them to put you in a neat little category and keep you there. (hooks, 1991, p. 90)

In our view these two choices are not always mutually exclusive. In different situations we make choices, sometimes consciously, sometimes unconsciously, depending on how comfortable or confident we are feeling in that context. All of this may mean that we frequently feel uncomfortable and ill at ease as we size up a situation and decide how to react. Even in conversations with colleagues or students we often have to decide whether to challenge them on something they have just said or whether to let it go. For example, phrases like 'the British mainland' illustrate how Britain has constructed itself in relation to Ireland. When English colleagues use this phrase in conversation it becomes important to point out the irony of a small island such as Britain constructing itself as a 'mainland'.

While it is hard to transcend the stereotypes of Irishness, it is also difficult to find a discourse or language to speak about our experiences as Irish women that does not have other resonances. For example, to speak of anti-Irish racism invokes anti-racist discourses that focus on colour. Although Irish people constitute the largest ethnic minority in Britain, it is only recently that we are officially becoming known as an ethnic minority. Yet the terms 'ethnic minority', 'Irish in Britain' or 'Irish communities' all have particular associations and assume homogeneity within these categories. None of these discourses adequately represents or names the experiences or identifications of Irish women in England. As Carole Boyce Davies (1994, p. 5) points out in relation to black women, each of the terms we use to name ourselves 'represents an original misnaming and the simultaneous constant striving of the dispossessed for full representation'. If we are to attempt to step outside of 'the narrow terms of the discourses in which we are inscribed' (*ibid.*), terms such as 'anti-Irish racism' will have to be used provisionally and constantly subjected to new analysis and questions.

In addition to dealing with stereotypes of how Irish women in higher education in England should behave, we also experience dilemmas in relation to assumed expertise. By this we mean that colleagues and students tend to assume that simply because one is Irish one is an expert on all matters relating to Ireland and Irish people – in England as well as in Ireland. This has a number of implications – in terms of resources it places expectations upon us that we can provide all sorts of useful materials to colleagues. In terms of teaching, it is also expected that if anything is to be done in relation to Ireland we are the obvious people to teach it. This has the effect not only of increasing our workload but also of 'passing the buck', so to speak, of placing the onus of responsibility onto us and not onto students or staff to develop an awareness of these issues. This tends to occur especially when we raise issues about the invisibility of Irish women/Irish people/Ireland in course content. If we point out these gaps then we should be prepared to fill them also. Obviously there is a paradox here for us. On the one hand, we want the invisibility of Irish women to be addressed and challenged. However, on the other hand, we do not feel that it is always appropriate for us to have to teach everything relating to Ireland and Irish women. One fear would be that, were we to leave our present institutions, the material on Irish women would cease to be taught because, after all, we were the only ones who could do it.

The Processes of Exclusion, Inclusion and Rendering Invisible of Irish Women in the English Higher Education System

Joan Scott (1992) suggests that by making 'visible the experience of a "different" group' as we tried to do at the beginning of this chapter, it is possible to expose 'the existence of repressive mechanisms, but not their *inner workings or logics*,' (Scott, 1992, p. 25). We attempt to expose the inner workings of how Irishness is constructed within the English higher education system by focusing on the ways in which cultural differences are articulated (Bhabha, 1994) and what Gayatri Spivak (1987) calls 'the mechanics of the constitution of the Other'. Cultural difference is employed sometimes to construct Irish women as *the same* as dominant constructions of white English, and at other times to construct us as outsiders and different from white middle-class English.

Differences are not all just differences, neither are relations of difference all the same. All relations of difference contain historical and political significance. They involve gender, neo-colonialism, 'race' and many other relations that are grounded in inequality. Why, for example, in certain circumstances in English higher education, is Irish represented as 'different' while middle-class white English is not? Cairns and Richards (1988) point out that the principle of difference is founded upon maintaining a distance which separates two identities. Polarization and the operation of dichotomies therefore tend to emphasize a difference which represents a distance between each identity. However, it is not just difference that we want to explore, but how difference is represented and acted upon in social relations which convert 'difference into oppression' (Maynard, 1994).

As colour difference and nationality become dominant signifiers of difference in England, the distance between Irish and English is lessened (see Hickman and Walter, 1995). Differences identified in terms of polarities and dichotomies such as black/white are more easily acknowledged and recognized than those that are less dichotomized. Because they are more easily recognized these differences are easily used to underpin inequality and oppressive social relations.

Unequal and oppressive social relations can also arise in cases where difference is not so polarized. Because most Irish people in England are white, their difference from dominant constructions of 'white English' is less defined than that of black people. This sometimes allows for Irish people to be included within dominant constructions of white English. This is often colluded with by many Irish people as it may coincide with their interests. However, others may feel that such inclusion renders them invisible and denies their identity and experiences. Irishness is constructed by the English media and state as really different when related to the violent nationalism of the IRA and when any transgressive acts are committed by Irish people. In such cases the boundaries between English and Irish are closely guarded and the civilized/uncivilized dichotomy is employed to maintain these boundaries.

When Irish people themselves assert their difference, the distance between white Englishness and white Irishness comes into question. The dominant myth of a unified whiteness is challenged and feelings of discomfort arise. The neutrality of whiteness and relations between Irish and English identities have to be confronted. In order to avoid the interrogation of whiteness and to maintain the myth of a unified white gaze, differences between Irish women and English women are either denied or heightened by strategies of inclusion and exclusion.

Attempting to Go Beyond the Inclusion/Exclusion Dichotomy

Inclusion can mean assimilation, a denial of difference, tokenism and disempowerment. In this section we discuss the possibilities of an 'inclusion' that recognizes difference and seeks to be proactive, challenging and empowering. There are problems with trying to merely add Irish women into the existing course structures. As we indicated earlier in relation to history and women's studies, this is not always possible or desirable because the existing ethos is so exclusive. To simply include a lecture on Irish women here or there does not work. It is not only tokenistic but also of little use to students. In the remainder of this section, one of us gives an account of her experiences of integrating Irish issues and Irish feminist activism into a range of courses. In a women's studies unit, I introduced the issue of Irish women in a fundamental way by examining the relationships between English feminism and Irish feminism. Because of the nature of this unit it lent itself quite well to such an innovation. By placing the relationship within the context of nationalism and imperialism, students were able to explore some of the key disagreements between the Irish and English suffragists. This session thus served the purpose not only of addressing Irish women and rendering them visible, but also of highlighting the ethnocentric nature of British feminism and of many recent feminist histories of the period. The students reacted positively to this move and many chose to do essays on this issue. Again resources proved a problem and I had to lend some of my own material to students. I also endeavoured to rectify the situation by ordering the relevant books and resources.

In another unit I changed my input to highlight the ways in which nationalism and imperialism have impacted on feminism. Here I use a comparison between the Irish and Indian suffrage movements to raise fundamental questions about Western feminists' critique of nationalism. Using these two case studies I attempt to show how feminists operating in a colonial context have engaged with nationalism. I use this study to illustrate how a Eurocentric focus on feminist activism leads to a narrow exclusivism and a misunderstanding of 'Third World' concerns. Highlighting the experiences of Irish women can pose interesting questions which confront students with new/alternative possibilities.

Concluding Thoughts

By speaking of our particular experiences, Irish women are seen as *creating* difference where none to speak of exists. Yet in other circumstances, as in the example of seeking funding, our difference is defined for us. Irish women's difference, then, is acceptable or unacceptable depending on who is defining it. Simple dichotomies of same/different, black/white, insider/outsider, maintain dominant constructions of white middle-class Englishness and the ideologies that underpin this identity within the higher education system in England. There is a need for more exchange of ideas and dialogue between English and Irish women within higher education in England. However, there are barriers to dialogue. These barriers include the terms of the dialogue itself (Gabriel, 1986), and the socio-historical context within which the dialogue takes place makes equal communication difficult. It is important to recognize that 'neutral dialogue' may be difficult to achieve. Gayatri Spivak (1990, p. 72) points out that the 'idea of neutral dialogue . . . denies history, denies structure, denies the positioning of subjects'. Spivak's view promises little hope as it seems to lock people into particular subject positions (colonizer and colonized, oppressor and victim) and does not account easily for changing contexts.

Our overall aim is to 'challenge the regulative mechanisms' (i.e. the processes by which difference is articulated and inclusion and exclusion take place) inherent in English higher education by finding ways of facilitating the development of Irish women's 'power knowledge' positions within higher education in England. This involves challenging colonial meanings and talking to our English women colleagues about the social relations that construct and maintain the inequalities between us.

Notes

We would like to thank Rosemary Deem, Wendy Langford and Bev Skeggs for helpful comments on earlier drafts of this chapter. However, we are responsible for all the views expressed here.

1 We focus on higher education in England because we have no experience of higher education in other parts of Britain.

2 In the past fifteen years Irish Studies Centres have been established within some higher education institutions in Britain. Until the late 1970s there were few courses with 'Irish' in the title (Hickman, 1990). Instead, according to Hickman (1990) the study of Ireland was taking place but rendered invisible by inclusion of Irish literature and history within broader English literature and British history courses. By the mid 1990s there were large Irish Studies Centres within at least three different institutions of higher education in England and the British Association for Irish Studies had been established to encourage the development of Irish studies at all levels within the education system. These are very important developments in making Ireland and Irish issues visible within higher education. However, their existence may also mean that other institutions and departments do not take responsibility for this area of study.

3 Seamus Heaney publicly protested at being included in an anthology of

British poets and objected in particular to his appropriation by the British establishment.
4 We acknowledge that Irishness and Englishness are not homogenous identities. We recognize that both are multifaceted and vary by class, gender, race political affiliation and other factors. However, in the context of this chapter we are looking at the ways in which Irishness is socially constructed within higher education in England.
5 In the absence of Irish Studies Centres these issues would remain largely invisible and unaddressed within higher education in England.

References

BELL, D. (1988) 'Ireland Without Frontiers: The Challenge of the Communications Revolution', in KEARNEY, R. (Ed.) *Across the Frontiers: Ireland in the 1980s*, Dublin, Wolfhound, pp. 219–30.

BELL, D. (1993) 'Culture and Politics in Ireland: Postmodern Revisions', *History of European Ideas*, 16, 1–3, pp. 141–6.

BHABHA, H. (1994) *The Location of Culture*, London, Routledge.

BHAVNANI, K. and COULSON, M. (1994) 'Transforming Socialist Feminism: The Challenge of Racism', in EVANS, M. (Ed.) *The Woman Question*, 2nd ed., London, Sage, pp. 334–44.

BRAH, A. (1988) Book Review (of ARNOT, M. and WEINER, G. (1987) *Gender and the Politics of Schooling*, London, Hutchinson; and WEINER, G. and ARNOT, M. (1987) *Gender under Scrutiny*, London, Hutchinson), *British Journal of Sociology of Education*, 9, 1, pp. 115–21.

BRAH, A. (1993) 'Reframing Europe: Engendered Racisms, Ethnicities and Nationalisms in Contemporary Western Europe', *Feminist Review*, 45 (Autumn), pp. 9–28.

BREEN, R., HANNON, D., ROTTMAN, D. and WHELAN, C. (Eds) (1990) *Understanding Contemporary Ireland: State, Class, and Development in the Republic of Ireland*, Dublin, Gill and Macmillan.

BRYSON, V. (1992) *Feminist Political Theory: An Introduction*, London, Macmillan.

BURTON, A. (1990) 'The White Woman's Burden', *Women's Studies International Forum*, 13, 4, pp. 295–308.

CAIRNS, D. and RICHARDS, S. (1988) *Writing Ireland: Colonialism, Nationalism and Culture*, Manchester and New York, Manchester University Press.

CLANCY, P., KELLY, M., WIATR, J. and ZOLTANIECKI, R. (Eds) (1992) *Ireland and Poland: Comparative Perspectives*, Dublin, Department of Sociology of University College, Dublin.

COULTER, C. (1993) *The Hidden Tradition*, Cork, Cork University Press.

CURTIN, C., JACKSON, P. and O'CONNOR, B. (Eds) (1987) *Gender in Irish Society*, Galway, Galway University Press.

CURTIS, L. (1984) *Nothing But the Same Old Story: The Roots of Anti-Irish Racism*, London, Information on Ireland.

DAVIES, C. B. (1994) *Black Women, Writing and Identity: Migrations of the Subject*, London and New York, Routledge.

GABRIEL, T. H. (1986) 'Colonialism and "Law and Order" Criticism', *Screen*, 27, 3–4, pp. 140–7.

GIBBONS, L. (1988) 'Coming Out of Hibernation? The Myth of Modernity in Irish Culture', in KEARNEY, R. (Ed.) *Across the Frontiers: Ireland in the 1980s*, Dublin, Wolfhound, pp. 205–18.

GREENSLADE, L. (1991) *Irish Migrants in Britain*, Liverpool, Institute of Irish Studies.

HAZELKORN, E. (1990) *Irish Immigrants Today*, London, Irish Studies Centre, University of North London.

HICKMAN, M. (1990) 'The Irish Studies Scene in Britain: Perceptions and Progress', *Text and Context*, IV (Autumn), pp. 18–22.

HICKMAN, M. and WALTER, B. (1995) 'Deconstructing Whiteness: Irish Women in Britain', *Feminist Review*, 50, pp. 5–19.

HOOKS, B. (1991) *Yearning: Race, Gender and Cultural Politics*, London, Turnaround Press.

IRISH CITIZEN (1912–1920), Dublin.

KEITH, M. (1991) 'Knowing Your Place: The Imagined Geographies of Racial Subordination', in PHILO, C. (Ed.) *New Words, New Worlds: Reconceptualising Social and Cultural Geography*, Aberystwyth, Cambrion Printers, pp. 108–13.

KELLS, M. (1995) *Ethnic Identity Amongst Young Irish Middle Class Migrants in London*, London, University of North London Press.

MAYNARD, M. (1994) 'Methods, Practice and Epistemology: The Debate about Feminism and Research', in MAYNARD, M. and PURVIS, J. (Eds) *Researching Women's Lives from a Feminist Perspective*, London, Taylor and Francis, pp. 10–26.

MOGHISSI, H. (1994) 'Racism and Sexism in Academic Practice', in AFSHAR, H. and MAYNARD, M. (Eds) *The Dynamics of 'Race' and Gender: Some Feminist Interventions*, London, Taylor and Francis, pp. 222–34.

O'CONNOR, B. and CRONIN, M. (Eds) (1993) *Tourism in Ireland – A Critical Analysis*, Cork, Cork University Press.

O'CONNOR, J. (1993) 'Introduction', in Bolger, D. (Ed.) *Ireland in Exile*, Dublin, New Island Books, pp. 11–18.

RADHAKRISHNAN, R. (1987) 'Ethnic Identity and Post-Structuralist Difference', *Cultural Critique*, 6, pp. 199–220.

REX, J. (1991) *Ethnic Identity and Ethnic Mobilisation in Britain*, Monograph in Ethnic Relations No. 5, Centre for Research in Ethnic Relations, Warwick.

SCOTT, J. W. (1992) '"Experience"', in BUTLER, J. and SCOTT, J. W. (Eds) *Feminists Theorize the Political*, London and New York, Routledge, pp. 22–40.

Smyth, A. (1994) 'Paying Our Disrespects to the Bloody States We're In: Women, Violence, Culture and the State', in Hester, M., Griffin, G., Rai, S. and Roseneil, S. (Eds) *Stirring It: Challlenges for Feminism* London, Taylor and Francis, pp. 13–39.

Spender, D. (1983) *Women of Ideas*, London, Ark.

Spivak, G. C. (1987) *In Other Worlds*, New York and London, Methuen.

Spivak, G. C. (with Threadgold, T. and Bartkowski, F.) (1990), 'The Intervention Interview', in Spivak, G. C. (Ed. S. Harasym) *The Post-Colonial Critic: Interviews, Strategies, Dialogues*, London and New York, Routledge, pp. 113–32.

Tovey, H. (1992) 'Development of the Field', *Irish Jouunal of Sociology*, 2, pp. 96–121.

Wainwright, M. (1994) 'British Like "Witty, Intelligent Irish" ', *Guardian*, 21 October, p. 5.

Walsh, B. (1991) 'Interpreting Modern Ireland: Time for a New View', *Studies*, 80, 320, pp. 400–11.

Walsh, B. (1993) 'Labour Force Participation in the Growth of Women's Employment, Ireland 1971–1991', *Economic and Social Review*, 22, 4, pp. 107–11.

Ward, M. (1991) *The Missing Sex: Putting Women into Irish History*, Dublin, Attic Press.

Chapter 10

Interrogating Patriarchy: The Challenges of Feminist Research

Louise Morley

This chapter critically examines developments in feminist research and raises questions about the problematic relationship between gender, power, method and epistemology. As assertions of 'knowledge' frequently both produce and guarantee domination and power, there is a problem as to how feminism can legitimately claim to be a site of knowledge about the oppression of women, without reproducing the power relations it questions. This produces tensions for feminist researchers. Participation in the social research industry can require a certain amount of collusion with the values that traditionally underpin it. In the market economy of the academy, this also involves a tacit acceptance of the juxtaposition of the economic with the aesthetic and intellectual. As a feminist academic, I share Fine's anxiety about 'how best to unleash ourselves from our central contradiction – being researchers and being active feminists' (1994, p. 13).

Perceptions of Feminist Research

Atkinson *et al.* (1993, p. 17) identify seven approaches that have been used in British educational qualitative research: symbolic interactionism, anthropology, sociolinguistics, ethnomethodology, qualitative evaluation, neo-Marxist ethnography and feminism.[1] A noticeable feature of their work is the extent to which feminism is dismissed in two paragraphs (compared to four for symbolic interactionism, and five for sociolinguistics). Whilst not a sociolinguist myself, I was able to detect the judgmentalism encapsulated in the use of the terms 'extreme', and 'exaggerated claims' (p. 25) when discussing feminist research. This reminded me of a research seminar I attended. My colleagues included a vicar researching Christian church services, maths teachers researching maths in the National Curriculum, and several others who followed their professional and ideological beliefs in their inquiries. Yet, I, as a feminist researcher researching the micropolitics of feminism, was the only member of the group pounced on for bias. I was told that there was danger of collusion and over-identification, even manipulation of my informants. Embedded in this interaction was the hidden discourse of purity and danger, with feminists perceived as pollutants of the otherwise hygienic research process. This strand has been theorized by several feminists. For example, Harding (1991, p. 114) highlighted how 'The social structure of the sciences remains hostile to women scientists, especially to researchers engaged in learning more about women and gender in ways directed by antisexist assumptions.'

Rose (1994, p. 67) points out how feminist researchers find out that their cultural capital is devalued when it comes to competing for academic posts. I have been asked, on many occasions, if I am able to write on subjects other than women. The implication is that I am so overwhelmed and distressed by my own grievances against patriarchy that my research is a kind of manic revenge, rather than legitimate academic inquiry. McRobbie (1982, p. 46) predicted this cultural response when she argued how the 'urgency and the polemics of politics . . . are . . . at odds with the traditional requirements of the scholarly mode'. Referring to feminist researchers, Fine (1992, p. 230) observes: 'Because we acknowledge that politics saturates all research but are usually the only ones who "come clean", we run the risk of being portrayed as distinctly "biased" and thus discounted.'

Social sciences cannot be value-neutral, according to Rosser (1988), because society is not neutral on issues such as gender, 'race' or sexual preference. Dubois (1983, p. 108) coined the term 'passionate scholarship' to describe the politically engaged premise of feminist research, a premise that breaches the academic rule of disembodiment. Fine (1992, p. 214) highlighted how researchers 'pronounce "truths" while whiting out their own authority, so as to be unlocatable and irresponsible'.

Braidotti developed de Beauvoir's earlier claims that the world is masculine but coded as universal. The result is the tendency to conflate 'the masculine viewpoint with the general "human" standpoint and the confinement of the feminine to the structural position of "other"'. Therefore the mark of sexual difference falls on women, 'marking them off as the second sex . . . whereas men are marked by the imperative of carrying the universal' (Braidotti, 1992, p. 26). This point is exemplified by Bhavnani (1993) who describes how, as a black feminist, her research on youth cultures was particularized, while influential ethnographies such as those undertaken by Willis (1978) became markers for universalistic insight. In social research, it seems as if only counter-hegemonic discourses such as feminism are described as standpoint theories. Standpoint theory involves the attribution of epistemic privilege to socially marginalized groups, enabling those who have otherwise been objectified to enter the research process as knowledge-makers (Harding, 1991). Standpoint theorists build in analysis of power relations and argue that 'science is part of a social order' (Henwood and Pidgeon, 1995, p. 14). But postmodernism, with its emphasis on pluralism, problematizes standpoint theory for its liberalist assumption that there is a unitary subject.

Feminist Critiques of Social Research

Feminist critiques of social research have shifted over the past two decades. Central to the debate has been the ongoing question of whether research can confront and act upon oppressive structures such as patriarchy, racism, the social class system, and if so, what this means for notions of validity, research relations, and possibilities for change (Gitlin, 1994; Holland and Ramazanoglu, 1995). Early thinking focused on androcentric approaches and the absence of subordinate groups both as researched and researchers. The concern was that even when power inequalities such as social class and youth culture were researched (Willis, 1978), other forms of inequality were omitted, like 'race', gender and sexuality. Oakley (1974) argued that this practice not only focuses attention on some areas of the social world, it also focuses attention away from others. She summarized this as 'a way of seeing is a way of not seeing' (p. 27). Interest in repressed knowledges meant that feminists wanted to discover the existence of voices of those who had been silenced or subordinated by or excluded from dominant discourses. 'The most simple and in many ways the most powerful criticism made of theory and practice within the social sciences is that, by and large, they omit or distort the experiences of women' (Stanley and Wise, 1993, p. 27).

Two decades ago, Stanley undertook a content analysis of three major British sociology journals (Stanley, 1974). She discovered that work reported generally focused on men and boys. In 1975, Chetwynd carried out a similar exercise, observing articles in psychology journals. She also found that psychology journals contained fewer females than males, generalized from male experience to the whole population, and also treated women as 'non-men'. This meant that the male experience was taken as the norm and that female experience fell at the other end of the bipolar scale, and so females are characterized as underachievers, because males are typified as achievers.

One remedy was an additive approach, with women appended to un-reconstructed studies, with little attention paid to the need to think differently about women. Research methods and identities of researchers remained the same, but the research sample would contain women. This caused more feminist concern and Reinharz (1979) used the term 'rape research' to describ what she perceived as exploitation, intrusiveness and objectification involved in patriarchal research, with researchers invading women's lives for purposes of their own career development, and with no thought for the impact of the research process on the participants. The debate became increasingly complex in the 1980s, when questions were asked about oppressive practices embedded in the research process itself (Stanley and Wise, 1983). Should research be on, by, for, or with members of subordinate groups? Were qualitative methods inherently more 'liberatory' then quantitative approaches? Does research automatically objectify the researched and privilege the researcher, who has the power to name, describe and frame questions and experiences?

So, including underrepresented groups was not in itself 'liberatory', if their inclusion was based on problematization and pathology. The insensitive application of inappropriate research methods meant that female, black and working-class people were researched in relation to the dominant group, and socially positioned as 'other'. As Neal (1995) illustrates, there has been a persistency of the sociology of deviance in the development of a research problem. For example, research on the alleged underachievement of black children in British schools made the issue of 'race' more visible in education, but its deficit perspective was felt to contribute to stereotyping and the negative social construction of a subordinate group. Theorists on policy archaeology have also inquired why certain issues come under the gaze of social researchers at particular political and historical moments, and they argue that social problems are social constructions (Scheurich, 1994).

McRobbie observed that 'No research is carried out in a vacuum. The very questions we ask are always informed by the historical moments we inhabit' (1982, p. 48). Sexist bias is reflected in how questions are phrased, the absence of categories and concepts that tap women's experiences, or inattention to variations in women's experiences by time and place (Billson, 1991). Feminist sociologist Smith (1987) drew attention to the 'peopling' of subordinate groups, and how generalization about a single society were made without sufficient differentiation on the grounds of 'race' and gender. A good example of this practice has been the sociological focus on the family, as the smallest social unit, with women's differentiated experiences submerged. Dubois (1983, p. 107) argues that this submergence rendered women not only unknown but, crucially, unknowable. Billson (1991) points out that insofar as women are isolated, marginal and dependent, it is inevitable that others will speak for them. Fonow and Cook (1991), Stanley and Wise (1993), and Patricia Hill Collins (1990) have all drawn attention to the issue of homogeneity, that is, the treatment of a marginalized group as one category of analysis, without attention to difference and diversity. Examples include studies on women which assume all women are heterosexual, or white, or mothers, or non-disabled. Thus, the practice of white, middle-class, heterosexual women retaining hegemonic control of the knowledge-producing process is steadily being challenged (Siraj-Blatchford, 1995).

Concern with power relations and democratization in the research process has not been confined to feminists. Harding (1991, p. viii) comments on 'the rising tide of critical analysis of the mental life and social relations of the modern, androcentric, imperial, bourgeois West'. While feminism has traditionally favoured collectivism and collaboration, rather than competition and hierarchies, other counter-hegemonic theorists raised similar questions about the notion of participation. Rowan and Reason (1981) contributed to the problematization of the knower to the known. Their New Paradigm theory suggested that action and subjectivity are essential elements of social change. For them cooperative inquiry was preferable, in which all those involved in the research contribute to the formation of the research question, choice of methods, analysis and dissemination.

A central premise in New Paradigm and feminist research has been a sensitivity to power relations which assumes the researcher has more cultural capital than the researched, reinforcing a traditional view that research focuses on disadvantage. Ball (1994), Walford (1994), and Neal (1995) acknowledge that while there is a paucity of inquiry into the ruling classes, the situation differs when the research gaze is upwards. When interviewing the elite, Neal cautions that collaborative research can rapidly degenerate into collusion. Phoenix (1994, p. 56) analyses the complexity of the reversal of traditional power relations in research studies when a black woman interviews white respondents. This subversion of traditional power relations can help make explicit the power relations within the research situation (Bhavnani, 1990, quoted in Phoenix, 1994, p. 56). According to Lather (1991, p. 53), research must produce emancipatory knowledge that will enable the oppressed to understand and change their own reality. This reading could imply a quasi-evangelical rescuer/victim relationship, with researchers discursively located as missionaries and saviours. Siraj-Blatchford (1995, p. 213) draws attention to the need to raise the consciousness of the oppressors as well as the oppressed in a researched context.

Tierney (1994, p. 98) argues that 'research is meant to be transformative'. The question of who or what is to be transformed remains ambiguous. The relationship between research and social change has long been a thorny issue, with an abundance of cultural clichés representing the academy's protected position from social problems. Publication in refereed international journals is the most prestigious outlet for research findings. Ladwig and Gore (1994, p. 234) ask 'how is writing a volume to be read by other academics going to contribute to the overall political concerns of the author?' Thus academic reflection becomes synonymous with introspection and is conceptualized in opposition to action. Kelly *et al.* (1994, p. 29) see this dichotomy as a 'masculinist hierarchy between theory and practice'. This poses challenges for feminist academics who have attempted to interrelate the two, via praxis, a concept developed by Gramsci. This can take the form of theoretically informed practice and vice versa, and places 'neither in a position of subservience to the other' (Gramsci, 1971, pp. 334–6). One methodology which attempts this is action research, a form of research carried out by practitioners into their own practices (Kemmis, 1993). In the tradition of Lewin (1948), the strong applied emphasis was perceived as an effective means of embedding change in the process of knowledge production. Siraj-Blatchford (1995, p. 218) extends earlier notions of action research, and states that what is needed at the present time is not simply practitioner action research but rather research pursued by organic intellectuals. Organic intellectuals,[2] according to Said (1993), are actively involved in society, constantly struggling to change minds and to expand the power and control of the group to which they are committed. The debate rarely extends to include the groups themselves in the research process, whether they are clients or service users. Another question that arises is whether feminists are automatically organic intellectuals and feminist research is inherently action research as it is committed to changing the position of women in society.

A further two questions frequently debated are whether all research undertaken by feminists is feminist research, and whether one has to be a feminist, or indeed a woman, to do feminist research. In response to the first question, I would suggest that there are limited opportunities for triangulation to verify how feminist the research felt for the researched. I have been interviewed by several self-proclaimed feminist researchers who have acted quite abusively in research situations, and have shown an alarming ignorance of the micropolitics of power in interpersonal transactions, by, for example, showing disrespect for boundaries I had set, and constantly pushing me for more information, more of my time. I have been asked crass closed questions and asked to commit to bipolarities not of my making. I have had confidential information referred to in social situations. I have had tape recorders set up without my permission, and no reassurances or information about how the tapes would be used. I have been pushed to reveal painful memories, with no consideration for the emotional consequences. In other words, I, as a feminist researcher, alert to power relations, have been left feeling dominated and angry. Without wishing to sound like superwoman, I have wondered, if I allowed this to happen to me, what happens to even more vulnerable members of the community?

The consequences of members of powerful groups researching the less powerful have preoccupied critics for some time. Skeggs argues that 'men cannot do feminist research because of the wider social relations they occupy which give them power to look at women' (1994a, p. 80). In his influential study of (male) youth culture, Willis (1978) described young women in relation to young men and described their responses to his questions as unforthcoming, unwilling to talk, and observed how they retreated, in giggles, into the background. Willis saw this as a symptom of the young women's social inadequacies, rather than a result of his presence as a male researcher.

Siraj-Blatchford (1995, p. 207) problematizes identity issues in relation to white researchers investigating 'race', recognizing on one hand that their 'oppressors' values' will influence the study. On the other hand, she believes it erroneous to assume that all black researchers have an anti-racist consciousness. I would go further to suggest that even when there is an anti-racist or anti-sexist consciousness, there is no guarantee that this miraculously transforms into process-sensitive interactions.

Is There a Feminist Methodology?

A fundamental question is what form feminism should take in textual terms (Stanley, 1991, p. 216). Smith (1992) maintains that social scientific inquiry ordinarily begins from a standpoint in a text-mediated discourse or organization. It could also be argued that the experience of sexist oppression is a valuable source of data for theorizing gender, exemplifying a postmodernist concept that power can be productively linked to knowledge (Giroux, 1983; Morley, 1995). While Stacey argues that 'there is no uniform canon of feminist research principles' (1988, p. 21), Stanley (1991) summarizes the basic tenets of what constitutes feminist research, emphasizing how feminist theory is derived from experience; the feminist researcher locates herself on the same critical plane as the researched, and there is a rejection of the dichotomous myth of subjectivity/objectivity. Stanley suggests that what these premises signify is actually better described as a feminist epistemology rather than a methodology. The debate on feminist research has misunderstood that what is being proposed is a different method or technique, rather than a specifically feminist theory of knowledge (Stanley, 1991, p. 208). Maynard (1993, p. 327) concludes that rather than the method *per se*, it is the questions asked, the way the researcher locates herself within the questions and the political purpose of the work which distinguishes feminist from other forms of research. While I would not argue for researchers taking on the role of counsellor or therapist, I would add that attention to process and an awareness of the complex interpersonal and intrapersonal dynamics activated by the research situation should be included in the taxonomy.

The problem of definition and quality assurance of feminist research has exercised many theorists. Kelly *et al.* (1992, p. 149) explored the central contradiction they perceived in the feminist rejection of binary oppositions and accompanying value hierarchies, and the way in which they felt many discussions of feminist methodology reproduced them, albeit reversing the value hierarchy. It is difficult to discuss feminist research and differentiate it from non-feminist research without also creating another bipolarity, with feminism a synonym for good practice. The very concept of good practice is itself problematic as it entails notions of standards, measurement and competence. There are competing views of what is good and it is not always clear what is meant by practice. Harding (1991, p. 113) argued that differentiation between feminist and non-feminist research is necessary and suggested that it was not possible simply to add feminism onto established research methodologies, because 'the two sets of beliefs contain tensions and contradictions'. Haraway (1988) believes that there are three central questions to pose in relation to whether research is feminist or not. Firstly, there is the issue of accountability, not just to the research participants, but to feminism in the wider sense. Researchers need to ask if the researched are reinscribed into prevailing notions of powerlessness. Secondly, in relation to sensitivity to the power relations embedded in the process, researchers should ask themselves if the micropolitics of the research relationship is discussed. Thirdly, in recognition that 'woman' is not a unifying category, researchers need to consider how their studies engage with questions of difference.

Early debate attempted to make the process more equitable, transparent, interactive, with emphasis on reciprocity and subjectivity (Finch, 1984; Roberts, 1981). As Maynard (1994, p. 23) demonstrates,

> One of the early driving forces of feminism was to challenge the passivity, subordination and silencing of women, by encouraging them to speak about their own condition and in so doing to confront the experts and dominant males with the limitations of their own knowledge and comprehension.

Stanley (1991, p. 207) draws attention to one criticism of feminist methodology that views it as essentialist, because it is 'concerned with an analytic exploration of "women's experiences"', thereby suggesting that women's experiences were homogeneous and innately different from those of men. In another analysis, which could also be described as essentialist in so far as it genders methods, Carlson (1972) used Bakan's (1966) distinction of 'agentic' and 'communal' to describe methodologies used by male and female researchers. Carlson argued that the agentic male features are 'separating', 'ordering', 'quantifying', 'manipulating', 'controlling', while the communal female features 'involve naturalistic observation, sensitivity to intrinsic and qualitative patterning of phenomena studies, and greater personal participation of the investigator' (quoted in Farnham, 1987, p. 101). In attempting to define how feminist research differs from the mainstream, Farnham asks, 'do feminists ask different questions?'

Skeggs (1994b) summarizes three areas to consider in relation to what constitutes feminist research: firstly, ontology, that is, what is knowable; secondly, epistemology, that is, what is knowledge and what is the relationship of the knower to the known; and thirdly, methodology, that is how we find things out. Skeggs argues that the ways in which these different questions are answered or ignored in the research process will demonstrate the different theoretical positions held by researchers. Differentiating feminist from non-feminist research, Skeggs (1994a, p. 77) claims that in response to the ontological question, 'feminist research begins from the premise that the nature of reality in western society is unequal and hierarchical'. This is not distinctly feminist, as socialist research could make the same claim, without necessarily paying attention to gender. Fine and Gordon (1991) believe that feminist research should involve the study of what is not, by disrupting prevailing notions of what is inevitable, what is seen to be natural and what is considered impossible.

Kelly *et al.* (1992, p. 150) maintain that what makes feminist research is not so much the method used, but rather how it is used, that is, its application and purpose. In their discussion of the use of quantitative approaches in a research project on sexual abuse, they believed that the survey method was one way of expanding understanding of the dimensions and complexities of the issues. They feel that, under certain circumstances, survey methods may be a preferred technique because they allow the researched anonymity in revealing distressing experiences. Ethical issues about the role of the researcher in inquiring into sensitive and difficult topics, such as domestic violence, have also been raised in relation to the idea of research as catharsis. In this instance, research can have a quasi-therapeutic effect, encouraging the researched to access occluded and painful memories, without ensuing support services.

Another example is how the compilation of statistics about the number of buildings in a city without access facilities for people with disabilities can be as consciousness-raising as interview data. Somehow, I can accept counting buildings more readily than incidents of sexual abuse. I felt distinctly uncomfortable reading Kelly *et al.*'s account of their research process. Whilst they display concern and sensitivity for any distress that might be activated by completion of the research questionnaires (for example, they produced resource sheets for follow-up support services etc.), the issue of entering young people's lives, opening up painful, and often occluded, memories, and then departing (albeit leaving them with information sheet in hand), raises numerous questions about the interrogation of human experiences for the purposes of knowledge production.[3]

The Anti-Positivism Campaign

Complex debates are frequently reduced to dichotomous preoccupation with qualitative versus quantitative modes of inquiry, with ethnographic methods such as interviewing and participant observation perceived as more 'liberatory' than surveys and statistics (Reinharz, 1983). This reductivism suggests that Enlightenment binary thinking continues to flourish in the academy. As Maynard (1993) points out, there is no point hankering after the old modernist notions such as truth, accuracy or legitimacy because their meaning is only relative to the form of discourse being used. Lately, critics have questioned whether there are any inherently 'liberatory' methods. Furthermore, liberation itself could be perceived as an Enlightenment concept, based on a rational linearity between intervention and outcome. There is also another distillation, suggesting that positivism and quantitative methods are synonymous and interchangeable. Hughes (1995, p. 396) explains how positivist views of science argue that an objective scientific method is powerful enough to eliminate social and political subjectivity. Feminists, Hughes reminds us, have argued that there is no objectivity disassociated from the social and economic politics of the inventors or users of specific scientific methods.

In social research, numbers have traditionally been perceived as the ultimate expression of objectivity. Maynard (1994, p. 13) challenges this view, stating that 'providing figures involves as much of an act of social construction as any other research'. Hughes (1995, p. 403) believes that statistical analysis becomes a powerful tool in constructing the Other, and that 'domination and exploitation would be impossible to sustain if difference was not created and maintained'.

> Quantitative approaches have foundationalist origins – they rest on an epistemological position which sees a single unseamed reality existing 'out there' which the special expertise of science can investigate and explain as it 'really' is, independent of observer effects. (Stanley and Wise, 1993, p. 6)

The positivistic imperative for 'objectivity' and the banishment of emotion from the research process has been heavily criticized and exposed for its dishonesty by a range of counter-hegemonic research theorists (Eichler, 1988; Fine, 1994; Lather, 1991; Rowan and Reason, 1981; Stanley and Wise, 1993). Harding (1991) and Haraway (1988) argue that objectivity has always been about a particular and specific embodiment. Therefore there can never be an unmediated account. Haraway (1991) describes the traditional positivist view of science as a 'God-trick', as it purports to see everything from nowhere. Haraway (1988) argued that feminist objectivity means quite simply situated knowledges. She suggests that feminists could view objectivity as a 'particular and specific embodiment', rather than as a 'false vision promising transcendence of all limits and responsibility' (pp. 581–2). Lather (1994, p. 47), citing Whitford (1991), observes that 'Embodiment is relegated to the female, freeing the phallocentric idea to transcend the material, creating the deadly split between epistemology and ethics'.

The challenge to the Enlightenment preoccupation with reason and rationality questions the very notion of how research can provide an objective, reliable and universal foundation for knowledge. Neutrality, according to Mies (1983), should be replaced by conscious partiality. Smith (1974) is critical of the social science norm of objectivity, which implies that subject and object can effectively be separated via the screen of 'clean' methodology. Identification with the social reality of the researched leads to allegations of bias. Skeggs (1994b, p. 78) highlights how 'Many male researchers are normalized in the process of research; they are able to leave their gender, and its accompanying institutional power positions, unquestioned'. Feminist research, however, repeatedly reminds us of our gender, both in its execution and content.

Feminist Ethnography

Stacey (1988) argues that ethnography appears to be particularly appropriate to feminist research as it emphasizes the experiential, with a contextual and interpersonal approach to knowledge. The term ethnography, borrowed from social anthropology, privileges the method of participant observation, and has been heavily influenced by the American sociologist Becker (1967). Stacey cites two major challenges for feminist ethnographers, the research process, and the research product, with possibilities for inequality, exploitation, and even betrayal endemic to ethnography. Her fear is that the intimacy involved in the ethnographic method ironically exposes subjects to far greater danger and exploitation than do positivist, abstract methods. This argument alludes to the notion of the feminist researcher as a kind of double agent, forging intimate relationships in order to acquire information to report back to base.

Stanley (1995, p. 185) describes feminist ethnography as 'critically aware, reflexively constituted, analytically and epistemologically positioned, aware of its own knowledge-claims and concerned to give readers as many textual means as possible of engaging with, disputing, even rejecting, the grounds for these as well as the claims themselves'. Morgan (1981, pp. 86–7) highlighted how ethnographic research has its 'own brand of machismo with its image of the male sociologist bringing back news from the fringes of society, the lower depths, the mean streets'. Metaphors many male ethnographers use to describe the process abound with images of danger and frontier-crossing, parodied by Ball: 'ethnography involves risk, uncertainty, and discomfort . . . researchers . . . must go unarmed, with no questionnaires, interview schedules, or observation protocols to stand between them and the cold winds of the raw real' (Ball, 1990, p. 157). The implication is that ethnography is not for the fainthearted or lily-livered. This stance could be in relation to accusations that qualitative research is 'soft', compared to the 'hardness' of statistics, with qualitative researchers trying to regain credibility by demonstrating how 'hard' the work is (Gherardi and Turner, 1987). But the issue of fabricating what can feel like fraudulent social relations in order to gather data and develop one's career remains problematic.

The Privileging of Experience

Holland and Ramazanoglu (1994, p. 130) believe that 'innovation in methodology has been through trying to grasp the parts that experience, emotion and subjectivity play in the research process, rather than seeing these as weaknesses to be controlled'. Whereas early thinking on feminist research insisted that knowledge claims must be grounded in women's experiences, more recently attention has been drawn to consideration that experience itself is shaped by social relations (Harding, 1991). Experience is increasingly perceived as partial, exclusionary and situated, with no automatic claims to authority and knowledge. Maynard and Purvis (1994, p. 6) argue that the notion of experience needs to be problematized, since individuals do not necessarily possess sufficient knowledge to explain everything in their lives. A popular view is that theory is the prerogative of the researcher who stands in disciplined intellectual tension against a glutinous mass of untheorized, unstructured experience. Stanley (1991, p. 208) disputes this construction, arguing that 'people theorize their own experience . . . and so researchers of the social are faced with an already "first order" theorized material social reality'. Challenging the theory/experience dichotomy, Stanley says that experience is not 'a morass of unformed inchoate sensation: people observe, categorize, analyse, reach conclusions – which is exactly what "theory" is' (*ibid.*).

Since all experience is mediated by a discourse, describing experience can culturally and discursively constitute it. Maynard (1993) indicates how the very act of describing experience involves inscribing it as well. In addition to uncertainties about interpretation, researchers also have to consider tacit knowledge, knowledge which is non-discursive. As Skeggs (1994b) indicates, whenever we speak or write about a reality, the language we use is not the reality to which we refer. It is questionable whether researchers can ever access women's experiences fully through verbal interactions, as language itself is inscribed with gendered power relations. Indeed, even to believe we can access the 'truth' of women's experiences is reminiscent of an Enlightenment project.

Reflexivity

Stanley and Wise (1991, p. 266) observe how the 'research process appears a very orderly and coherent process'. They term this absence of personal statements 'hygienic research', or research as described rather than experienced. Reflexivity demands a type of emotional literacy on the part of the researcher, who can sensitively engage with the research study while/because s/he is aware of her/his own responses, values, beliefs, and prejudices (Morley, 1995). Hammersley and Atkinson (1983, p. 234) believe that reflexivity involves the 'explicit recognition of the fact that the social researcher, and the research act itself, are part and parcel of the social world under investigation'. Reflexivity can be part of the research process, with researchers feeding back transcriptions and interpretations to the researched for comment. Stanley (1991, pp. 209–10) talks about 'alienated knowledge', and discusses how traditional scientistic knowledge hides, through a series of textual means, its labour process. Reflexivity, she argues, acknowledges that our descriptions are mutually constitutive. Indexicality of knowledge, she writes, demonstrates that it is contextually dependent: 'abstract generalized theoretical knowledge is actually contextually-dependent knowledge which has been stripped, by semantic and textual means, of its context'.

Holland and Ramazanoglu (1995, p. 281) argue that while feminists can 'aim at reflexivity . . . we cannot break out of the social constraints on our ways of knowing simply by wanting to'. Henwood and Pidgeon (1995) remind us that the practice of reflexivity will not automatically strengthen the credibility of an account, and that the outcomes of feminist research also tend to be evaluated within a still generally unreflexive discipline.

Reflexivity can also mean hesitancy, uncertainty and caution as a result of being acquainted with the theoretical complexities of the subject. Cain (1990) argues that there is a difference between personal and theoretical reflexivity, the former being seen as the individualized thoughts, feelings and responses of the researcher, the latter a theoretical understanding of the site from which one works. Reflexivity is often discursively located in opposition to the concept of ventriloquy. Ventriloquy, according to Fine (1992) requires a denial of politics in social research, a refusal to use 'I' and treating subjects as objects while calling them subjects. A reflexive concern with its own production can lead to accusations of feminist research being introspective and narcissistic. Preoccupation with 'I' can reduce the research process to a cathartic exercise in which the researcher abuses the uninterrupted attention of the text/reader to 'client' on unresolved personal material.

Grounded Theory

A popular qualitative research methodology is grounded theory (Strauss and Corbin, 1990). Central to this process is the belief that the researcher starts with a *tabula rasa*, and elicits theory from the data. The aim is for theory to follow data rather than precede it. This approach was developed in opposition to the positivistic notion of hypothesis testing and deductivism, in which a predetermined theory was used with the rigidity of a grid on the research data. Lather (1986) described grounded theory as an attempt to minimize researcher-imposed definitions, and avoid the problem of conceptual overdeterminism and theoretical imposition. Reinharz (1983) advocates not undertaking an extensive literature search before an investigation, in order to avoid self-fulfilling prophecies. Strauss and Corbin (1990) claim that the research question in grounded theory study is a statement that identifies the phenomenon to be studied, with insight and understanding increasing with data interaction. Grounded theoreticians are advised to maintain an attitude of scepticism as all theoretical explanations should be regarded as provisional. Everything should be checked out, played against the actual data and never accepted as fact. Grounded theory, according to Strauss and Corbin (p. 55) should 'help the analyst to break through biases and assumptions brought to, and that can develop during, the research process'. The researcher's perspectives are altered by the logic of the data.

At one time, grounded theory was seen as highly compatible with feminism as, firstly, it was concerned to locate theory in participants' worlds and secondly, it aided the process of breaking out of the confines of androcentric theory (Henwood and Pidgeon, 1995). Many feminist researchers who initially rejected deductivism now reject grounded theory, on the basis that no feminist study can be politically neutral, completely inductive or solely based on grounded theory, as all work is theoretically grounded (Maynard, 1994). Kelly *et al.* (1992, p. 156) believe that 'As feminists we cannot argue that theory emerges from research, since we start from a theoretical perspective that takes gender as a fundamental organizer of social life'. Holland and Ramazanoglu

(1995) argue that we cannot read meaning in texts, allowing them to pose their own meanings, without also reading into them.

One complexity of data-led theorizing is articulated in the term 'false consciouness'. Lather (1986, p. 269) points out how 'Sole reliance on the participants' perceptions of their situation is misguided because, as neo-Marxists point out, false consciousness and ideological mystification may be present'. Applying Gramsci's theories of hegemony (Gramsci, 1971), Lather (1986) emphasizes how most people to some extent identify with and/or accept ideologies which do not serve their best interests. Smith (1992) argues that since knowledge is essentially socially organized, it can never be an act or an attribute of individual consciousness. This poses challenges both for grounded theory and for the feminist researcher working with non-feminist informants. If informants deny or exclude discussion of the existence of patriarchal dominance in their lives, does this mean that it does not exist, or that the informant is suffering from false consciousness, or that the informant is micropolitically enacting macropolitical power relations?

Interpretation and Artefact

The question of whether an artificial and patriarchal order is being put on the raw data is a recurring theme in feminist research. Feminists in the 1990s have argued that there is an inherent fragmentation and fabrication in the research process as people's lives are dissected according to the researcher's frame of reference. Maynard (1994, p. 11) indicates how

> Only one part of experience is abstracted as the focus for attention and this is done in both a static and an atemporal fashion. Often the result of such an approach is a simple matrix of standardized variables which is unable to convey an in-depth understanding of, or feeling for, the people under study.

Fine (1994, p. 22) draws attention to how social research invariably involves 'carving out pieces of narrative evidence that we select, edit, and deploy to border our arguments'. She also indicates how this can mean politicizing perspectives narrated by people who have tried to represent themselves as non-political (Fine, 1992, p. 218). A further concern is that feminist researchers dissect women's narratives and subject them to an analysis heavily influenced by male theorists of social science. The categorization implies a forced reading and assignment to the tick boxes of patriarchy. Smith (1989, pp. 35–6) drew attention to the dangers of feminists turning talk into texts and texts into sociology. Holland and Ramazanoglu (1995, p. 274) comment that even if the researcher identifies politically with women, this does not necessarily give us the methodological tools with which to avoid the conceptual distancing of women from their experiences. They highlight how feminists have had to accept that there is 'no technique of analysis or methodological logic that can neutralise the social nature of interpretation' (*ibid.*, p. 281). The difference with feminist research is that it admits it!

Celebrating Women's Diversity

In 1984, Finch asserted that there is an added dimension when women interview women, because 'both parties have a subordinate structural position by virtue of their gender' (p. 76). Lather (1988, p. 571) asserted that 'to do feminist research is to put the social construction of gender at the centre of one's inquiry'. A criticism of this approach has been the exclusion of differences among women. In the 1990s, this has been challenged, recognizing that there are hierarchies and hegemonies between women. For example, Patricia Hill Collins (1990, p. 26) discusses the absence of black women from gendered research, observing how 'Groups unequal in power are correspondingly unequal in their ability to make their standpoint known to themselves and others'.

There is also widespread rejection of the notion of double or triple disadvantage when researching, for example, disabled women. The research can itself be part of images of disadvantage. Morris (1995) believes that, as far as disabled women are concerned, research is alienated knowledge, because the researcher/theorist has not grounded herself as a non-disabled person holding certain cultural assumptions about disability. Disability and old age, according to Morris, are identities with which gender is very much entwined but which have been almost entirely ignored by feminist researchers.

Siraj-Blatchford (1995) believes that researchers need to be reflexive regarding the representativeness of their data. But Maynard (1994, p. 24) argues that 'It is not always necessary to include women who are white, black, working-class, lesbian or disabled in our research to be able to say something about racism, classism, heterosexism and disableism'. This approach differentiates between the tokenistic practice of adjusting the research sample, and the need to conceptualize and embed consideration of the structures of inequality into the research project itself.

Postmodernism

Postmodern theory is also highly critical of social research. Lather (1991) argued that the tradition of grand narratives with their totalizing and universalizing theories must be rejected. Tierney (1994, p. 99) maintains that 'The postmodern world . . . is one that rejects the positivist definition of "objectivity", or that a singular "truth" exists that awaits to be discovered'. He also highlights how 'postmodernism has shown us the fallacy of the modernist belief that science will lead to human perfection' (*ibid.*, p. 112). A feature of postmodernist thought is the disruption of certainties, and the formerly firm foundations on which knowledge claims were based (Gipps, 1993). This has clear implications for knowledge production as it confronts the search for absolutes and for certainty in our ways of knowing.

Maynard indicates how for postmodern feminism

> the social world is pictured as so fragmented, so individualistic, so totally in a state of flux that any attempt to present a more structured alternative, which, by its very nature, much social research does, is regarded as, *a priori*, mistaken. (Maynard, 1994, p. 22)

One postmodernist view would suggest that research is part of the technology of regulation. Maynard (1993) questions whether it is possible to develop research techniques which do not involve the researcher in strategies of control and surveillance. Foucault suggested that if you want to understand how power works, you should look at the knowledge, self-understandings, and struggles of those whom powerful groups have cast off as the other (Best and Keller, 1991). Social research can contribute to the misinformation about subordinate groups, which is internalized and reproduced.

So . . .

As we have seen, feminist theorizing of research has developed in complexity and sophistication, from early concerns with exclusion and distortion, to current debates on epistemology and methodologies. Differentiating feminist from non-feminist research is part of the evolutionary process, but can collapse into modernist bipolarities. Labelling work feminist research is not like providing a 'kitemark' which ensures particular qualities, as there is a range of interpretations and interests contained within the term. For three decades, there has been a lively discussion drawing attention to the need for us to notice the patriarchal paradigms sedimented in our research practices. There has been an increasing emphasis on what constitutes knowledge, and how to access it without further oppressing both researchers and researched. What surprises me, however, is that while much of the theory is very challenging to mainstream canons, the debate still takes place within the discourse which assumes research is a useful exercise. Hence, we have endless deliberations on how to do it better and less oppressively. Nobody, however, suggests that we stop the activity altogether!

Notes

1 The emphasis on qualitative approaches in the chapter by Atkinson *et al.* excludes discussion of quantitative methods such as the psychometric indus-

try and the obsession with mathematical measurement which has dominated educational research.
2 This was a term developed earlier by Gramsci and describes the important role played by intellectuals in the process of social change.
3 It could also be argued that statistical evidence can be used to influence public policy and ensuing service provision.

References

ATKINSON, P., DELAMONT, S. and HAMMERSLEY, M. (1993) 'Qualitative Research Traditions', in HAMMERSLEY, M. (Ed.) *Educational Research*, London, Paul Chapman, pp. 16–31.
BAKAN, D. (1966) *The Duality of Human Existence: An Essay on Psychology and Religion*, Chicago, Rand McNally.
BALL, S. (1990) 'Self-Doubt and Soft Data: Social and Technical Trajectories in Ethnographic Fieldwork', *Qualitative Studies in Education*, 3, 2, pp. 157–71.
BALL, S. (1994) 'Researching Inside the State: Issues in the Interpretation of Elite Interviews', in HALPIN, D. and TROYNA, B. (Eds) *Researching Education Policy*, London, Falmer Press, pp. 107–20.
BECKER. H. (Ed.) (1967) *Sociological Work*, London, Allen and Unwin.
BEST, S. and KELLER, D. (1991) *Postmodern Theory*, New York, Macmillan.
BHAVNANI, K-K. (1990) 'What's Power Got to Do with It? Empowerment and Social Research', in PARKER, I. and SHOTTER, J. (Eds) *Deconstructing Social Psychology*, London, Routledge.
BHAVNANI, K-K. (1993) 'Tracing the Contours: Feminist Research and Feminist Objectivity', *Women's Studies International Forum*, 16, 2, pp. 95–104.
BILLSON, J. M. (1991) 'The Progressive Verification Method: Toward a Feminist Methodology for Studying Women Cross-Culturally', *Women's Studies International Forum*, 14, 3, pp. 201–15.
BRAIDOTTI, R. (1992) 'Origin and Development of Gender Studies in Western Europe', in European Network for Women's Studies Workshop, *Establishing Gender Studies in Central and Eastern European Countries*, Wassenar, The Netherlands, Nov. 5–8, pp. 23–32.
CAIN, M. (1990) 'Realist Philosophy and Standpoint Epistemologies OR Feminist Criminology as a Successor Science', in GELSTHORPE, L. and MORRIS, A. (Eds) *Feminist Perspectives in Criminology*, Milton Keynes, Open University Press, pp. 124–40.
CARLSON, R. (1972) 'Understanding Women: Implications for Personality Theory and Research', *Journal of Social Issues*, 28, pp. 17–32.
CHETWYND, J. (Ed.) (1975) 'The Role of Psychology in the Propagation of Female Stereotypes', *Proceedings of the BPS Symposium*, Nottingham.
COLLINS, P. H. (1990) *Black Feminist Thought: Knowledge, Consciousness and the Politics of Empowerment*, London, Routledge.

DUBOIS, B. (1983) 'Passionate Scholarship: Notes on Values, Knowing and Method in Feminist Social Science', in BOWLES, G. and KLEIN, R. D. (Eds) *Theories of Women's Studies*, London, Routledge and Kegan Paul, pp. 105–16.

EICHLER, M. (1988) *Non-Sexist Research Methods*, London, Allen and Unwin.

FARNHAM, C. (1987) *The Impact of Feminist Research in the Academy*, Bloomington, University of Indiana Press.

FINCH, J. (1984) 'It's Great Having Someone to Talk To: The Ethics and Politics of Interviewing Women', in BELL, C. and ROBERTS, H. (Eds) *Social Researching: Politics, Problems and Practice*, London, Routledge and Kegan Paul, pp. 70–87.

FINE, M. (1992) *Disruptive Voices*, Ann Arbor, University of Michigan Press.

FINE, M. (1994) 'Dis-stance and Other Stances: Negotiations of Power Inside Feminist Research', in GITLIN, A. (Ed.) *Power and Method: Political Activism and Educational Research*, London, Routledge, pp. 13–35.

FINE, M. and GORDON, S. M. (1991) 'Effacing the Center and the Margins', *Feminism and Psychology*, 1, 1, pp. 19–25.

FONOW, M. and COOK, J. (Eds) (1991) *Beyond Methodology: Feminist Scholarship as Lived Research*, Bloomington, Indiana University Press.

GHERARDI, S. and TURNER, B. (1987) *Real Men Don't Collect Soft Data* (Quaderno 13), Trento, Universita di Trento, Dipartimento della Politica Sociale.

GIPPS, C. (1993) 'The Profession of Educational Research', *British Educational Research Journal*, 19, pp. 3–16.

GIROUX, H. (1983) *Theory and Resistance in Education*, London, Heinemann Educational.

GITLIN, A. (Ed.) (1994) *Power and Method: Political Activism and Educational Research*, London, Routledge.

GRAMSCI, A. (1971) *Selections from the Prison Notebooks*, HOARE, Q. and NOWELL-SMITH, G., (Eds) London, Lawrence and Wishart.

HAMMERSLEY, M. and ATKINSON, P. (1983) *Ethnography: Principles in Practice*, London, Tavistock.

HARAWAY, D. (1988) 'Situated Knowledges: The Science Question in Feminism and the Privilege of the Partial Perspective', *Feminist Studies*, 14, 3 (Fall), pp. 573–99.

HARAWAY, D. (1991) *Simians, Cyborgs and Women: The Reinvention of Nature*, New York, Routledge.

HARDING, S. (1991) *Whose Science? Whose Knowledge?*, Milton Keynes, Open University Press.

HENWOOD, K. and PIDGEON, N. (1995) 'Remaking the Link: Qualitative Research and Feminist Standpoint Theory', *Feminism and Psychology*, 5, 1, pp. 7–30.

HOLLAND, J. and RAMAZANOGLU, C. (1994) 'Coming to Conclusions: Power and Interpretation in Researching Young Women's Sexuality', in

MAYNARD, M. and PURVIS, J. (Eds) (1994) *Researching Women's Lives from a Feminist Perspective*, London, Taylor and Francis, pp. 125–48.

HOLLAND, J. and RAMAZANOGLU, C. (1995) 'Accounting for Sexuality, Living Sexual Politics. Can Feminist Research be Valid?', in HOLLAND, J., BLAIR, M. and SHELDON, S. (Eds) *Debates and Issues in Feminist Research and Pedagogy*, Clevedon, Multilingual Matters/Open University, pp. 273–91.

HUGHES, D. (1995) 'Significant Differences: The Construction of Knowledge, Objectivity, and Dominance', *Women's Studies International Forum*, 18, 4, pp. 395–406.

KELLY, L., REGAN, L. and BURTON, S. (1992) 'Defending the Indefensible? Quantitative Methods and Feminist Research', in HINDS, H., PHOENIX, A. and STACEY, J. (Eds) *Working Out: New Directions for Women's Studies*, London, Falmer Press, pp. 149–60.

KELLY, L., BURTON, S. and REGAN, L. (1994) 'Researching Women's Lives or Studying Women's Oppression? Reflections on What Constitutes Feminist Research', in MAYNARD, M. and PURVIS, J. (Eds) *Researching Women's Lives from a Feminist Perspective*, London, Taylor and Francis, pp. 27–48.

KEMMIS, S. (1993) 'Action Research', in HAMMERSLEY, M. (Ed.) *Educational Research*, Buckingham, Open University Press, pp. 177–90.

LADWIG, J. G. and GORE, J. M. (1994) 'Extending Power and Specifying Method Within the Discourse of Activist Research', in GITLIN, A. (Ed.) *Power and Method: Political Activism and Educational Research*, London: Routledge, pp. 227–38.

LATHER, P. (1986) 'Research as Praxis', *Harvard Educational Review*, 56, 3, pp. 257–77.

LATHER, P. (1988) 'Feminist Perspectives on Empowering Research Methodologies', *Women's Studies International Forum*, 11, 6, pp. 569–81.

LATHER, P. (1991) *Getting Smart: Feminist Research and Pedagogy With/in the Postmodern*, New York, Routledge.

LATHER, P. (1994) 'Fertile Obsession: Validity after Poststructuralism', in GITLIN, A. (Ed.) (1994) *Power and Method: Political Activism and Educational Research*, London, Routledge, pp. 36–60.

LEWIN, K. (1948) *Resolving Social Conflicts*, New York, Harper.

MAYNARD, M. (1993) 'Feminism and the Possibilities of a Postmodern Research Practice', *British Journal of Sociology of Education*, 14, 3, pp. 327–31.

MAYNARD, M. (1994) 'Methods, Practice and Epistemology: The Debate about Feminism and Research', in MAYNARD, M. and PURVIS, J. (Eds) *Researching Women's Lives from a Feminist Perspective*, London, Taylor and Francis, pp. 10–26.

MAYNARD, M. and PURVIS, J. (Eds) (1994) *Researching Women's Lives from a Feminist Perspective*, London, Taylor and Francis.

MCROBBIE, A. (1982) *The Politics of Feminist Research*, *Feminist Review*, 12, pp. 46–57.

Mies, M. (1983) 'Towards a Methodology for Feminist Research', in Bowles, G. and Klein, R. D. (Eds) *Theories of Women's Studies*, London, Routledge, pp. 117–39.

Morgan, D. (1981) 'Men, Masculinity and the Process of Sociological Inquiry', in Roberts, H. (Ed.) *Doing Feminist Research*, London, Routledge, pp. 83–113.

Morley, L. (1995) 'Measuring the Muse: Creativity and Career Development in Higher Education', in Morley, L. and Walsh, V. A. (Eds) *Feminist Academics: Creative Agents for Change*, London, Taylor and Francis, pp. 116–30.

Morris, J. (1995) 'Personal and Political: A Feminist Perspective on Researching Physical Disability', in Holland, J., Blair, M. and Sheldon, S. (Eds) *Debates and Issues in Feminist Research and Pedagogy*, Clevedon, Multilingual Matters/Open University, pp. 262–72.

Neal, S. (1995) 'Researching Powerful People from a Feminist and Anti-Racist Perspective: A Note on Gender, Collusion and Marginality', *British Educational Research Journal*, 21, 4, pp. 517–31.

Oakley, A. (1974) *The Sociology of Housework*, London, Martin Robertson.

Phoenix, A. (1994) 'Practising Feminist Research: The Intersection of Gender and "Race" in the Research Process', in Maynard, M. and Purvis, J. (Eds) *Researching Women's Lives from a Feminist Perspective*, London, Taylor and Francis, pp. 49–71.

Reinharz, S. (1979) *On Becoming a Social Scientist*, San Francisco, Jossey Bass.

Reinharz, S. (1983) 'Experiential Analysis: A Contribution to Feminist Research', in Bowles, G. and Klein, R. D. (Eds) *Theories of Women's Studies*, London, Routledge, pp. 162–91.

Roberts, H. (Ed.) (1981) *Doing Feminist Research*, London, Routledge and Kegan Paul.

Rose, H. (1994) *Love, Power and Knowledge: Towards a Feminist Transformation of the Sciences*, Cambridge, Polity Press.

Rosser, S. (1988) 'Good Science: Can it Ever Be Gender Free?', *Women's Studies International Forum*, 11, 1, pp. 13–19.

Rowan, J. and Reason, P. (Eds) (1981) *Human Inquiry*, Chichester: Wiley.

Said, E. (1993) 'Representations of the Intellectual' (the 1993 Reith Lecture), *Guardian*, 24 June.

Scheurich, J. (1994) 'Policy Archaeology: A New Policy Studies Methodology', *Journal of Education Policy*, 9, 4, pp. 297–316.

Siraj-Blatchford, I. (1995) 'Critical Social Research and the Academy: The Role of Organic Intellectuals in Educational Research', *British Journal of Social Research*, 16, 2, pp. 205–20.

Skeggs, B. (1994a) 'The Constraints of Neutrality: The 1988 Education Reform Act and Feminist Research', in Halpin, D. and Troyna, B. (Eds) *Researching Education Policy: Ethical and Methodological Issues*, London, Falmer Press, pp. 75–93.

SKEGGS, B. (1994b) 'Situating the Production of Feminist Ethnography', in MAYNARD, M. and PURVIS, J. (Eds) *Researching Women's Lives from a Feminist Perspective*, London, Taylor and Francis, pp. 72–92.

SMITH, D. (1974) 'Women's Perspective as a Radical Critique of Sociology', *Sociological Quarterly*, 44, pp. 7–13.

SMITH, D. (1987) *The Everyday World as Problematic*, Milton Keynes, Open University Press.

SMITH, D. (1989) 'Sociological Theory: Methods of Writing Patriarchy', in WALLACE, R. (Ed.) *Feminism and Sociological Theory*, London, Sage, pp. 34–64.

SMITH, D. (1992) 'Sociology from Women's Experience: A Reaffirmation', *Sociological Theory*, 10, 1, pp. 88–98.

STACEY, J. (1988) 'Can There Be a Feminist Ethnography?', *Women's Studies International Forum*, 11, 1, pp. 21–7.

STANLEY, L. (1974) 'Sexual Politics in Sociology: A Content Analysis of Three Sociology Journals,' unpublished paper, University of Salford.

STANLEY, L. (1991) 'Feminist Auto/Biography and Feminist Epistemology', in AARON, J. and WALBY, S. (Eds) *Out of the Margins*, London, Falmer Press, pp. 204–19.

STANLEY, L. (1995) 'My Mother's Voice? On Being a "Native" in Academia', in MORLEY, L. and WALSH, V. A. (Eds) *Feminist Academics: Creative Agents for Change*, London, Taylor and Francis, pp. 183–93.

STANLEY, L. and WISE, S. (1983) *Breaking Out*, London, Routledge.

STANLEY, L. and WISE, S. (1991) 'Feminist Research, Feminist Consciousness and Experiences of Sexism', in FONOW, M. and COOK, J. (Eds) *Beyond Methodology: Feminist Scholarship as Lived Research*, Bloomington, Indiana University Press, pp. 265–83.

STANLEY, L. and WISE, S. (1993) *Breaking Out Again*, London, Routledge.

STRAUSS, A. and CORBIN, J. (1990) *Basics of Qualitative Research: Grounded Theory Prcedures and Techniques*, London, Sage.

TIERNEY, W. G. (1994) 'On Method and Hope', in GITLIN, A. (Ed.) *Power and Method: Political Activism and Educational Research*, London, Routledge, pp. 97–115.

WALFORD, G. (Ed.) (1994) *Researching the Powerful in Education*, London, UCL Press.

WHITFORD, M. (1991) *Luce Irigaray: Philosophy in the Feminine*, London, Routledge.

WILLIS, P. (1978) *Profane Culture*, London, Routledge and Kegan Paul.

Chapter 11

Interdisciplinary Ideals and Institutional Impediments: A Case Study of Postgraduate Provision

Elizabeth Bird

Origins of the MSc in Gender and Social Policy

In the early 1970s a group of women, some of whom held academic posts at the Universities of Bristol and Bath, and all of whom were involved in a variety of groups in the women's movement, began to offer courses in what became known as women's studies. These courses were provided through the then Department of Extra-Mural Studies at the University of Bristol and they were able to grow in strength and number because they proved attractive to students and brought new kinds of students into the university. During the 1970s, the scope of the courses developed both intellectually, as they drew upon a growing body of published work, and geographically, with courses being established in centres beyond Bristol, such as Swindon, Bridgwater, Taunton, Stroud, and Cheltenham. The courses were all 'beyond the walls' in the sense of being outside the formal academic curriculum of the University of Bristol, open to anyone, involving no formal assessment, with the opportunity to challenge both academic boundaries and the conventional relationships between teacher and taught. The group of women who had been involved in teaching the courses were collectively involved in editing the book *Half the Sky: An Introduction to Women's Studies* (Bristol Women's Studies Group, 1979). I was a member of the group and was also, from 1976, the academic responsible for the programme of courses, as I had been appointed Staff Tutor in Sociology in the Department of Extra-Mural Studies in 1976.

During the 1980s, the original forays outside the walls slowly moved within the walls. Those women who were on the academic staff of the university began to teach courses on 'women' or 'gender' to undergraduates or postgraduates. They also published in this area and became increasingly recognized outside the institution if not within. Lack of internal recognition, as shown through failures to achieve promotion or appointments, led to increasing frustration, with some key women leaving the institution, and relationships between colleagues were sometimes uneasy. The rewards came from teaching and a growing number of postgraduates doing research into 'women' or 'gender'. In the late 1980s the Faculty of Social Sciences adopted a policy of increasing postgraduate numbers and the then Graduate Studies Officer of the Faculty invited a group of women academics to develop a postgraduate taught masters course. The invitation was framed in terms of a market – it was felt to be a popular and fashionable topic – and as a way of utilizing some quite well-known 'experts' who happened to be on the staff of the university. One of them had been on a government 'think-tank' and had been awarded a readership.

A group of women members of academic staff got together and drew up a course programme. From the outset we were fairly clear about certain issues. We had heard tales about another university, where a women's studies MA had supposedly run into problems in trying to reconcile the contradictions of academic curricula and the conventions of student/staff relationships with the revolutionary and subversive agenda of women's studies as the academic branch of the women's movement. At the time there was much debate about whether academic women were betraying or had betrayed their sisters. We resolved that we would aim for a 'Southern Bradford', comparing ourselves with the MSc at the University of Bradford, in that we would focus on social policy and would call it 'gender' because we wanted to look at masculinity as well. We also thought that women's studies might be too threatening for the Social Sciences Faculty Board, but our reasons were not primarily pragmatic.

In the event we did not avoid conflict with either staff or students, but that is not my prime focus in this chapter. Suffice it to say that there were concerted attacks at all stages of its approval within the Faculty of Social Sciences resulting in progress through majority votes rather than the norm of consensus. This is in sharp contrast to the progress in the Summer Term of 1994 of an MSc in Women's Studies which proceeded without any debate. As my focus in this chapter is on interdisciplinarity, the relationship of the course to the Department and Faculty is the most relevant aspect of how it was established. At the time – 1988–89 – the University of Bristol was in the process of setting up a system of devolved resource allocation. The Faculty had decided to allocate ten FTEs (full-time student equivalents) to the new MSc in Gender and Social Policy. The women involved in planning and teaching the course were drawn from eight departments, comprising seven budget centres. As we intended eventually to offer five options, we arrived at what seemed like a sensible solution of allocating the student numbers pro rata to the departments in which the women teaching the option were located, on the basis of each option equalling 20 per cent of student numbers. Heads of Departments, whose approval was felt to be needed, agreed to academic staff being involved, although the necessity for the approval of the Head of Department was somewhat vague. This was all before the days of Quality Assurance and systems of scrutiny for new courses. The course outlines did not require departmental approval as they were presented direct to the Faculty's Graduate Studies Committee, the chair of which had been responsible for suggesting the new MSc. As eight departments were involved, including two which were not even in the Faculty of Social Sciences (one in Medicine and one in Law), it was decided that the course would be 'faculty-wide'. Interdisciplinarity was being promoted as a 'good thing' and we secured a grant of £500 from a new central university committee which was given 'top-sliced' money to distribute to departments for innovation in teaching.

Problems in Administration

After the course had finally been approved we had to start by recruiting students. This required resources/money to pay for advertising, printing leaflets, postage etc. There was no money, as the devolved budget did not come into effect until year one plus one, and, as the course was not located in a department, there were no departmental resources. The faculty had no budget but somehow we managed to get leaflets printed internally and charge it to some account. This problem was more acute because we had no departmental account, but when the Sociology Department started a new MSc in sociology two years later, they also had difficulties in obtaining any allocation for start-up and the costs of publicity and printing were actually met by the other higher education institution which was a partner in the MSc. We had the £500 from the Teaching Committee, and an invaluable friend and ally in the Clerk to the Faculty of Social Sciences who was very good at finding ways and means.

The problems of start-up were symptomatic of the difficulties to come in relation to budgets. Throughout the whole first six years of the MSc, i.e. from 1988 to 1994, the problem of identifying a budget was never resolved. Had we known this when we started we might never have had sufficient resolve. The reasons for the problems are complex and lie in three separate but interrelated factors: the supremacy of the individual department in terms of how the university works; the withdrawal of the original system of devolved budgeting; and the relative powerlessness of the women involved in teaching on the MSc programme. Before the time when the student load income was to have been accredited to the participating departments, i.e. year one plus one, the devolved budget system was withdrawn, due to internal reorganization following an unexpected institutional deficit of £4 million.[1] In the aftermath of this reorganization, departments returned to historical resource allocations, where academic staff salaries were paid for centrally but other costs such as postage, photocopying or additional teaching fell on departmental budgets.

As our MSc had no departmental home we had no budget. We did need money however, for advertising and recruitment and for student bursaries. Departments were told they could award bursaries to reduce the fee the student had to pay if they wished. Under the devolved budget system this was worth it as the income per student more than met the cost of a 50 per cent fee reduction, but when devolved budgets disappeared, departments found that they were charged for the bursaries but received no income as the central finance office kept all income related to students.

In the case of bursaries awarded to our MSc students, there was no-one to charge. When charges were made on the participating departments along the same lines as the student income had been allocated, Heads of Department realized that rather than the net income which they had been promised when Gender and Social Policy was begun, they were actually having to pay out money to the central administration. By this time the course had been running successfully for two years and had exceeded its target of ten full-time equivalent students. The heads of the departments in which the women were based began to question whether they should be allowed to continue to teach on the programme. Moreover, because the Registry had to register the student numbers in a single department, that department found that its postgraduate student numbers were distorted and it was being charged for expenditure on advertising.

The problems eased for a period of three years during which a supporter of the MSc became Dean of the Faculty of Social Sciences and under his Deanship, together with the supportive Clerk of the Faculty, the dean placed the so-called faculty-wide course on his minimal and nominal budget and found enough money for a limited number of bursaries and to pay the advertising bills. That dean was succeeded by another in the triennial rotation and the Clerk moved on to another post, and as fees to external examiners have now been placed on departmental budgets, the external examiner had to wait over six months before anyone could agree who was able to authorize for her to be paid.

This extended washing of dirty linen in public is not intended to scandalize, nor do I wish to apportion blame, but rather to demonstrate the gulf between the theory of interdisciplinarity and the reality of institutional practice. The nub of the problem as far as the University of Bristol is concerned is departmental autonomy and the power of Heads of Department. That having been said, no Head of Department could be said to have abused his/her power and no member of the Gender and Social Policy teaching staff has been prevented from teaching on the course. Because postgraduate courses are examined at faculty level, there are no problems with assessment and the course runs itself by means of a Staff/Student Academic Committee. The students find the lack of a departmental home a disadvantage when it comes to common-room facilities and other such resource issues, but an advantage in that they 'own' the course in ways which they would not do if it were based in a Department. This also has advantages for the teaching staff, as they are able to run the course in a fairly autonomous way. The disadvantages are that the work is often not recognized by Heads of Department either as part of teaching loads or for promotion purposes.

Given the composition of the promotion committees in the past, it is possible that success in either teaching or researching gender, specifically women, would not have counted for a great deal even if the Heads of Department had been aware of it. The position for some of the staff teaching on the course is not that different from ten years ago – they may be well-known

outside the institution but feel ignored and unrecognized within their departments. The questions of recognition and academic worth raise much broader
issues about both interdisciplinary work and feminist scholarship which I
discuss below. Before leaving the institutional impediments of the University
of Bristol it would be interesting to know how common these are. I suspect
that departmental autonomy is the predominant model in most of the 'old'
universities, leaving aside collegiate institutions such as Oxford and Cambridge which have their own complications. In 'new' universities, Deans and
Faculties have more power, and modular frameworks and degree 'pathways'
are well established, as they are also in the United States of America. Undergraduate, as opposed to postgraduate, programmes in women's studies are
also better established in UK 'new' universities and are almost universal in the
USA.[2] A modular framework for undergraduate degrees has now been introduced at the University of Bristol and a new devolved budgeting system
(Resource Allocation Mechanism) has been introduced. The specific problems
of the MSc in Gender and Social Policy have been resolved by locating it
within the Department for Continuing Education. As from 1994, both student
registrations and student fee income are being credited to the Department for
Continuing Education. As head of the department I can both authorize expenditure and have an income out of which to meet expenditure. The new MSc
in Women's Studies is attempting to work with the new resource allocation
framework and it will be interesting to see whether that is a model which can
cope with cross-departmental teaching and expenditure.

HEFCE – Quality Assurance and Research Selectivity

The Higher Education Funding Council for England (HEFCE) (together with
the Scottish and Welsh equivalents) has established two methods of quality
control, the Research Assessment Exercise and the Teaching Quality Assessment, which affect funding. That of research selectivity has existed for several
years and has had a direct and significant effect on funding; that of teaching
quality assessment is relatively recent and its effect on funding is not yet
known. Both have implications for interdisciplinary work and their impact on
women's studies is yet to be established. Teaching quality assessments are
taking place on a rolling programme. Academic *subjects* are inspected which
means that departments are the focus, and quality assurance mechanisms,
linked to both the HEFCE teaching assessments and the Higher Education
Quality Council (HEQC) quality assessment, are based on *departmental* au-
dits. All courses have to belong to departments and when the various auditors
do their inspections, they inspect departments. Ultimately, it will become
almost impossible for courses not to be based in a department, which, at the
University of Bristol and elsewhere, means based in a discipline. What then
happens to interdisciplinary work? Does this mean that in order for women's
studies or gender studies to be studied, they must become subjects/disciplines/

academic departments? Many North American universities now have depart-ments of women's studies. In the United Kingdom, such departments are rare although they do exist, at York and Roehampton for example. Controversy erupted when Mary Evans had to fight for the title of Professor of Women's Studies when the University of Kent awarded her a personal chair in 1991[3] but since then five other Professors of Women's Studies have been appointed at UK institutions of higher education. Most of these are 'personal' chairs, i.e. they are attached to the individual, and do not indicate the establishment of a *department* of women's studies. If we do have departments of women's studies where do they belong? In what faculty? What subject?

The Research Assessment Exercise throws up similar questions. The consultation process for the next round in 1996 is still taking place and the list of Units of Assessment have been published. This contained the curious recommendation that women's studies and gender studies be assessed as part of the Politics and International Studies Unit of Assessment.[4] Thanks to interventions by the Women's Studies Network (UK) Association and other parties this was subsequently changed and there is now to be a sub-panel on women's studies whose assessments will be submitted to the main Sociology panel. The consequences of research selectivity are considerable for the fund-ing of institutions and thus of departments. A high rating last time round of 4 or 5 resulted in more resources for the institution as compared to those with lower scores and some of this resource may be allocated to high-scoring departments. Research productivity, measured by publications which are in turn given differential weight depending on where they are published, has become the measure of academic worth. The implications for feminist re-search are considerable and are discussed further below. The research selectiv-ity consultation document admits that interdisciplinary work raises problems but is not clear about how these can be solved.[5]

Discussion and Conclusion

I wrote this chapter as a descriptive case study and delivered it as such at the WHEN conference in 1994. In revising it for publication I shall attempt to add a more analytic and reflective conclusion. I feel better equipped to do this now than when I originally gave the paper, as in the interim I participated in an evaluation commissioned by the DG XXII of the European Commission. This involved writing a national report on the state of women's studies in higher education in the UK and working in collaboration with colleagues represent-ing all the member states of the European Union and other European coun-tries participating in the Erasmus Programme. I have written a comparative analysis (Bird, 1996) and will draw on this in my discussion. It is never possible to make any claims for representativeness on the part of a single case study, but the Bristol example can usefully be discussed in relationship to innovation and change within the academy, the position of women's studies and gender studies within academic subjects or disciplines, and what is meant by interdisciplinarity.

Within the United Kingdom, one of the most significant changes in higher education in the last fifteen years has been the rapid expansion in undergraduate and postgraduate numbers, without a commensurate growth in resources. This has been accompanied by an increase in managerialism, linked to the perceived need for both efficiency and savings, as prescribed for the 'old' university sector by the Jarratt Report (CVCP, 1985). More recently, the Further and Higher Education Act of 1992 resulted in the abolition of the 'binary line' and the creation of 'new' universities out of the former polytechnics. As others have noted (Adkins and Leonard, 1992; Rose, 1994), one result of expansion was the need to recruit more students and it has been claimed that the growth in women's studies courses is a direct result of their popularity in the market place. The HMI report on Women's Studies courses in seven institutions in the then public sector opens its summary thus: 'Women's Studies courses are popular with students' (HMI, 1993).

It is not so long ago that student popularity would never have been seen as a recommendation but this is a reflection of another shift (well documented in recent theorizing about pedagogy in higher education – see Bocock and Watson, 1994), from teaching to learning, from staff to student. As we have seen, the motives for establishing the Bristol MSc were connected to the market as, although Bristol has yet to experience any difficulties in recruiting at the undergraduate level, historically its postgraduate numbers have been comparatively low for a research institution.

Market demand is not however a sufficient explanation for the overall growth in students studying women's studies and gender studies, which is a world-wide phenomenon. A recent study of seventeen countries across the world showed that women's studies had been established in universities in all except two of those countries (Stiver Lie *et al.*, 1994), and the European evaluation project showed that all European Erasmus universities had women's studies programmes (Bird, 1996; Van der Steen and Levin, 1993). Most commentators agree that the rise in women's studies stems out of the women's movement, but the connections between grass roots activism and academic research is by no means straightforward. Some have argued that in being assimilated into the academy women's studies, or specifically feminism, loses its political force and is diluted or taken over and the change of name from women's to gender studies may signify this dilution (Richardson and Robinson, 1994).

In countries where curricula and institutions are more determined by the local or national state than in the UK, there has been direct political intervention to establish women's studies teaching and research (Rose, 1994; Bird, 1996). Curricular innovation in higher education has not been the subject of much research (Squires, 1990). One exception is the work of Becher, who identifies several ways in which academics defend their disciplines (Becher, 1989) and, drawing on the work of Elzinga (1987), he cites peace and conflict research, environmental research and women's studies as examples of 'new fields of investigation crystallising around . . . ideological discourse in society' (Becher, 1989, p. 141). Becher argues that new disciplines face rivalry, jealousy and suspicion, but that these may be lessened in times of expansion.

In terms of British higher education, a previous period of expansion saw the creation of seven 'new' universities. A special number of the *Higher Education Quarterly* was published in 1991 to celebrate twenty-five years since their founding and contributors to that volume reflected on the influence of the American model of California in leading the new universities of the 1960s to abandon subject-based departments in favour of multidisciplinary schools (Briggs, 1991; Scott, 1991). The first research centres in Women's Studies in the United Kingdom were all located in these old-new universities (York, Kent, Lancaster, Warwick). The rapid growth in undergraduate programmes in Women's Studies in both the USA and the new-new universities of the United Kingdom may be due as much to a system of higher education which is flexible and modular as to grass roots political activism.

I should like to conclude by reflecting on just what I mean by 'interdisciplinary ideals' in my title. I suspect this is mainly an alliterative attraction, as I do not think I really know what these 'ideals' might be. There is little agreement on what constitutes interdisciplinarity as opposed to multi-disciplinarity or intradisciplinarity. Within women's studies the question has been linked to the question of integration, i.e. studying within an established discipline, versus autonomy, i.e. women's studies as a separate subject or discipline. While some recent commentators suggest that women's studies has moved into the 'malestream' (Aaron and Walby, 1991) from the margins, others argue that it should be established as an autonomous discipline, particularly in respect of research funding (Evans *et al.*, 1994; Rose, 1994). The contributors to the European evaluation project were divided on this question, some viewing a separate women's studies discipline as a dangerous ghetto (Bird, 1996). In terms of career advancement within the academy for women academics teaching or researching women's studies, there is mixed evidence (Morley, 1995; Davies and Holloway, 1995; Brown Packer, 1995; Rose, 1994). Undoubtedly, having to allocate women's studies to a single category for the HEFCE Research Assessment Exercise may make it difficult for women's studies research to be properly evaluated. Against this, there are some subject panels (e.g. French, Sociology) on which active feminist researchers are well-represented.

I think that what we in Bristol meant by interdisciplinary ideals was the opportunity to recruit students from a variety of subject backgrounds and to work together as a team without undue interference from our colleagues and heads of department. We have undoubtedly achieved this ideal despite the institutional impediments. Whether because of a strong institutional policy on equal opportunities (see West and Lyon, 1995), or the belated recognition of academic excellence, the situation at Bristol in 1996 is very different from that prevailing in 1987 when we began planning our MSc. Then, only one member of the nine original staff had been promoted to a readership; now, four of the course team are professors, one is a head of department, and three others are senior lecturers. Life certainly seems less embattled, though this sounds too complacent. The absence of conflict surrounding the new MSc in Women's Studies may in itself be a reflection of the removal of debate from academic institutions as observed by Evans (1995). The opportunities for recruiting students and for publishing work in women's studies are still immeasurably better than for those working in less innovative fields of academic endeavour, and everyone involved in women's studies or feminist research is now part of a world-wide community of scholars and students.

Notes

The opinions and account are those of the author. They have not been agreed by other staff involved in the programme, nor do they represent the views of the University of Bristol.

1 University of Bristol, 'Report of the Sub-Committee on Financial Controls', adopted by Council 22 February 1991. An external report by Coopers Lybrand Deloitte was presented in May 1991.
2 An article in the *Independent on Sunday* (23 October 1994) stated that there were twelve BA programmes in the UK, with a total of ninety courses, and two chairs in Women's Studies, at North London University and the University of Kent. The extent of courses in the United States of America can be seen in the *Women's Studies Quarterly* (vol. XXII, nos. 1 and 2, Spring/ Summer 1994) listings which take up thirty-four pages and include courses at all levels and in all sectors of American higher education from Ivy League to Community College.
3 See Griffiths, 1991.
4 Higher Education Funding Council for England, *Conduct of the 1996 Research Assessment Exercise: Panel Membership and Units of Assessment*, consultation paper, June 1994, RAE96 2/94. The proposed Unit of Assessment number 40 also includes peace studies.
5 Higher Education Funding Council for England *1996 Research Assessment Exercise* Circular June 1994 RAE96 1/94 Para 14: 'there is some concern that adequate expertise has not always been brought to bear on all parts of interdisciplinary submissions'.

References

AARON, J. and WALBY, S. (Eds) (1991) *Out of the Margins: Women's Studies in the Nineties*, London, Falmer Press.

ADKINS, L. and LEONARD, D. (1992) 'From Academia to the Education Marketplace: United Kingdom Women's Studies in the 1990s', *Women's Studies Quarterly*, 3 & 4, pp. 28–37.

BECHER, T. (1989) *Academic Tribes and Territories: Intellectual Enquiry and the Cultures of Disciplines*, Milton Keynes, SRHE/Open University Press.

BIRD, E. (1996) 'Women's Studies in European Higher Education', *European Journal of Women's Studies*, 3, pp. 151–65.

BOCOCK, J. and WATSON, D. (Eds) (1994) *Managing the University Curriculum: Making Common Cause*, Buckingham, SRHE/Open University Press.

BRIGGS, A. (1991) 'A Founding Father Reflects', *Higher Education Quarterly*, 45, 4, pp. 311–22.

BRISTOL WOMEN'S STUDIES GROUP (Eds) (1979) *Half the Sky: An Introduction to Women's Studies*, London, Virago.

BROWN PACKER, B. (1995) 'Irrigating the Sacred Grove: Stages of Gender Equity Development', in MORLEY, L. and WALSH, V. (Eds) *Feminist Academics: Creative Agents for Change*, London, Taylor and Francis, pp. 42–55.

COMMITTEE OF VICE-CHANCELLORS AND PRINCIPALS (CVCP) (1985) *Report of the Steering Committee for Efficiency Studies in Universities* (Chairman Sir. A. Jarratt), London, CVCP.

DAVIES, C. and HOLLOWAY, P. (1995) 'Troubling Transformations: Gender Regimes and Organizational Culture in the Academy', in MORLEY, L. and WALSH, V. (Eds) *Feminist Academics: Creative Agents for Change*, London, Taylor and Francis, pp. 7–21.

ELZINGA, A. (1987) 'Internal and External Regulatives in Research and Higher Education Systems', in PREMFORS, R. (Ed.) *Disciplinary Perspectives in Higher Education and Research*, Report 37, Stockholm, University of Stockholm, GSHR.

EVANS, M. (1995) 'Ivory Towers and Life in the Mind', in MORLEY, L. and WALSH, V. (Eds) *Feminist Academics: Creative Agents for Change*, London, Taylor and Francis, pp. 73–85.

EVANS, M., GOSLING, J. and SELLAR, A. (Eds) (1994) *Agenda for Gender*, Canterbury, University of Kent (Women's Studies Committee).

GRIFFITHS, S. (1991) 'MA Pioneer Charges Kent with Sexism', *The Higher (THES)*, 29 Nov., p. 6.

HMI (1993) *Aspects of Women's Studies Courses in Higher Education April 1991 – March 1992* 371/92/NS, London, DFE/HMSO.

MORLEY, L. (1995) 'Measuring the Muse: Feminism, Creativity and Career Development in Higher Education', in MORLEY, L. and WALSH, V. (Eds) *Feminist Academics: Creative Agents for Change*, London, Taylor and Francis, pp. 116–30.

RICHARDSON, D. and ROBINSON, V. (1994) 'Theorizing Women's Studies, Gender Studies and Masculinity: The Politics of Naming', *European Journal of Women's Studies*, 1, 1, pp. 11–27.

ROSE, H. (1994) *Love, Power and Knowledge: Towards a Feminist Transformation of the Sciences*, Cambridge, Polity Press.

SCOTT, P. (1991) 'Opportunities Gained, Lost and to be Grasped', *Higher Education Quarterly*, 45, 4, pp. 367–81.

SQUIRES, G. (1990) *First Degree: The Undergraduate Curriculum*, Buckingham, SRHE/Open University Press.

STIVER, LIE, S., MALIK, L. and HARRIS, D. (Eds) (1994) *The Gender Gap in Higher Education*, World Yearbook of Education, London and Philadelphia, Kogan Page.

VAN DER STEEN, M. and LEVIN, T. (Eds) (1993) *European Women's Studies Guide*, Utrecht, WISE.

WEST, J. and LYON, K. (1995) 'The Trouble with Equal Opportunities: The Case of Women Academics', *Gender and Education*, 7, 1, pp. 51–68.

Chapter 12

The Power of Numbers: Quantitative Data and Equal Opportunities Research

Máiréad Dunne

Much research concerned with equal opportunities issues has adopted qualitative approaches. In this chapter I discuss the contribution of quantitative methods to such research. More specifically, the complementarity of qualitative and quantitative research methods is raised through a discussion of the use of quantitative data to inform equal opportunities work. I explore the theoretical contradictions produced by the use of established statistical categories, alongside reconceptualized notions of class, 'race' and gender relations. These tensions are discussed with reference to a recently completed year-long study in four co-educational state comprehensive schools (Dunne, 1994). In the broadest terms, this research was designed as a qualitative study to explore the production of differentiated educational experiences and unequal educational outcomes by focusing upon classroom relations. It developed, however, to include significant amounts of quantitative data.

My position as a researcher in higher education is fundamentally significant to the focus and design of my research. Positioning myself as a feminist researcher demanded that I regard my own experiences and social location as central to the construction of the research in the initial stages. For me, it also meant a continual self-consciousness and reflexivity throughout the process of the research. In this particular research project the social descriptors of class, 'race' and gender were highlighted as significant elements in an exploration of differential educational experience and performance. The physical location of this research in terms of these social categories was critical to the satisfactory exploration and analysis of the research questions. The relatively technical question about the identification of appropriate research locations, however, raised serious difficulties. In the process of searching for schools to take part in my research, I became aware of the poorly informed perceptions of the educational context, by those in significant institutional positions. This raises critical issues for the continuing struggle for anti-oppressive education in practical and theoretical terms. As a direct consequence, I began to engage in quantitative research as part of what had been designed as a qualitative research project. A range of these issues is addressed in this chapter, using the research project to illustrate the argument.

I start by briefly outlining the substantive, methodological and theoretical frameworks of the research project. I then describe the practical problems of finding appropriate research sites which influenced the initial conception of the research design. I then summarize the methodological and theoretical difficulties raised by this shift. Using examples from my research, I discuss some critiques of quantitative research and its methods. Following this I illustrate how such data might contribute to the development of equal opportunities work. In developing these points, important theoretical issues are addressed. I reflect upon the broader implications for research by considering the methodological difficulties and theoretical tensions raised by the quantitative/qualitative oppositions.

In accordance with the confidentiality assurances given to teachers, pupils, schools and the LEA, all names used in this paper are pseudonyms. The intention of this paper is not to mount a critique of the Middlington city council, which has often been cited as exemplary with regard to efforts towards social justice in its educational and other services. In this respect Middlington is more of a critical case, suggesting that the situation in other local councils might be, at best, fairly similar to those described in this chapter.

The Research Project: An Overview

Substantive Concerns

My research started from questions about equal opportunities in mathematics education. At a fundamental level these questions developed from my own experiences and observations of unequal outcomes of schooling with particular reference to mathematics and science. They were also an expression of my frustration. The development of policy documents to address issues of equal opportunities within various institutions had undoubtedly raised general awareness, particularly of sexism and racism (Rattansi, 1992). The potential challenge of equal opportunities to existing institutional organization, however, seemed to have produced limited change in the day-to-day functioning within schools (Acker, 1988) and a fairly superficial effect upon the participation and performance of girls, ethnic minorities and working-class pupils (Cole, 1992; Davies *et al.*, 1990; Delpit, 1988; Demaine, 1988). Further, there was little evidence of improved employment or social conditions of these social groups (Anthias and Yuval-Davis, 1993). The connections between schooling and future social location were explicit within my initial research concern. This included the relationship between certification at the end of compulsory schooling and post-16 opportunities, as well as social positioning in which gendered, racialized and classed identities limit the occupational possibilities of individual pupils. The concentration on mathematics was a recognition of its function as a critical filter to exclude individuals from particular opportunities and career pathways. Higher education institutions in particular continue to use a pass in GCSE mathematics as an entry requirement irrespective of the course of study. My specific focus was on the mediation of equal opportunities policies at the local level, which was articulated in the question: 'What is going on inside the mathematics classroom to produce unequal outcomes in terms of gender, "race" and class?'

Methodological Position

From the outset epistemological questions about the construction and legitimation of knowledge in educational research were key problematics that influenced the development of my methodological position. Feminist work has made these explicit by questioning the production of knowledge in the positivist tradition and re-examining its claims to objectivity (see for example, Harding, 1986, 1991; Lather, 1986, 1991, 1992; Oakley, 1981; Roberts, 1981; Stanley and Wise, 1983). Traditional methodologies associated with the natural sciences were critiqued by certain feminists as part of a masculine perspective and agenda (Dunne and Johnston, 1994; Hodge, 1988; Jayaratne and Stewart, 1991; Ramazanoglu, 1992; Stanley and Wise, 1990). Locating my research within this epistemological position meant, rather than a search for the 'true account', my efforts to understand what was going on, primarily focused upon participants' meanings. It is in this light that the qualitative emphasis of the research was seen as appropriate. Another methodological element, reflexivity about my research practice, often emphasized in feminist literature, was influential in the development of this research.

There is an explicit link between the substantive concern with equal opportunities and my methodological position. Implicit in a social constructionist position there is a recognition of the viability of other knowledges and multiple interpretations. This potentially provides powerful arguments for issues of social justice in education. The focus upon the actors' meanings at the local level is consistent with this position (Bryman, 1988). The study developed from collaboration and the sharing of meanings, through explicitly addressing the relations between society and schooling in what Hollands (1985) describes as a structural ethnography.

In summary, as my research question suggests, the centre of the empirical work was located within schools and had a qualitative rather than a quantitative emphasis. Despite feminist critiques of some of its elements (see for example Fraser, 1989), the ethnographic study was framed from a combination of a qualitative emphasis in the research, a focus at the local level, a collaborative/emancipatory methodology, the centrality of the meanings of those in the researched arena, and a personal commitment to legitimate insiders' knowledge of schooling (Dunne and Mac an Ghaill, 1991). Understanding the research participants' cultures and meanings in the arena of the school was of central epistemological importance to the development of analyses that could begin to address my research question.

Theoretical Frameworks

As a starting point of my research, I acknowledged teacher and pupil class-room experiences as significant to the pupils' future mathematics education opportunities and thus examination results. In turn these are important to post-16 options, higher education possibilities and the future social location of individuals. Within schools, teachers are ascribed institutional power, but as most teachers realize, this is limited by the ways in which it is contested by the pupils. In these terms, and as they often describe, teachers are neither uni-formly powerful nor powerless in relation to schooling. As the work of other educational researchers has highlighted, pupils' resistance and collusion are integral to the social relations of schooling (see for example, Griffin, 1985; Mac an Ghaill, 1988, 1994). The active part played by teachers and pupils in con-structing classroom conditions was an explicit consideration in my research. Further, it could be expected that these classroom relations contribute to the construction of teachers' views of appropriate mathematics education experi-ences for pupils at later stages of their schooling.

As with other sociological work, the task of my analysis of the substantive issues was to make problematic the common sense of the teachers' accounts of schooling (Burgess, 1988). Rather than reproduce the cultural deficit view of educationally marginalized pupils, I set out to analyse critically the teachers' accounts. For example, in my research, and as previously described by Dubberley (1988), the notion of the pupils' mathematical ability, described as an essential, personal quality, was fundamental to the teachers' justification for differentiation and the distribution of educational opportunities. From my theoretical frame the pupils' mathematical ability is produced within the class-room as the teachers read meanings from social interactions framed by par-ticular theoretical considerations. In Walkerdine's terms, '"the child" is an object of pedagogic and psychological discourses' (1988, p. 202). Rather than presenting essentialized and unitary subjectivities, I am arguing that pupil identities are constructed, multiple and relational. Within this framework, both classroom relations and the teachers' theoretical frameworks for under-standing those relations are of central significance to the construction of ability. As Walkerdine suggests, 'the "truth" about children's "mathematical development" is produced in the classroom' (1988, p. 9). Rather than the causes of the apparent reproduction of social stratification through schooling being externalized, the classroom is conceptualized as an arena of contesta-tion. Such a conceptualization transforms questions about educational policy, laying emphasis upon the micropolitical relations in particular contexts (Morley, 1995). The older dichotomized perspective which represents the oppressed as acted upon, the victims of the oppressors or oppressive social structures, is described by Foucault (1978) as a reification of power relations. Using this poststructuralist framework, power is conceptualized as being con-tinually constructed through social relations, rather than unilaterally evident in social structures such as patriarchy or racism. This alternative theory of power suggests that it is through relations of conformity and resistance within a particular context that structured relations of dominance and subordination operate or are contested.

My theoretical framework clearly draws on a poststructuralist perspective in the acknowledgment of the complexity of power relations, their productive capacity and notions of individual collusion or resistance within discursive practices. This thread runs through all elements of my research. At the methodological level my experience, observations and frustrations influenced a revision in my research methods, that is, they were productive of creative academic practice. In itself, this represents my own resistance and collusion with established traditions of research within higher education. Similarly, in substantive terms, relating the construction of each pupil's ability to the distribution of educational opportunity, within my research, social stratification is conceptualized as actively produced within the classroom, rather than being externally structured and passively reproduced in schooling (Grosz, 1990). At the same time, the persistent educational marginalization of certain social groups suggests patterns of social relations which are difficult to explain from this poststructuralist position. It has been important, therefore, for me to recognize patterns of social location, and to hold on to notions of the material conditions of schooling as centrally significant to classroom social relations and to analyses of particular social arenas. Notions of collusion and resistance with social structure provide some explanatory mechanism for my hybrid theoretical position. As Mehan explains,

> Casting the relationship between features of social structure and interactional process in reflexive terms offers the possibility of transcending the macro-micro or structure-agency dualism that has plagued the sociology of education. Doing so encourages us to demonstrate the situated relevance of social structures in the practical activities of people in social interaction, rather than to treat social structure as a reified abstraction and social processes in situated and historical isolation. (Mehan, 1992, p. 17)

Locating the Research

The location of this research in terms of class, 'race' and gender was critical to the satisfactory exploration and analysis of the research questions. In order to maximize opportunities to observe and analyse the intersections of these social categories within each school context and to provide specific contextual contrasts, research sites for qualitative empirical work had to be carefully selected. The final selection of the participating schools was based upon pupil intake characteristics, together with the gender, ethnic group and teaching experience of the volunteer teachers.

In the process of selecting particular schools and teachers to participate in my research, I made preliminary visits to thirteen schools that were regarded as appropriate by Middlington LEA schools advisers, university Education Department staff and some local teachers. These recommendations were all made on the basis of impressions of different schools without reference to statistical evidence. It soon became apparent that although the implementation of equal opportunities initiatives was generally supported by education personnel, this support was based on vague impressions of the magnitude of the populations affected, or the depth of that effect. Indeed this experience, supported by informal, ad hoc surveys, strongly indicated that many of the common-sense and widely held notions of, for example, the size of ethnic minority populations, are often grossly exaggerated (Gaine, 1995). Estimates often quadrupled the composite black proportions of the population. Most immediately this presented me with problems of selecting appropriate schools to participate in the research. Of more global importance, such impressions are ultimately significant to perceptions and evaluations of current equal opportunities work and future developments.

The difficulties of identifying appropriate schools to participate in the research prompted me to survey available quantitative data to clarify the situation in Middlington. The practical difficulties of locating research sites has caused me to reconsider the predominant methodological frameworks informing research on equity issues. It led me to reflect upon the value of such quantitative methods for anti-oppressive education movements in particular, and research development more generally. Using data from my research, I sketch out how this pseudo-methodological opposition has worked against the combination of quantitative and qualitative data in research to support initiatives in anti-oppressive education. I also consider some of the theoretical difficulties and possibilities raised by this combination of methods in social research.

Methodological and Theoretical Tensions

It is worth exploring briefly why, within much equal opportunities research, qualitative methods predominate. It is clear that quantitative and qualitative methods represent different traditions in research. The increasingly broad acceptance of qualitative work is significant and has developed from the critique of positivism, most notably, for me, by feminist scholars (Maynard, 1994). Perhaps as a by-product, these methods have been dichotomized. Supported by common practice in higher education research methodology courses, these methods are set in opposition to one another. This is further substantiated in academic practice as methodological position is often reduced to a description of either one of these two methods. Quantitative methods, not without foundation, have tended to be associated with the 'evils' of positivism. It would seem that in the process there has been a conflation of methods and methodology (Layder, 1988), with 'methods' often used to signify different methodological positions. Alongside others I would claim that the methodological position, as concerned with theory and analysis of the research process, is of greater significance to interpretation than any particular method or data-gathering technique used in research (Bulmer, 1988; Platt, 1984). The combination of methods thus does not necessarily present a problem, rather, as I am arguing in this paper, they may be complementary if the strengths and limitations of each tradition are acknowledged.

At the theoretical level, too, there is an increasing confusion in which earlier models of social life with their more simplistic and unidimensional explanations are being replaced by more complex and contingent frameworks for analysis. This move away from the deterministic models of reproduction theory (see for example Bowles and Gintis, 1976) has demanded a re-conceptualization of the notion that schooling passively reflects the social patterns of the broader society. This reworking has taken cognizance of the social construction of identity and difference, highlighting the active and productive social arena of the classroom. Although these frameworks potentially offer more enriched and powerful explanations, they also introduce further complexities in analyses of social life. In theoretical terms, the more fragmented and relational notions of social behaviour produce unpredictable and contingent social relations which in poststructuralist accounts place emphasis upon the context. This shift has produced a theoretical tension for me which remains unresolved. As other researchers have suggested (see for example Apple, 1993; Epstein, 1993; Kemmis, 1991; Mac an Ghaill, 1994) the problem with a poststructuralist framework is the tendency to relativism. On the one hand, I acknowledge the possibilities in individual relations, particularly for teachers. Schools have made and can make a difference as pupils and teachers actively make meanings and construct identities (Epstein, 1993; Mac an Ghaill, 1992; Mehan, 1992). Despite this, there is continuing evidence of the reproduction of educational disadvantage of the same social groups. Indeed it is this observation that framed the initial research question.

The Statistical Data: Some Critical Comments

Statistical Categories

The preparation for any statistical work requires the definition of categories within which the data are to be gathered and presented. The absence beyond a category label, within the Middlington city council data, suggests assumptions about category boundaries and their applicability have been made. The continued use of certain categories seems to be a historical legacy rather than the result of any continued reflection upon their appropriateness. Indeed, changes in statistical categories affect the assumed power of the data to describe a social setting. This difficulty is accentuated in longitudinal studies and monitoring, from which much of the data in my study was taken. The apparent fixity of categories is rationalized in practical terms and stands against the changing city context and theoretical developments in anti-oppressive work.

The use of established categories tends to limit the conception of society as complex and dynamic. It not only militates against a critical re-examination of the categories but it also confers a static and discontinuous quality upon people in the categorized social groups. These stand in opposition to the more recent sociological debates in this area, as the unidimensional categorization implies essential characteristics of these social groups and their individual members hiding the relational nature and contextual contingency of social interactions. Although this point is taken to represent a major disjuncture between quantitative and qualitative research traditions, such critiques are also applicable to much qualitative work (Kelly *et al.*, 1995). In the following sub-sections I will elaborate how the use of ethnic and social class categories has been limited in practical terms and has thus been distanced from the immediate context it intends to describe and the theoretical developments that could inform such descriptions.

Ethnicity

The use of ethnic categories in Middlington city council statistics tends to be based on four ethnic categories, Asian, African-Caribbean, white and other. In many of the tables this was reduced to the three largest categories as information on the 'other' ethnic groups often either was unavailable or referred to very small proportions. In some schools and in the city council Careers Office, however, there has been some expansion of the one Asian category into anything from four to seven groups, or the finer stipulation of some groups in the 'other' category to include for example, Vietnamese, Chinese, African, etc. Nevertheless, in order to gain continuity and comparability in my research I had to use the lowest common denominator across all the institutions, that is, the basic four categories listed above.

The limited conception of ethnicity, perpetuated in the use of these categories, is problematic and has provoked extended academic debate concerning associated issues such as culture, identity and 'other-ing'. The discussion here will be confined to the use of ethnic categories in the context of Middlington, in reference to the two conglomerate categories 'Asian' and 'white'. In particular, different Asian groups have different histories of immigration, educational capital, occupational status and material conditions of life. To collect and present data within the category 'Asian' is to treat as collective the separate histories, cultures, national affiliations and religions of quite different social groups (Dickinson, 1982; Hiro, 1991; Modood, 1992; Rex, 1991). As Modood suggests, 'if Sunni Muslim, Shia Muslim, Hindu, Sikh were to be used as sociological and equality monitoring categories, they

would reveal that by most socio-economic measures there is a major divide'
(Modood, 1992, p. 33).

Derived from the census data, Table 12.1 shows the Asian population of
the wards within which the schools participating in my research were situated.
They are listed from most to least affluent ward. The proportion of Asians as
a percentage of the total population ranges from 1.4 per cent to 40 per cent.
Comparison of Tower Grange's ward in the inner city with Claremont Court's
ward, in an outer suburban location, with better social and material conditions,
shows that the Asian proportion of their populations are fairly equal at around
40 per cent. However, once the conglomerate category of Asian is separated
it becomes clear that most of those living in the poorer, inner-city area are
Pakistani. Those in the more affluent areas are Indian.

These figures substantiate the point made by Modood (1992) that the
social stratification of the Asian groups is concealed by the use of the conglomerate term. Interpretation of these statistics at the broader level is inevitably
skewed and misrepresents the context. It is extremely important to note that
educational statistics in Middlington use only the larger 'Asian' category and
thus cannot tell us anything about the differential experience or outcomes
of schooling for those populations who are categorized as the subgroups.
This averaging of the 'Asian' experience has the effect of ameliorating the
extremes of material and educational disadvantage experienced by the most
marginalized sectors. The focus of equal opportunities work if based upon
information about the 'Asian' population as a whole is likely to inappropri-
ately target certain groups and individuals, that is, to treat as equal those
groups which patently are not.

The category 'white' similarly distorts the data collection and its interpretation especially for equal opportunities research. Again the historical, cul-

Table 12.1 Asian populations in Middlington wards

School ward	Asians	% total pop.	Indian	% Asian pop.	Pakistani	% Asian pop.	Bangladeshi	% Asian pop.	East African	% Asian pop.
Ashbourne	439	1.4%	309	70.4%	77	17.5%	18	4.1%	35	8.0%
Claremont Court	10892	40.0%	9227	84.7%	900	8.3%	397	3.6%	368	3.4%
Broxton Park	5271	21.3%	3185	60.4%	1850	35.1%	84	1.6%	152	2.9%
Tower Grange	8611	37.7%	256	3.0%	7341	85.3%	780	9.1%	234	2.7%

Source: Government Publications, 1991.

tural, and religious variations of different white ethnic groups cannot be examined by the use of this term. In effect this has meant the concentration of the equal opportunities debate upon black ethnic groups, often emphasizing African-Caribbeans, one of the smaller black ethnic minority groups. Concomitantly, this has resulted in a relative denial of white ethnicities, whether dominant or subordinate. For Middlington, as for England as a whole, the largest ethnic minority group, the Irish, are rarely monitored or the subject of comment in social statistics or in terms of equality of opportunity (Jeffcoate, 1984; Miles, 1989). More recently, however, under pressure from Irish community groups, some local councils have recognized the ethnic minority status of the Irish. These groups have also made representations to the Office of Population Censuses and Surveys in anticipation for the 2001 census as the 1991 form did not include the Irish in its questionnaire about ethnic minority status (*Irish Post*, 1996). The invisibility of these groups critically affects the perceptions, development and remit of the equal opportunities movement across the broad spectrum of social institutions. Removal of, for example, the Irish from the aggregated 'white' group is also likely to produce different contrasts between all ethnic minority groups and the ethnic majority. At the theoretical level this invisibility has stunted the conceptual development of notions of discrimination, racisms and anti-racism in the UK context.

Social Class

The tendency to essentialize and biologically to frame gender and ethnic categories is more tentative in relation to social class. In different city council offices, the collection of statistics in this latter category has been particularly problematic and more variable. For example, the educational statisticians and schools rely heavily upon free school dinner uptake, despite their personal acknowledgment of the limits of this parameter to differentiate individuals and groups who live in quite different material and social conditions. In contrast to this weak indicator of class used in educational statistics, my informal contacts with various individuals involved with schools in Middlington suggest a high degree of consensus about the socio-economic classification of particular school populations. In Bourdieu's (1987) terms social class is a 'folk category' which remains despite its unpopularity and decline as an analytical construct in the academy. Social class has long been a controversial social descriptor, in monitoring and empirical studies. It has almost been abandoned in academic circles, ironically, despite the glaring differences in the material resources of certain groups of people, which have become more marked over the last fifteen years (Brindle, 1993). At the same time as this theoretical neglect, there have been calls from various educationalists (notably those within Middlington LEA) for a measure of 'value added' to include alongside the publication of schools' examination results. This is an implicit acknowledgment of the influence of these factors upon academic achievement and an attempt to account for the different social and material conditions of pupils and teachers.

The significance of socio-economic factors is referred to in the Middlington Education Reports for 1989, 1991 and 1992. By 1991 the relationship was graphed showing a strong correlation between poverty and poor GCSE results. The collection and analysis of educational data was however meagre in this regard, both in the LEA and within the schools. Registration for free school meals was the only measure of social class. This was in itself problematic, as entitlement was only given to those pupils whose families were on income support and who had applied. Not only was take-up estimated as much lower than entitlement, but there are acknowledged limitations in the use of income support as an indicator of poverty. Figures for 1992 showed registration for free school meals at 36.3 per cent in the primary sector and at 28.6 per cent in secondary schools. Suggestions to explain this difference by LEA statisticians, teachers and school secretaries or administrators centred on the stigma attached to having free school meals, becoming a more sensitive issue for the older school pupils.

In my research, socio-economic status was a central social justice issue. The contextual account had thus to draw on a variety of statistics to extend the unreliable free school meal data. These were available in the 1991 Census. In particular, the housing information, unemployment statistics and information on domestic conditions were used to develop broader descriptions of the schools, wards and city. Going beyond the point made earlier about the reliability of the 1991 Census at a general level, these data were not without their own difficulties. Housing tenure and general domestic conditions in any ward are amongst the standard social indicators as they quite clearly are a measure of affluence in each ward. The more questionable indicator of material deprivation, over-crowding, produced some unexpected figures. Although extremely over-crowded housing is obviously an indicator of economic marginalization, in some senses the notion of space and personal distance from others in a household is deeply cultural. The two wards with the most over-crowded households were those with the high Asian populations, but these contained families of very different socio-economic status in other terms. It could be argued that the measure used in the 1991 Census reflects Anglo-centric cultural attitudes around family, community and personal space. Crudely, there is an implied connection made between increased wealth and personal isolation in the domestic situation.

As with free school dinners, there were certain difficulties with the unemployment statistics as they relied upon registration for benefits. For example, the female unemployment figures were consistently lower than for males. This reflects a problem with female non-claimants which relates to traditions of their unwaged, domestic labour. In general, too, there have been considerable changes in the categories for claiming benefit which have affected the official unemployment figures regionally and nationally. Nevertheless, in relative terms the data showed a clear distinction between the two inner-city schools and those in the outer city. They ranged between the Ashourne school ward with less than the city average unemployment rate and the Tower Grange ward with nearly half of its over-16 population economically inactive (retired persons under pensionable age, permanently sick and students) and almost a third of the economically active population being unemployed. In statistical terms there are other difficulties relating to the collection of data at different levels of generality.

There are several difficulties both with ethnic and social class quantitative descriptions of education contexts. These not only refer to the problems of the monitoring process but also to the conceptual clarity about social classifications and intersections of these as well as the relationship to equal opportunities initiatives. For example, the high ethnic minority populations in the more economically marginalized wards indicated a significant but complex relationship between social class and ethnicity. However, the most socially and economically marginalized ward in my research had a majority white population. This important connection has not been emphasized either in equal opportunities work in education or in theoretical developments. Higher education institutions have an important contribution and responsibility in this respect. The limited social class data is related to poorly developed theoretical constructs that could reciprocally inform monitoring and social analysis.

Further implications for higher education from my research concern the organization and presentation of research methodology courses in higher education, which has contributed to the polarization of quantitative and qualitative methods presenting another set of obstructions to theoretical advance. At the same time the emphasis on methods deflects attention away from the more significant issues of methodology. Finally, although my illustrative examples focus upon the secondary education sector, there have been parallel developments in all sectors of public education. The rise of managerialism, institutional restructuring and financial accountability, as part of the new educational agenda, are just as evident in higher education as elsewhere. These environments, which are increasingly hostile to efforts for social justice, have exacerbated common problems with monitoring and the already poor levels of awareness.

Engagement with quantitative data can enable an internal critique of such monitoring to improve the systems of information-building and develop creative partnerships between different groups of professionals. In the next section I will illustrate the contribution of quantitative data

- in providing clearer descriptions of specific contexts for all parties concerned with education (teachers, Heads, policy-makers);

- to communicate in statistical terms the need for a continuation of equal opportunities work;

- in monitoring, evaluation and re-direction of equal opportunities work.

The Contribution of Quantitative Data

Grounding Equal Opportunities Activities

In terms of issues of equal opportunity, a central starting point of my research, the statistics provide a quantitative account of the situation as it obtains in the broad context and in the specific research sites. Although these statistics do not tell the whole story and cannot convey the qualitative aspects of gender, class and 'race' inequities, they do inform us of the magnitude of the social issues. They can provide descriptions of the leafy suburb and the inner city, portraying the heterogeneity of school contexts that are often homogenized.

Entering Statistical Discourse

Equal opportunities activities in education have been under attack since the restructuring of education through the 1988 Education Reform Act (see, for example, Johnson, 1991a, 1991b). Further, the effect of the publication of school league tables has been to reduce the significance of schooling to exami-

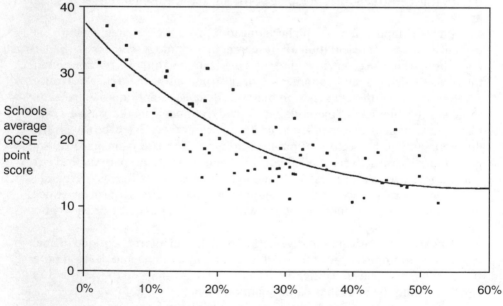

Correlation Coefficient $R = 0.74$ (significant at the 1% level)
Source: Middlington City Council, 1992a.

Figure 12.1 *The relationship between attainment at GCSE and poverty as measured by free school meals registration in Middlington*
Source: Middlington City Council, 1992a.

nation results. Anti-oppressive education movements need to develop some counter-discourses to broaden this narrow conception of schooling for examination and to re-emphasize the diversity of schools being compared. In Middlington LEA, for example, the Education Committee Reports have been used to raise significant questions. These reports include statistics to show that all urban areas similar to and including Middlington consistently achieved lower GCSE pass rates than the national average. Direct connections were made also between these GCSE results and poverty levels within the city; between social deprivation and poor examination results (see Figure 12.1). Two reports raised the controversy associated with the compulsory publication of raw examination results and called for the development of a measure of 'value added' (Middlington City Council, 1992a, 1992b). The opportunity was taken to emphasize the point that crude comparisons of examination results of the vastly different schools and LEAs had left deprived urban areas comprising all of the bottom thirty LEAs in the 1992 league tables (Barber, 1993). For example, in 1988, Middlington ranked in the bottom 25 per cent out of ninety-six LEAs on raw data but within the top 20 per cent when adjusted for socio-economic factors (DFE, 1992; Middlington City Council, 1989). Subsequently although obviously not solely related, the interim report by Sir Ron Dearing, chief adviser on curriculum and testing, persuaded the government to sanction detailed research into 'value-added' approaches to school performance (Meikle, 1993).

It is evident that the use of statistics can provide important information which may be used to forward efforts in anti-oppressive education and help to guide the locus of those efforts. In particular, the social and educational marginalization of particular sectors of the population may be highlighted more clearly. It is important therefore to engage in the statistical evidence that supports any particular rationale for educational change. At the same time, this engagement will enable the development of certain critiques of this evidence, as discussed above. Given the prevailing political and economic climate with its marginalization of equity issues and emphasis on financial accountability, this engagement would seem to be imperative. The increasingly hostile environment is influencing all sectors of public education including higher education, which has a dual responsibility in the education of students and the development of theory and research. It is inevitable that priorities will be made and information about marginalized communities should be included to inform decision-makers as a bid to secure resources. As suggested earlier, such data could make an important contribution to the directing of equal opportunities initiatives. A wider dissemination of this information also seems appropriate, given that it was its absence that prompted significant changes to my initial research intentions and the development of this paper.

To avoid misinterpretation, I want to make clear that this is not an argument to diminish the significance of, for example, racism experienced by a relatively small social group; not least because such studies of racism or sexism can tell us as much or more about the general societal/institutional context, dominant group or individual who engage in such discriminatory practice as they do about the subjects of these acts. This raises another related point about the emphasis in research, upon the subordinate group culture. This focus is evident particularly in qualitative empirical studies and in this process has encouraged the framing of these groups as problematic. Paradoxically, as the poststructuralist critique suggests, this slips easily into a reconstruction of deficit within a normative frame of reference, which reasserts rather than disrupts the power relations (Morley, 1995). This 'making' of research problems has to be addressed by both traditions of research. The argument I am making is for a critical engagement with quantitative data and statistical representations of the social world, to construct and critique this data in order to support efforts for social justice. If we are to improve our understanding of society it would seem that this might appropriately be initiated in research studies that combine quantitative and qualitative methods and contribute to the development of theory which in turn may help with work on the ground to improve the general conditions of the marginalized groups.

Monitoring and Re-direction

Continual monitoring of the situation is needed to gauge developments. Evidence about the effects of policy changes in quantitative terms is often more acceptable to policy-makers. Such information would enable the successes of equal opportunities work to be recognized, the re-direction of initiatives and the anticipation of future work. Further, if an aim of equal opportunities work in the education system is to attain equal participation of all social groups, then these statistics will assist in quantitative descriptions of what might be expected.

Conclusions

At the preliminary and more straightforward level improved monitoring within LEAs would provide a clearer picture of the local educational context. This would serve as an important reminder of the enormous variety of pupils and institutions that tend to be homogenized in educational debate and policy. In turn this would present convincing data to support the continuation of initiatives to promote social justice. Examples from Middlington indicate some such possibilities. It is clear, however, that questions of how such data might best be collected and used need to be addressed and reviewed in relation to theoretical advances and practical concerns. More broadly we must be conscious that the emphasis on specific sectors or social categories is partly forged by the interplay of practical and theoretical concerns. The need for partnership between different interested groups, i.e. researchers, academics, administrators, managers and activists, is clear. The problems of research could be helped by coordination and sharing between agencies concerned with policy, practice and research.

There is a critical role for higher education in the creative construction of frameworks for research in both methodological and substantive terms. Advances in both come from the productive process of reflection upon theoretical tensions. My efforts in this paper have focused upon developing a counter to the binary oppositional location ascribed to quantitative and qualitative research methods. It is within the institutional power of higher education to sustain or transcend this divide. At the very least there is a responsibility to reflect critically upon the organization and presentation of research methodology courses. There are parallel arguments about the responsibilities of higher education in substantive issues. The limited data on social class in the LEAs in some ways reflects and is reflected in a similar absence in the sociology of education. It seems evident to me that there is work to be done in advancing understanding of social class, especially in view of its widespread but 'quiet' usage by educationalists across all levels. In Bourdieu's (1987) terms this may be described as transforming a 'folk category' back into an 'analytical construct'.

The more fluid conception of identity formation and social relations presents particular problems for statistical data. The establishment of fixed categories reifies and essentializes social groups. The newer theories demand a fresh look at gender, 'race' and class variables which could contribute to a more comprehensive theorization of anti-oppressive schooling. These clearer conceptualizations would include the social majorities and non-essentialized understandings of all social categories. There is a need to develop statistical descriptions and analyses that can explore the intersections of class, 'race' and gender relations. The broad communication of such developments would encourage theoretical advances in the conceptions of social life and the focus of equal opportunities work. Theoretically this represents a move beyond single issues and the hierarchies of oppressions to a more 'whole', coherent perspective on all oppressive relations, the complexities of identity formation and the contingencies of specific contexts (Rattansi, 1992).

The difficulties with statistical data are brought sharply into focus against such reconceptualizations of social life. Exploring the intersections of class, 'race' and gender is made more difficult by the unsophisticated methods used to gauge social class. Ironically, this is the single most significant factor in educational achievement and experience. At the same time, it has receive little attention within equal opportunities work (Cordingley, 1993). Reclaiming social class and making explicit, through qualitative and quantitative methods, the relationships with 'race' and gender would assist us in our understanding of the complexities of the social categories and their intersections. Quantitative methods undoubtedly could contribute to an appropriate refocusing of our efforts towards anti-oppressive education.

Note

I would like to thank the teachers and pupils at Ashbourne, Claremont Court, Broxton Park and Tower Grange for their cooperation and interest in my research. Similarly thanks go to Middlington City Council officials who unhesitatingly assisted me with the collection and analysis of the quantitative data. Ashok in the LEA and Robin in the Careers Office deserve particular mention. Finally I would like to extend thanks to Barry Cooper, John Pryor, Máirtín Mac an Ghaill and Christian Haywood for their engagement in debate and their comments on earlier drafts of this paper.

References

ACKER, S. (1988) 'Teachers, Gender and Resistance', *British Journal of Sociology of Education*, 9, 3, pp. 307–22.

ANTHIAS, F. and YUVAL-DAVIS, N. (1993) *Racialized Boundaries*, London, Routledge.

APPLE, M. (1993) 'What Post-modernists Forget: Cultural Capital and Official Knowledge', *Curriculum Studies*, 1, 3, pp. 301–16.

BARBER, M. (1993) 'Recipe for Success in the Inner Cities', *Guardian, Education*, 6, July, p. 7.

BOURDIEU, P. (1987) 'What Makes Social Class? On the Theoretical and Practical Existence of Groups', *Berkeley Journal of Sociology*, 22, pp. 1–17.

BOWLES, S. and GINTIS, H. (1976) *Schooling in Capitalist America*, London, Routledge and Kegan Paul.

BRINDLE, D. (1993) 'Safety Net Fails More Families', *Guardian*, 20, July, p. 3.

BRYMAN, A. (1988) *Quantity and Quality in Social Research*, London, Unwin Hyman.

BULMER, M. (1988) 'A Comment on: The Relation of Theory and Method: Causal Relatedness, Historical Contingency and Beyond', *Sociological Review*, 36, pp. 470–4.

BURGESS, R. G. (1988) 'Doing School Ethnography', *Social Studies Review*, 3, 5, pp. 190–3.

COLE, M. (1992) 'Winding Up the Studies Business', *Guardian*, 18 February, p. 21.

CORDINGLEY, P. (1993) 'What about the Class Angle?', *Times Educational Supplement*, 5, November, p. 22.

DAVIES, A. M., HOLLAND, J. and MINHAS, R. (1990) *Equal Opportunities in the new ERA*, Hillcole Paper 2, London, Tufnell Press.

DELPIT, L. (1988) 'The Silenced Dialogue: Power and Pedagogy in Educating Other People's Children', *Harvard Educational Review*, 58, 3, pp. 280–98.

DEMAINE, J. (1988) 'Teachers' Work, Curriculum and the New Right', *British Journal of Sociology of Education*, 9, 3, pp. 247–64.

DEPARTMENT FOR EDUCATION (1992) *School Performance Tables. Public Examination Results 1992*, London, Department for Education.

DICKINSON, P. (1982) 'Facts and Figures: Some Myths', in TIERNEY J. (Ed.) *Race, Migration and Schooling*, London, Rinehart and Winston, pp. 58–86.

DUBBERLEY, W. (1988) 'Social Class and the Process of Schooling – A Case Study of a Comprehensive School in a Mining Community', in GREEN, A. and BALL, S. J. (Eds) *Progress and Inequality in Comprehensive Education*, London, Routledge, pp. 179–201.

DUNNE, M. (1994) 'The Construction of Ability: A Critical Exploration of Mathematics Teachers' Accounts', unpublished PhD thesis, University of Birmingham.

DUNNE, M. and JOHNSTON, J. (1994) 'Gender Research in Mathematics Education: The Production of Difference', in ERNEST, P. (Ed.) *Mathematics, Philosophy and Education: An International Perspective*, London, Falmer Press, pp. 221–30.

DUNNE, M. and MAC AN GHAILL, M. (1991) 'Whose Account Counts? Epistemology, Power and Skill within the Research Process', presentation at British Educational Research Association Conference, Nottingham, August.

EPSTEIN, D. (1993) *Changing Classroom Cultures*, Stoke-on-Trent, Trentham Books.

FOUCAULT, M. (1978) *The History of Sexuality, Volume 1, An Introduction* (trans. A. Sheridan), Harmondsworth, Penguin.

FRASER, N. (1989) *Unruly Practices: Power, Discourse and Gender in Contemporary Social Theory*, London, Polity Press.

GAINE, C. (1995) *Still No Problem Here*, Stoke-on-Trent, Trentham Books.

GOVERNMENT PUBLICATIONS (1991) *Census Statistics 1991*, London, HMSO.

GRIFFIN, C. (1985) *Typical Girls?: Young Women from School to the Job Market*, London, Routledge and Kegan Paul.

GROSZ, E. (1990) 'Conclusion: A Note on Essentialism and Difference', in GUNEW, S. (Ed.) *Feminist Knowledge: Critique and Construct*, London, Routledge, pp. 332–44.

HARDING, S. (1986) *The Science Question in Feminism*, Milton Keynes, Open University Press.

HARDING, S. (1991) *Whose Science? Whose Knowledge?* Milton Keynes, Open University Press.

HIRO, D. (1991) *Black British, White British: A History of Race Relations in Britain*, London, Griffin Books.

HODGE, J. (1988) 'Subject, Body and the Exclusion of Women from Philosophy', in GRIFFITHS, M. and WHITFORD, M. (Eds) *Feminist Perspectives in Philosophy*, London, Macmillan Press, pp. 46–61.

HOLLANDS, R. G. (1985) *Working for the Best Ethnography*, Stencilled Occasional Paper SP No. 79, Birmingham, Centre for Contemporary Cultural Studies, University of Birmingham.

IRISH POST (1996) 'Warning on an Irish Category in Next Census', 20 January, p. 7.

JAYARATNE, T. and STEWART, A. (1991) 'Methods in the Social Sciences', in FONOW, M. M. and COOK, J. A. (Eds) *Beyond Methodology*, Bloomington, Indiana University Press, pp. 81–106.

JEFFCOATE, R. (1984) *Ethnic Minorities and Education*, London, Harper and Row.

JOHNSON, R. (1991a) 'A New Road to Serfdom? A Critical History of the 1988 Act', in Department of Cultural Studies, University of Birmingham, Education Group II, *Education Limited: Schooling, Training and the New Right in England since 1979*, London, Unwin Hyman, pp. 31–86.

JOHNSON, R. (1991b) 'My New Right Education', in Department of Cultural Studies, University of Birmingham, Education Group II, *Education Limited: Schooling, Training and the New Right in England since 1979*, London, Unwin Hyman, pp. 87–113.

KELLY, L., REGAN, L. and BURTON, S. (1995) 'Defending the Indefensible? Quantitative Methods and Feminist Research', in HOLLAND, J. and BLAIR, M. with SHELDON, S. (Eds) *Debates and Issues in Feminist Research and Pedagogy*, Clevedon, Multilingual Matters/Open University, pp. 235–47.

KEMMIS, S. (1991) 'Emancipatory Action Research and Postmodernisms', *Curriculum Perspectives*, 11, 4, pp. 59–65.

LATHER, P. (1986) 'Research as Praxis', *Harvard Educational Review*, 56, 3, pp. 257–77.

LATHER, P. (1991) *Getting Smart*, London, Routledge.

LATHER, P. (1992) 'Qualitative Issues in Educational Research', *Theory into Practice*, XXXI, 2, pp. 87–99.

LAYDER, D. (1988) 'The Relation of Theory and Method: Causal Relatedness, Historical Contingency and Beyond', *Sociological Review*, 36, pp. 441–64.

MAC AN GHAILL, M. (1988) *Young, Gifted and Black*, Milton Keynes, Open University Press.

MAC AN GHAILL, M. (1992) 'Student Perspectives on Curriculum Innovation and Change in an English Secondary School: An Empirical Study', *British Educational Research Journal*, 18, 3, pp. 221–34.

MAC AN GHAILL, M. (1994) *The Making of Men: Masculinities, Sexualities and Schooling*, Buckingham, Open University Press.

MAYNARD, M. (1994) 'Methods, Practice and Epistemology: The Debate about Feminism and Research', in MAYNARD, M. and PURVIS, J. (Eds) *Researching Women's Lives from a Feminist Perspective*, London, Taylor and Francis, pp. 10–26.

MEHAN, H. (1992) 'Understanding Inequality in Schools: The Contribution of Interpretive Studies', *Sociology of Education*, 65, 2, pp. 1–20.

MEIKLE, J. (1993) 'Minister To Go On Retreat To Rescue Education Policy', *Guardian*, August 3, p. 1.

MIDDLINGTON CITY COUNCIL (1989) Education (Policy and Finance Sub-

Committee) Report of the Chief Education Officer: Examination Results 1989.

MIDDLINGTON CITY COUNCIL (1992a) Report of the Chief Education Officer, Education Committee: GCSE and A/AS Level Examination Results 1991.

MIDDLINGTON CITY COUNCIL (1992b) Report of the Chief Education Officer, Education Committee: Examination Results 1992.

MIDDLINGTON CITY COUNCIL CAREERS SERVICE (1991) *Destinations of Year 11 School Leavers in Middlington 1991: A 'Snapshot' Survey*, Middlington, Middlington City Council.

MILES, R. (1989) *Racism*, London, Routledge.

MODOOD, T. (1992) *Not Easy Being British: Colour, Culture and Citizenship*, Stoke on Trent, Runnymede Trust and Trentham Books.

MORLEY, L. (1995) 'The Micropolitics of Women's Studies: Feminism and Organizational Change in the Academy', in MAYNARD, M. and PURVIS, J. (Eds) *(Hetero)sexual Politics*, London, Taylor and Francis, pp. 171–85.

OAKLEY, A. (1981) 'Interviewing Women: A Contradiction in Terms', in ROBERTS, H. (Ed.) *Doing Feminist Research*, London, Routledge, pp. 30–61.

PLATT, J. (1984) 'Functionalism and the Survey: The Relation of Theory and Method', *Sociological Review*, 34, pp. 501–36.

RAMAZANOGLU, C. (1992) 'On Feminist Methodology: Male Reason versus Female Empowerment', *Sociology*, 26, 2, pp. 207–12.

RATTANSI, A. (1992) 'Changing the Subject? Racism, Culture and Education', in RATTANSI, A. and REEDER, D. (Eds) *Rethinking Radical Education*, London, Lawrence and Wishart, pp. 52–95.

REX, J. (1991) *Ethnic Identity and Ethnic Mobilisation in Britain*, Monograph in Ethnic Relations No. 5 (new series), ESRC and Centre for Research in Ethnic Relations, University of Warwick.

ROBERTS, H. (Ed.) (1981) *Doing Feminist Research*, London, Routledge.

STANLEY, L. and WISE, S. (1983) *Breaking Out: Feminist Consciousness and Feminist Research*, London, Routledge and Kegan Paul.

STANLEY, L. and WISE, S. (1990) 'Method, Methodology and Epistemology in Feminist Research Processes', in STANLEY, L. (Ed.) *Feminist Praxis*, London, Routledge, pp. 20–56.

WALKERDINE, V. (1988) *The Mastery of Reason: Cognitive Development and the Production of Rationality*, London, Routledge.

Chapter 13

Women and Disability in Higher Education: A Literature Search

Alessandra Iantaffi

When I agreed to write a brief summary of my literature search on the situation of Women and Disability within higher education, I realized that, first of all, I needed a clear definition of key terms, and in relation to these I had to decide whether to use the term 'women with disabilities' or 'disabled women'. Disability can be seen in different ways by different people, and while non-disabled professionals tend to see it as an illness, a drama and a problem, others, like Hannaford (1985), French (1994) and Thomson (1994), view it as a 'social construction' (Thomson, 1994, p. 584), with society itself, in our case Western society, perceived as disabling. Subscribing to the latter view I have decided to refer to 'disabled women' and not 'women with disabilities', as it is impossible, in my opinion, to *have* something without owning, controlling and choosing it. It is, indeed, not disabled women, but society that owns those environments, controls and chooses those policies that disable them. Those women, therefore, *are* disabled by physical, legal and educational structures that are unsuitable to their situation. Hannaford (1985) has a powerful description of how disability was, in fact, imposed on her by other people's changed perception of her, rather than by her accident.

> On leaving hospital, and finding the mantle of 'disabled' placed firmly upon my unwilling shoulders, I entered a world which was alien, absurd and ultimately defeating. My weak grasp on my identity was no real match for the massed forces of society, who firmly believed themselves as 'normal' and myself just as firmly as 'abnormal'. I found myself inhabiting a stereotype. (Hannaford, 1985, p. 10)

This 'mantle' of disability, although placed both on men and women, affects women in a particular and unique way, as disability, gender and other factors, like race, culture, creed, class, sexuality, and age, interact, creating a layered and complex type of oppression experienced by disabled women. I defined this type of oppression as 'layered', rather than as a 'double' disadvantage (Hannaford, 1985; Lonsdale, 1990; Matthews, 1994) because the discriminations disabled women experience operate 'simultaneously' (Lloyd, 1994, pp. 218–19), creating a 'dilemma of identity' (*ibid*., p. 211), but also characterizing disabled women as an oppressed minority in their own right (Hannaford, 1985). Identifying disabled women as a political group rather than a pathological one (Thomson, 1994; Morris, 1993; Cornwall, 1995) is, indeed, of vital importance if their experiences are to be seen as meaningful at policy-making level. 'Our dissatisfaction with our lives is not a personality defect but a sane response to the oppression which we experience' (Morris, 1993, p. 67).

Morris, supporting this argument, describes how retaining the concept of the 'double disadvantage' can hinder the struggle for equity, reinforcing the negative and passive image of disabled women that society promotes through the media: 'There is a tendency when describing the "double disadvantage" that disabled women experience to shift the attention away from nondisabled people and social institutions as being the problem and onto disabled women as passive victims of oppression' (*ibid.*, p. 63).

Can disabled women be seen as a minority, when the composition of their group is so varied in its membership, including black and working-class women, lesbians, catholics, younger, older and many other women? Is the disability, the gender, or a combination of both, the common factor among them all? As Hannaford points out it is the 'societal reaction and non-action which causes disablement' (Hannaford, 1985, p. 10), and this is, in my opinion, the common factor that can and does bring together disabled women from different walks of life. Every woman has her own particular situation, but her experience added to all the other women's experiences of 'disablement' becomes, in this context, a political tool of change and cause for celebration and pride (Morris, 1991). Individual accounts of experiences of disability also acquire value, creating spaces for those 'absent voices' (Morris, 1995) that have been absent from public discourse for too long. Anti-essentialist critics have, in fact, disqualified the legitimacy of personal reports, silencing 'the voice of many who have never yet been heard' (Potts and Price, 1995, p. 112). Such accounts can become, on the contrary, a starting point for future research, since they provide us with a wealth of information and resources, as Shildrick and Price point out:

> The move towards embodied selves need not threaten a new dead end of essentialism; it can speak both to the refusal to split body and mind, and to the refusal to allow ourselves to be fragmented and pathologized. At the same time to stress particularity *and* substantiality for the female body challenges the universalized male standard and opens up for us new possibilities of healthy being-in-the-world. (Shildrick and Price, 1994, pp. 176–7)

In this framework my decision to focus on higher education has a reason that is both personal and political. As a woman studying at university, I soon realized how Western academia seemed to have, among its other functions, the important tasks of educating the next ruling class, and educating those whose job it is to teach the rest of us to support the ruling class. At the same time, I also noticed that not all members of society were represented equally within this system. The absence of disabled women as students, researchers, and academics (Morris, 1993, p. 66), in this establishment where knowledge is produced, supported, criticized or rejected, and where attitudes can be challenged or reinforced, was and is too conspicuous to be ignored (Cornwall, 1995). Any eventual presence of a disabled woman at university becomes therefore a 'special and exceptional', rather than a legitimate and rightful, case:

> Access for people with disabilities, and access meant in the widest of senses, is seen as a 'special' concession, a charitable act. This perspective obscures the position that people with disabilities are undoubtedly in; that of a minority group within the dominant culture. A minority group in terms of social and economic power. (Hannaford, 1985, p. 14)

Even when and where disabled women are present in higher education, they are not always visible and the materiality of their bodies is often ignored or perceived as conflictual and uncomfortable in an environment where 'well-functioning' bodies are taken for granted and are often seen as a prerequisite for academic endeavours.

> You need to be able to take it for granted that your legs will transport your mind to the places it needs to go – to the means of academic production such as the library, the photocopier, etc. (Potts and Price, 1995, p. 102)

Academia seems to be trying to preserve this Cartesian 'life of the mind' (*ibid*., p. 104), not acknowledging the 'materiality of its own production' (*ibid*., p. 102), and therefore ignoring the bodies that support and increment its existence. The presence of disability, and even more so of gendered disability, becomes threatening: 'Disability issues challenge academic, professional and scientific ethics, parts of our cultural heritage, our attitudes, and often require additional resources or direct affirmative action' (Cornwall, 1995, p. 397).

Those 'additional resources' are, however, often lacking, or deficient, causing the limited access to education that disabled women have. Where access is provided, and a disabled woman finds herself in a position of power as a member of staff, her body still contradicts her position and her authority, challenging the assumptions of students and other members of staff, creating a conflict between the mental image people behold when thinking of an academic and her actual 'abnormal' body (Hannaford, 1985, p. 45). In the case of hidden impairments, this visibility is sometimes acquired through the use of technical or human support. Deaf people who use sign language interpreters, for example, are often faced with the task of asserting their own authority through someone else, having to clarify to their students, or classmates, that the interpreter is only a means to enable them to communicate, and not a mark of 'dumbness' or of their assumed inability to speak. In this context, non-disabled people are constantly challenged to look and listen to the person rather than the disability, visible through the communication support worker, the wheelchair or their bodies.

> Going into a teaching situation, my body is marked. . . . The identity from which I am seen to speak is 'read off' my body, my accent, my movements and gestures. . . . My body may also act to disrupt expectations and call my authority into question from the moment I enter a room. I am female, disabled and teaching. . . . The way in which my body enters into and affects the teaching situation as disabled and female highlights how the disruptive materiality of any of our particular bodies becomes most marked at the points when we resist or destabilize the discursive norms of academia. . . . It is precisely the implication that bodies can be 'taken-for-granted' within the academy that should alert us to the often unspoken but highly disruptive role played by the presence of particular women's bodies. (Potts and Price, 1995, pp. 108–9)

Disabled women in academia often find that their disruptive presence causes various forms of 'handicapism . . . even if it is masked with condescension' (Hannaford, 1985, p. 121), in an attempt to make them feel inferior and to remind them of their place as unable beings and recipients of charity:

> I am made to feel that if a student cannot adjust to the institute's plan or curriculum, one is not 'worthy' to study the subject, and one is not interesting enough to be given time for a talk. (Student quoted in Reindal, 1995, p. 237)

> When physical impairment means that there are things that someone cannot do for themselves, daily living tasks which they need help with, the assumption is that this person is 'dependent'. And in western culture to be dependent is to be subordinate, to be subject to the control of others. . . . Those who cannot do things for themselves are assumed to be unable to control their lives. (Morris, 1995, p. 74)

Physical dependency, therefore, provokes prejudice and the 'refusal to identify with a person's reality' (Morris, 1995, p. 69), in an attempt to set disability 'apart from common humanity' (*ibid.*). As Morris (1993) and Matthews (1994) remind us, anyway, disability is not alien to, but an integral part of life and humanity, although society has depicted it in such a way that it becomes an experience to be feared and kept at a distance. Disability is feared because it is seen as a hopeless situation of passivity, lack of control and of happiness. Distress, ugliness and other negative values are also associated with it. The way society views dependency and independence affects also the academy, and, since academics are seen as independent people, this negative image of disability as a state of dependency does not 'fit in' with society's image of higher education. We try, therefore, through action, or non-action, to keep this experience away from the intellectual life led within this establishment, in order to preserve this from any kind of contamination that disabled women's bodies, with all their associated negative values, might bring (Potts and Price, 1995). The presence and the experiences of disabled women are often ignored, and this can be clearly noticed when searching, as I am trying to do, written material on this subject. I kept finding, in fact, materials on disability *or* women *or* higher education, but, when I put the three terms together, I found very little on many databases available on CD-ROM or on-line, and, even then, I only found isolated articles and chapters, as can be seen from the references list of this chapter. Disabled women are, however, present within academia, as women like Matthews, Potts, Price and many others, remind us through their lives and writings, even if academia does not seem to be ready to acknowledge them.

In the light of these considerations, can the experience of higher education ever be a positive, emancipatory experience for disabled women? Academia can certainly prove to be a stimulating and challenging environment, on condition that it stops asking itself 'what people cannot do' (French, 1994, p. 136) and it starts acting on 'how society can be changed to enable disabled people to participate fully within it' (*ibid.*). Among others, two areas that can prove to be liberating for disabled women are research and women's studies. Research that is participatory and emancipatory (French, 1994; Morris, 1995), led by and conducted with disabled women is, indeed, the first step toward a more articulate and public awareness and understanding of this group, whose members, as a result, will also become more powerful and influential in relation to policy-making. At present, unfortunately, French highlights how far from ideal the situation of disability research is: 'A major problem regarding disability research is that, other than being "subjects", disabled people are rarely involved in it, and that this situation leads to inappropriate questions being asked and unsuitable services being developed' (1994, p. 141).

Women's studies can already be the place where disabled women meet, make strategic alliances with nondisabled researchers (Morris, 1993, 1995) and strengthen their identities to then go out and lead the research on disability. As Kennedy *et al.* (1993) clearly express, women's studies 'can activate new ways of being in the Academy, new ways of knowing, new ways of organizing' (p. xiv) and disabled women have a new perspective and new ideas to offer to and to take from this discipline.

Therefore, putting disability on the agenda must be seen in a positive
light, as an action that brings change and empowerment to all

women. Breaking down the barriers of fear and guilt is sometimes painful. In some ways, it is like starting a journey that you think will never end; but when you begin the sense of relief is rewarding. . . . Women must identify with each other, and find strength in our differences! (Matthews and Thompson, 1993, pp. 135, 138)

I hope that this chapter can also be a small contribution to this 'journey' that academia is just starting to explore, and that my further studies will also allow me to find new data and information on disabled women in higher education, cooperating to expand and promote research in this field.

References

CORNWALL, J. (1995) 'Psychology, Disability and Equal Opportunity', *The Psychologist*, 8, 9, pp. 396–7.

FRENCH, S. (1994) 'Researching Disability', in FRENCH, S. (Ed.) *On Equal Terms: Working with Disabled People*, Oxford, Butterworth-Heinemann, pp. 136–47.

HANNAFORD, S. (1985) *Living Outside Inside: A Disabled Woman's Experience*, Berkeley, CA, Canterbury Press.

KENNEDY, M., LUBELSKA, C. and WALSH, V. (1993) 'Introduction', in KENNEDY, M., LUBELSKA, C. and WALSH, V. (Eds) *Making Connections: Women's Studies, Women's Movements, Women's Lives*, London, Taylor and Francis, pp. ix–xvi.

LLOYD, M. (1994) 'Does She Boil Eggs? Towards a Feminist Model of Disability', in BLAIR, M., HOLLAND, J. and SHELDON, S. (Eds) *Identity and Diversity*, Clevedon, Multilingual Matters, pp. 211–24.

LONSDALE, S. (1990) *Women and Disability: The Experience of Physical Disability among Women*, Basingstoke, Macmillan.

MATTHEWS, J. (1994) 'Empowering Disabled Women in Higher Education', in DAVIES, S., LUBELSKA, C. and QUINN, J. (Eds) *Changing the Subject: Women in Higher Education*, London, Taylor and Francis, pp. 138–45.

MATTHEWS, J. and THOMPSON, L. (1993) 'Disability as a Focus for Innovation in Women's Studies and Access Strategies in Higher Education', in KENNEDY, M., LUBELSKA, C. and WALSH, V. (Eds) *Making Connections: Women's Studies, Women's Movements, Women's Lives*, London, Taylor and Francis, pp. 130–41.

MORRIS, J. (1991) *Pride Against Prejudice: Transforming Attitudes to Disability*, London, The Women's Press.

MORRIS, J. (1993) 'Feminism and Disability', *Feminist Review*, 43, pp. 57–70.

MORRIS, J. (1995) 'Creating a Space for Absent Voices: Disabled Women's Experience of Receiving Assistance with Daily Living Activities', *Feminist Review*, 51, pp. 68–93.

POTTS, T. and PRICE, J. (1995) 'Out of the Blood and Spirit of Our Lives: The Place of the Body in Academic Feminism', in MORLEY, L. and WALSH, V. (Eds) *Feminist Academics: Creative Agents for Change*, London, Taylor and Francis, pp. 102–15.

REINDAL, S. M. (1995) 'Some Problems Encountered by Disabled Students at the University of Oslo: Whose Responsibility?', *European Journal of Special Needs Education*, 10, 3, pp. 227–41.

SHILDRICK, M. and PRICE, J. (1994) 'Splitting the Difference: Adventures in the Anatomy and Embodiment of Women', in GRIFFIN, G., HESTER, M., RAI, S. and ROSENEIL, S. (Eds) *Stirring it: Challenges for Feminism*, London, Taylor and Francis, pp. 156–79.

THOMSON, R. G. (1994) 'Readrawing the Boundaries of Feminist Disability Studies', *Feminist Studies*, 20, 3, pp. 583–95.

Chapter 14

Terms of Engagement: Pedagogy as a Healing Politic

Val Walsh

... life depends upon interlocking circuits of contingency...
(Bateson, 1978, p. 118)

In contrast to Western binary thinking, within which reason and rationality are opposed and superior to feeling and the somatic, a holistic perspective eschews hierarchical and totalizing theory or 'solutions', emphasizing instead relational process and multiplicity as continuous, dynamic and creative: the loop or spiral of living process. Renewal, maintenance and breakdown are not in linear or polarized relation, but weave a web of connections/meanings. Structures and processes are not dichotomized and put in opposition to each other as explanatory devices, but can be considered together and in their connections, avoiding 'the production of universals as normative, and difference therefore as pathological' (Walkerdine, 1990, p. 193). Holistic practice undermines 'Reason's Dream' (Rotman, cited in Walkerdine, 1990, p. 188), which Valerie Walkerdine describes as 'a fantasy of equality, an attempt to create "normal subjects" while failing to tackle fundamental oppressions and exploitations'.

In this chapter I advocate a holistic perspective in relation to women's contradictory presence and position in the academy, as students and tutors; an epistemology of connection as opposed to separation (Collins, 1991, p. 217). This involves dialogue across boundaries and demarcations of power: disciplines, discourses, identities, social locations, roles. This practice is seen as foundational to the creation of 'knowledge that fosters resistance' (*ibid.* p. 207), in an increasingly competitive, individualistic culture, which actively encourages us to cancel each other out. Dialogue involves disclosure / exposure, and the attendant risks of conflict, hostility, even abuse. Yet without dialogue there can be no identification or alliance, for example between women from different class, ethnic, religious, or cultural backgrounds; between disabled women and non-disabled women; between younger women and older women; between lesbians, bisexual and heterosexual women; between child-free women and mothers. And without alliance women remain dispersed, strangers to each other: potential enemies.

Pedagogy, as the theory and practice of institutional education, has lacked 'as clear a knowledge base as engineering or medicine' (Craft, 1996a, p. 11), and its position and function in the academy has been historically insecure, even marginal, and continues to be contested. Is this in part because of its hybrid indeterminacy and unstable, ambiguously genderized identity, as a complex mix of stereotypically 'female' and 'male'-identified practices? I am conscious of the contradictions which inhere in conceiving pedagogy as an institutional practice capable of resisting institutionalization, and as anti-oppressive practice, a discourse of empowerment – and in trying to speak of and out of those contradictions. I suggest that a significant feature of this problematic, and of pedagogic practice itself, is the tension between the sexualized polarity of therapeutic and political concepts and discourses, as relatively unofficial, even taboo: in, but not of, the academy. I draw on the testimony of recent graduates, who, in assessing their own undergraduate experiences, weave academic theory with holistic, therapeutic and political concepts and concerns. Those whose place is not reserved as of right or privilege in higher education hunger after meaning, and soar as we make it, for ourselves and with each other, be we students or tutors. Higher education remains one of the crucial sites of struggle for those who, in order to survive and thrive, need to construct alternative epistemologies and other validation processes (Collins, 1991, p. 204). Reconceiving empowerment in terms of co/creativity allows contradictions to become productive rather than destructive. This chapter attempts to locate pedagogy at the centre of what is a continuing process of salvage and renewal in and of the academy.

Being Is Meaning/ful

Much of my formal academic training has been designed to show me that I must alienate myself from my communities, my family, and even my own self in order to produce credible intellectual work. (Collins, 1991, p. xiii)

Going into higher education was the most amazing thing that ever happened to me, but it was also one of the most painful because it couldn't deal with the conflict that I wanted to theorise, which was class. It gave me some amazing tools, though, which I'll always have.... (Spence, 1995, p. 209)

Running through the witness of these feminists – a black American and a white British woman of working-class origin – is an understanding of higher education as painful, damaging, useful and exciting: as both 'empowering' and 'disempowering'. The sense of rupture and displacement which marks their words is both social and psychic. It suggests that education means different things to different people, at least partly as a function of social identities and locations we bring with us, for example the complex mingling of age, class, disability, ethnicity, gender, and sexuality. Subjectivities are forged first in the mess and pressure of the world outside academia, and so bear the marks of those struggles for being and meaning, which are so entwined. The theoretical physicist, David Bohm, believed that being is meaning, according to Dossey (1993). He put forward 'a new way of thinking, consistent with modern physics, that does not divide mind from matter or subject from object. . . . Meaning, which is simultaneously mental and physical, can serve as the link or bridge between realms' (Bohm, quoted in Dossey, 1993, p. 99).

The academy has not, historically, paid much attention to being and meanings in relation to the education of its students. This is in sharp contrast to students themselves, perhaps particularly mature students (see below, pp. 195–201). In recent life history interviews with women from white working-class backgrounds,[1] I have noticed the way meanings feature prominently within their narratives, as preoccupation, source of pleasure, and as central to self-understandings. Perhaps oppression and social marginalization are analogous to illness, another social construct with considerable personal impact? Dossey has noted the way in which shifts of consciousness occur during illness, which give patients what he calls a 'feeling for the organism' (Dossey, 1993, p. 22). He suggests that 'This is one reason why so many patients seem to understand deeply the role of meaning in the world' (*ibid.*). Perhaps being on the margins – whether as a result of age, class, ethnicity, disability, poverty, sexuality or illness, for example – intensifies meanings, even produces a crisis of meaning? – is in itself an epiphany? – providing, that is, that these liminal locations have not already destroyed you.

In the academy, scholarly research has been the priority (particularly in the 'old' universities), and being and meaning have been *conceptual* subjects for specialist attention – academic philosophy – rather than a basis for pedagogy. But recently, theories of mind and the universe, epistemological theories, theories of identity and subjectivity, philosophy and politics, bear witness to a growing and widespread move towards more holistic practices: the 'big' and the 'little', the universe and the person, nature and psyche, are not unrelated concerns (Bateson, 1978; Bohm, 1981; Capra, 1983; Collins, 1991; Griffiths, 1995; Lancaster, 1991; Lancaster and Claxton, 1995; Nye, 1994; Roszak, 1993; Stanley, 1990, 1992). The move away from separation and splitting, towards connection, integration and healing, is also evident in practices which, until recently, lay largely outside the academy, for example feminist and holistic art practices, (social) ecology, environmentalism, holistic health and spirituality (Dossey, 1993; Gablik, 1991; Gibson, 1995; Goodison, 1990; Hardy, 1996; Hill and Stears, 1995; Mellor, 1992; Mies and Shiva, 1993; Shiva, 1989).[2] These shifts in consciousness provide new frameworks for feminist process in education, towards a holistic pedagogy which reformulates the relation between, for example, body / mind / spirit, and therapeutic and political purposes and practices.

Empowerment?

> Many professors have intensely hostile responses to the vision of
> liberatory education that connects the will to know with the will to
> become. (hooks, 1994, pp. 18–19)

Feminist philosopher Morwenna Griffiths argues that self-creation is political,
and that reflection on experience using theory produces 'understanding of how
gender (and race, class, sexuality, nation) are all implicated in self-creation'
(Griffiths, 1995, p. 133). She goes further: 'Becoming aware of the political
influences on processes of self-creation leads to empowerment' (*ibid.*). Here,
empowerment is predicated on the development of political consciousness,
which enables students and tutors, for example, to remove 'the blinkers which
they had previously disregarded' (*ibid.*). This process of politicization is, therefore, also both an ontological matter (an important feature of becoming) and
an educational matter, in that education plays its part in the effort to answer
the questions Griffiths poses: 'How did I come to be myself? And is what I take
to be myself my real self?' (Griffiths, 1995, p. 173). For those on the margins,
or from the margins, these are likely to be persistently poignant, provocative
and urgent questions, despite postmodern pressure to disperse and relinquish
subject identity as a personal/political project (Brodribb, 1992; Butler, 1990):
questions of 'self' and 'selves' in relation to authenticity and validity remain on
the emotional and political agenda (Griffiths, 1995, pp. 174–85; Sparkes, 1995,
pp. 97–8).

The process of 'answering' these questions will never, however, be merely
a 'head thing'. Any 'meaning-rich emotion' (Dossey, 1993, p. 101), such as
fear, anxiety, joy, exultation, will be imbricated and influential. Therefore
empowerment includes recognition of, and working through, *damage*: the
ways in which power relations in society become internalized as, for example,
shame, self-loathing, inferiority, powerlessness. Empowerment is currently
fashionable, and has become a feature of educational, liberatory, feminist,
management and new right discourses. In the absence of a politicized context,
the discourse of empowerment could lead to new forms of domination
(Morley, 1995). Empowerment connotes a certain inner confidence (not certainty), self-knowledge and courage, but it also pertains to the power relations
which constrain access to material, social and cultural resources (for example,
discursive space). Empowerment is contested territory: it has *both* therapeutic
and political resonance. Either way, it cannot be conceived or practised as
something done (by the powerful) to others (less powerful). It happens in the
context of and with the help of relevant others, including some we do not know
(Griffiths, 1995, p. 120).

For those who are members of stigmatized and marginalized groups,
education is therefore *borderline*: a liminal location which hovers between
politics and therapy. It is a fine line, in every sense, and presents a disturbance
in higher education, where both the therapeutic and the political are seen as

pollutants of academic work and purpose. Here, I follow Mary Douglas, in 'treating all pollution behaviour as the reaction to any event likely to confuse or contradict cherished classifications (Douglas, 1966a, p. 51; also 1966b). This may be why some traditional academics find it so unacceptable, even threatening, to *their* identity and status, which of course it is, as long as they see their own identities and social positionings as fixed and immutable. This stance is both a defence of existing power relations and privilege, and a denial that they, like the rest of us, are always in a state of 'becoming' (Bohm, 1981; Griffiths, 1995; Dossey, 1993). Empowerment is perhaps best seen as a possibility in contexts which, for example, help reduce fear, self-loathing and shame, increase open and responsible communication in groups, and generally allow for equal and meaningful participation, rather than just listening or observing (Griffiths, 1995, pp. 165–7).

Women's pleasure in knowledge and learning is evident in the increasingly widespread women's studies courses, and the continuing expansion of publications by women, in particular about women and for women. These achievements are all the more remarkable in a culture 'which flourishes on the inculcation of inadequacy and shame' (Spence, 1995, p. 140), and where 'the behaviour of women who do not accept their inferiority is experienced as violence against men' (Ramazanoglu, 1987, p. 63). Feminism starts with the fact that constraint and damage feature prominently, even routinely, in women's lives (Brodribb, 1992; Faludi, 1992; French, 1992; Hanmer and Maynard, 1987; hooks, 1989, 1993). The academic work of feminists is therefore distinct from its malestream counterparts, in being produced at, in spite of, and in opposition to, the conjunction of both social and cultural pressures outside academia, as well as structures of discrimination inside (Bacchi, 1992; Bagilhole, 1993; Caplan, 1994; Carter and Jeffs, 1995; Morley, 1994; Morley and Walsh, 1995; Ramazanoglu, 1987; Spurling, 1990; Stiver Lie and O'Leary, 1990; Walsh, 1994; this book). Feminist knowledges are thus *impure* at source (in their liminal locations), as well as in intent: they are the result of more than just academic interests and aptitudes. Liminality / 'impurity' / hybridity mark both their roots and creativity. Students' and tutors' internalized narratives of oppression will therefore variously frame, inform and determine our lives and work. This in turn calls for pedagogic methods and 'terms of engagement' (hooks, 1989, p. 53) which depart from the university norm.

Pedagogy: Hybrid, Multiple, Relational – and Sexually Ambiguous

For hundreds of years, higher education was thoroughly white and male: young men sitting at the feet (literally or metaphorically) of older male scholars, who were not expected to have or need any teaching skills which were not 'natural'. This certainty and sense of continuity – of status, purpose and roles – have been eroded. A more diversified student population has put pressure on traditional university identities, and on demarcations between academics and students. New constituencies in higher education have also made themselves felt through the curriculum, via, for example, women's studies, black studies, lesbian and gay studies, and Irish studies. In addition, information and communication technologies present the means to separate or integrate student and tutor interests in yet further ways. Distance learning, networked and on-line course materials, for example, promise reliable access for all students, including disabled students, but to a package. The interactive possibilities of new information technologies are being fiercely promoted, and a technology-led teaching revolution is being predicted (Barber and Preston, 1996, p. v). The increasing emphasis on technical 'competences' has also been accompanied by 'the demonisation of social science and the loss of an equal opportunities perspective' (Craft, 1996a, p. 11).

In suggesting that pedagogy and pedagogic relationships be 'reinstated' as the core of academic culture, alongside and equal to research and writing, I am going against the grain of recent changes in higher education. In the wake (I think that is the right word here) of restructuring, managerialism and under-funded mass higher education, the traditional lack of status and resources accorded pedagogy is being intensified (Davies and Holloway, 1995; Evans, Gosling and Seller, 1994; Morley and Walsh, 1995). In the 1960s and 1970s, pedagogy emerged as a body of intellectual and professional theory and practice, which is now being systematically eroded and excluded in Britain by government decree (Craft, 1996a, p. 11).

Historically, very few university tutors have undertaken professional education as teachers: it has not been part of the person specification. Yet among the detrimental effects of the 1992 Research Assessment Exercise, sociologists cite 'more emphasis on publication at any cost, and still less appreciation of committed and effective teaching' (Warde, 1996, p. 2).

> This new 'teaching machine' university, in which in some institutions the old supermarket slogan of 'pack them in and pile them high' seems to have been adopted as the institutional motto, is an essential part of *any* discussion of women and higher education. (Evans, 1995, p. 74, citing Spivak, 1993)

It is vital that pedagogic relationships attract some tender loving care, in a climate designed to destroy them as the heart of higher education.

Pedagogy as a concept is problematic, as it seems to imply that the relation between 'teaching' and 'learning' is straightforward – the one the result of the other; that the complex and mutually interactive processes involved – cognitive, interpersonal, emotional, for example – can be systematized as a linear sequence, and reduced to questions of methods. A holistic perspective interrupts such closure, by resisting binary and hierarchical demarcations (even within feminism), for example by recognizing and connecting the position and experience of female students *and* female tutors, inside *and* outside academia. Only then can empowerment be reconceived as simultaneously co/creativity / therapy / politics. For this, female students and tutors must go beyond merely rejecting what Freire called 'banking education' (1972, pp. 46–7), within which roles, hierarchy and power are clearly demarcated and observed, and information and knowledge flow in one direction, from tutor to student (Gore, 1992; Weiler, 1991).

The non-subject-based skills involved in effective teaching might be summarized in terms of, for example, ideational, interpersonal, communication, diagnostic and counselling skills; curriculum design, teaching methods, an understanding of group dynamics; technology in education; a grounding in the psychology and philosophy of education; an understanding of, and commitment to, equal opportunities. Political understanding might be added, as relevant to the contextualization of academic subjects, within the curriculum and society, and within organizational structures and cultures in higher education institutions. It is clear then, that pedagogy is not a *pure* subject, but a complex hybrid. Perhaps the academy's indifference to pedagogy is also ambivalence, even deep unease, at its hybrid disciplinary, class and gender-bending identity: its *sexual ambiguity*. The differential status of its contributing skills and discourses depends on the genderized hierarchy of knowledge and disciplines in the academy.

For example, the intellectual and organizational, being more associated with rationality, control and therefore élite masculinity, overshadow what are seen as applied skills (for example, teaching methods and curriculum design), following the historically persistent polarization of 'pure' and applied knowledge / the intellectual and the manual / mind and body / male and female, in Western epistemologies. In Britain, these are also class demarcations. Interpersonal skills and communication have until recently been marginalized as 'natural' and associated with the 'private', 'the maternal space', as opposed to the world of paid employment and public enterprise. Diagnostic, counselling, and group dynamics skills are likely to be variously associated with clinical, medical or alternative therapies, whose identities and status are clouded by doubleness: both public as professions (therefore male), and private, in their caring functions (therefore female). Therapeutic practices are coded female in their associations with the unconscious, with 'madness'. Together with a perceived proximity to 'deviance' and social failure, this makes any 'therapy' fiercely demarcated and opposed to matters academic, except as an object of study, as material, for example within medicine or psychology. This hostility is embraced by some feminists. In one feminist dictionary, for example, 'therapist' is succinctly defined in two words: 'the/rapist' (Mary Daly, 1978, cited in Kramarae and Treichler, 1992, p. 448). This perhaps points to the value in differentiating between the very real problems women experience at the hands of professional therapists, and the ensuing distrust for the institution of therapy (Kitzinger and Perkins, 1993); and the fact that for many women, therapeutic is not an 'ideology – a way of seeing the world that enlarges the personal, with no agenda for the political' (Armstrong, 1996, p. 12).[3] It is rather, spiritual and/or, political, *or both*, and connotes healing, and/or sustaining well-being /immunity /meaningfulness, as opposed to damaging or undermining. So 'damage' is understood as a social and political construct. The tension produced by the sexualized polarity of therapeutic and political concepts and practices is thus evident in both the academy and feminism. For example, asking, 'Do I need therapy *or* feminism?' replays the binary without reworking it .

Contextual skills – relating and connecting, for example, the academic, the social and the cultural – are conscious, critical and political. Challenging rather than nurturing, they connote masculinity. But they are also value-laden, so despite their male-identified credentials, contextual skills are suspect: their roots lie in the partnership between early sociology and class politics. They therefore lack purity and objectivity, being contaminated by their declared ties to what lies outside the academic sanctuary (as in the case of women's studies, for example). Last but not least, equal opportunities is obviously and irredeemably associated with all society's (and the academy's) Others, and therefore, of course, with women and feminists.

Therapeutic and political processes are equally, in their various manifestations, about access to and processes of meaning, well-being, power and change, and, as Dossey has pointed out, 'However meaning is approached, the answers are almost always laden with emotion' (Dossey, 1993, p. 14). Emotion itself has until recently been officially out of bounds for academics, a sign of manly 'failure' or distress, rather than purpose or commitment. In relation to the production of rationality, Walkerdine has suggested that 'this so-called natural process of mastery entails considerable and complex suppression' (Walkerdine, 1990, p. 186): 'inscribed with domination [it is] the bid for a world freed from clouding emotions' (*ibid.*). Stephen Fineman has noted how 'the facade of rationality' (Fineman, 1994, p. 1) has prevented understanding and scrutiny of 'organisations as emotional arenas' (*ibid.*, p. 9). The politics of emotion and its gendered subtexts are fairly recent areas of academic interest (Griffiths, 1995, pp. 94–111).

It becomes apparent that gender and class pervade and are produced by these classifications and discourses. If gender attributes are performative (Butler, 1990, p. 141), pedagogy begins to look like more than just an unruly performance. In its interdisciplinary transdisciplinarity, and its blend of 'female' and 'male', it appears androgynous / bisexual / 'queer'. The consequence is an academic identity which cannot easily (if at all?) be authorized by or as part of existing genderized academic categories and practices, not least because 'we regularly punish those who fail to do their gender right' (Butler, 1990, p. 140). For female students and tutors, perhaps feminists even more so, pedagogy may therefore prove to be one more route to marginalization, and not just influence, and grounds for our ambivalence as academics.

Changing Lives

> To make a revolutionary feminist epistemology, we must relinquish
> our ties to traditional ways of teaching that reinforce domination . . .
> we must first focus on the teacher-student relationship and the issue
> of power. (hooks, 1989, p. 52)

Pedagogy produces social relations as much as knowledge. In re-examining
questionnaire responses a group of graduates completed at least one year after
graduation, I notice two things relevant to this discussion. They deploy language and theory derived from their degree studies, in retrospectively and
reflexively describing and evaluating their undergraduate experiences, but
they also conspicuously fail to describe and evaluate these in *pure, academic*
terms.[4] They mix therapeutic and political awareness, giving priority to holistic
values concerning the whole person. For example, *relationships*, with tutors
and other students, and the role of *feeling* in their learning process, predominate. There is explicit awareness of the problem of *power relations*, particularly between student and tutor, and connections are made between power
relations and *teaching/learning methods*. The issue of *authority* and how it
is deployed is significant. So too are the students' own expectations about
authority on entering higher education, that is, the way many of them have
internalized patriarchal authority as natural, normal, and right. For example,
James, a young man brought up as middle class, who subsequently came out as
gay as a postgraduate student, comments on his undergraduate experience:

> On entering higher education, I more or less accepted without ques-
> tion authority, existing power relations (social, political, economic
> and institutional) as 'natural' and in some cases as correct. Truly, *I
> thought I knew myself* and even the world! (emphasis added)

This was a shift *away from certainty*. James moved through 'initial confusion'
towards 'inward confidence' (which is not the same as certainty), summing up
his feelings at the end of his degree:

> There are still many questions unanswered but a positive step has
> been taken towards '*liberation*' and '*wholeness*'. (emphasis added)

He evaluates his undergraduate experience in terms of concepts drawn from
political, holistic and *therapeutic* discourses, implicitly linking these.

Margaret, a single mother from a working-class background, who had
been a mature student, also felt constraints at the start, but in contrast to
James, she entered higher education conscious of her 'deficit' position:

> I was very aware of my age, class and gender, and *not feeling like a
> real student* . . . I believed I would come out in three years with some

absolute knowledge, an ultimate truth, which I had previously not owned. *I never had viewed myself as a creative being.* (emphasis added)

At the end of her degree three years later, she felt differently:

I accept myself a lot more and value myself and others a lot more, am more accepting of others. I have not found any absolute truths . . . I am more aware of the fragility of humanity, more angry at oppression and inappropriate power . . . I believe I move in and out of *health* and *creativity*. (emphasis added)

She has achieved – through experience and study – useful knowledge about health and creativity, and the relation between them. She now sees these as aspects of her own identity, which is itself now more a process than a fixed location. But health and creativity are not conventional academic goals. The changes in herself, which she values, and her sense of self within the larger contexts of society, the universe, world-wide oppression and injustice, seem to be connected, even a function of, her developing relationships with others, and not just the academic subjects she is studying. And the certainty she sought on entry has receded as a preoccupation or goal.

For many women students and tutors, education is coded: as 'breaking out', 'getting on', 'overcoming', etc. Entering higher education, Debbie, a young woman, spoke of her 'feelings of excitement, of having achieved something myself, feeling that I was going somewhere, thirsty for knowledge, expecting a new life to open up'. Once a student, however, ' as a working-class person I felt inferior, having to prove my worth'. Class shame is a powerful disincentive and trigger of inadequacy. Power relations and course methods are seen as mutually linked to this dynamic, forming part of a 'hidden curriculum'. Transgressing traditional boundaries, replacing them with links and conjunctions, may take the form of interdisciplinary methods, transdisciplinary goals and multi-media work (Lubelska, 1991; Walsh, 1995a).

Another young woman, Rosemary, highlights the impact of interactive and participatory methods (for example, joint and small group tasks, and the use of technology):

A course which demanded you think through your opinions and reasons, and to be able to discuss them, and being able to socialize with peers of similar interests and academic ability (roughly) stimulated conversation and debate, which provided a safe environment in which to grow in confidence . . . It was almost impossible not to get involved because of the nature of the course.

Many women have now experienced the personal / political / social / intellectual / therapeutic benefits of networking and collaboration, and might agree that 'dialogue is a powerful gesture of love' (hooks, 1993, p. 122), vital to the construction of community. Yet dialogue is not 'natural', but an acquired skill, which can be acquired and valued by men as well as women. As pedagogic process, dialogue seems familiar. Akin to conversation, it lacks academic status and credibility – which are, after all, what students and tutors expect of higher education. The lack of status afforded conversation is, of course, essential to the construction of the academic voice and its separation from ordinary life, and in particular, perhaps, 'women's talk'. Rosalind Edwards has shown how mature women students face a situation in which 'their knowledge, gained within the private sphere, was often not acceptable as a legitimate way of knowing within academia (irrespective of whether or not they themselves wished to use local and particular knowledge in this way)' (Edwards, 1993, p. 137).

Through dialogue we can give and share testimony, and construct a basis for alliance and friendship. However, whether students or tutors, women may feel hesitant about skills and values drawn from our lives outside the academy, because this sphere is coded 'feminine' and 'domestic', and subordinate to the public world of which the academy is a part. It may seem like regression, to be looking 'back' to this life we are 'leaving behind', to this maternal space, for materials, values and skills (Walsh, 1995b). The academy is, after all, constructed in opposition to that world of nature/body/feeling (Brodribb, 1992). But empowerment may depend on precisely such feeling and friendship. Bobbie, a middle-class mother who had been a mature student, declares:

> Being valued, energized and empowered changes people's lives forever, not just for the period they are studying . . . It has taught me the value of true friendship and support that only women are capable of giving freely to each other.

And Val, a working-class mother and former mature student, finds her heterosexuality qualified by her experience as a student, and new possibilities of friendship opened up:

> Heterosexual still and long-time married, but now able to look at women differently. My eyes now opened, I can feel it acceptable to find other women (a) intellectually and personality-wise attractive, (b) physically beautiful and attractive . . .

She acknowledges her homophobia, which, as it comes into view, begins to disperse.

Feeling Safe *and* Adventurous

The academy produces specialized knowledge, and 'the relationship between everyday and specialised thought' (Collins, 1991, p. 32) is one of its determining functions, producing a binary opposition which denies the relevance and value of those (the majority) not defined as 'experts'. It is easy to slip into this mode, because it is so dominant and pervasive within the academy, and because it seems to afford a measure of status and safety. However, where student and tutor form a binary opposition, *identification* is lost, and student and tutor remain at a distance and out of touch. The subtext for conceiving empowerment as simultaneously self-creation, healing and politicization, is *co/creativity* (Gablik, 1991; Walsh, forthcoming). Once we engage with each other as mutual learners and teachers, when the process starts to spark, we take pleasure in each other, our work and ideas. Individualism and competitiveness are not rewarded, but individuals are openly valued: 'This theme of talking with the heart taps the ethic of caring, another dimension of an alternative epistemology used by African-American women' (Collins, 1991, p. 215). The separation of feeling from thinking, 'the pressure to separate thought from action – particularly political activism' (*ibid.*, p. 31) find no place within the tradition of black feminist thought, while the Western academy makes a feature of it. So when conventional boundaries and demarcations are replaced by fluidity, even uncertainty, this can be daunting. Students may feel both excitement and alarm.

Marion, a single mother from a working-class background, who was a mature student, draws a vivid contrast between two courses using different methods:

> In the first year I found this course safe, with lectures, seminars and traditional attitudes and prescriptions of expectations. My role was listener, notetaker and a regurgitator of information. Participation was not part of this course . . . I could stay in the background, *I was safe.* (her emphasis)

Here, safety equates with invisibility, conformity and dependence. The passivity and compliance required are continuous with the idea of the modest and demure female. By contrast, on another course:

> The first year was a terrifying ordeal. I was expected to participate. I was noticed. *I was not safe.* Help! I was encouraged, I was listened to, I was never made to feel that my voice / words were anything but important and maybe worth something. To my total surprise I did not *drown*: I grew . . . I never again felt isolated because of my knowledge or feelings. (her emphasis)

Here, safety is reformulated: intellectual and emotional challenge become integrated, to create a new and different threshold of pain and pleasure! Marion's experience demonstrates how pedagogic methods actively constitute power relations, and either resist or collude with, in this case, age, class and gender stereotypes.

The reflections of these graduates refute binary thinking. For example, they speak of 'feelings of oppression, subordination, uncertainty and confusion' as *both* negative *and* potentially productive. They speak of the importance of working through difficulties, of working through feelings. For men, too, it can be an undoing of damage, rejection and coercive socialization. Gerard, a white gay man and also dyslexic, had been a mature student. He evoked and articulated his revolution in a final-year project which he undertook explicitly as an evaluation of his undergraduate experience:

> This referencing of my awakening knowledge and meaning has incorporated the realization that theory is a living, active, multi-dimensional practice, that affects, influences and describes, various oppressions and emancipation. This definition was offered to me by my relationship with the people I studied with, not in an academic constructed lecture but in an open communal environment, where social context (eating and drinking) became part of the natural codes and interaction of self-disclosure. This deconstructed theory into personal experience, through oral networks of trust, honesty, and politically codified narratives.

The sense of mutuality and reciprocity which are important aspects of these relations may be unfamiliar, even scary or annoying at times. For others, impatient for a realization of a feminist and/or anti-racist agenda, for example, these terms of engagement may foster expectations which exceed what is possible in the academic environment. The simultaneous construction of *safety* (stereotypically associated with *home*: the maternal / therapeutic / psychological) and *challenge* (understood as *away:* science / mountains / masculinity / the public sphere) may take students by surprise, not just because such integration is unfamiliar. Coded – perhaps stereotyped – as variously 'informal' / 'friendly' / 'feminine' / 'feminist'/ 'aggressive' / 'authoritative' – these methods (and the tutors) may be perceived as non-academic, non-professional and political. A stance which avoids an authoritarian mode of address, which relates to students as also persons (women or men), may be seen as too personal, and as making demands for an unacceptable level of intellectual involvement (connoting masculinity) and personal commitment (connoting femininity). If gender attributes are performative (Butler, 1990, p. 141), breaking the normative binary boundaries of gender in one's pedagogic performances may be deeply and *sexually* challenging for students, being neither 'female' nor 'male'. The consequences for female or feminist tutors (and students) may be particularly challenging, as while the female man is historically a feature of patriarchal culture, women who depart from emphasized femininity (that is, the pure heterosexual sign) remain at best an enigma, at worst deviant failures (Battersby, 1989; Butler, 1990; Walsh, 1995a (pp. 52–5), 1995c).

Affiliation and Reconciliation as Academic Virtues

Reconceiving and enacting pedagogic process as an alliance between student and tutor makes fundamental changes to our epistemological systems, as well as our pedagogic methods. An epistemology of separation – the either/or mentality – constitutes (sexual) hierarchy as fundamental to thinking and social order. This reiterates patriarchal authority and oppression as 'natural', incontestable, and sex as binary (Butler, 1990). What is valued by these students is 'a shift of vision' (Collins, 1991, p. 29) which allows continuity between the various facets of their lives. An epistemology of connection can help students and tutors make sense, of ourselves in relation to our academic work and each other, for example, and can obviate the need to deny or suppress aspects of our other social identities (Collins, 1991, p. 217; Hollway, 1994; Kennedy *et al.*, 1993; Watt and Cook, 1991).

Anna is a lesbian from a working-class background. She was a mature student not studying in her first language. Socially, therefore, like many other students, she was multiply a marginal. One of her degree subjects was an interdisciplinary and multi-media course with an explicit equal opportunities policy, which shaped course content, methods and ethos. Comparing this experience with other, more traditionally organized subjects, she declared:

> It was different in the way daylight is different from night!!! You see,
> I believe it is not enough to be presented with a plain academic
> theoretical framework in which you are positioned as an unauthor-
> ized outsider, where you are not allowed to write in a personal mode
> in essays and you have to keep your political personal life to yourself.
> Well, this course authorized mainly all outsiders to a voice.

A student with a sensory impairment had a very different experience on another 'equal opportunities' course, devoted to race issues. Val was left to challenge the oppressive and insulting behaviour of other students in a class, when they refused to use the technology which was essential for her participation. The students and tutors saw themselves as equal opportunities activists, but on this occasion they behaved as badly as any racist, with the result that the student left the course to find somewhere safer: 'I felt robbed but also worried about having these professionals in society', she wrote. The concept of purity (either/or, singularity) can be perpetuated within and by identity politics, producing a hierarchy of oppression, within which some are seen as more 'human' than others, and have more rights. Val was a very able and creative student, who went on to achieve national recognition. However, reflecting on her undergraduate experience, she remembered:

> My self-esteem was low and a (proven) turn-off to other
> students ... I became more aware of my impairment and sense of

isolation . . . I felt almost invisible at times . . . Even other disabled
students rejected me. I wanted us to form a group, but they said our
needs were so dissimilar it was useless.

Equal opportunities activism, policies and curriculum can leave oppression untouched. The healing and creative space women need in higher education cannot be constructed from one side only, by students *or* tutors. However,
without a fundamental belief in the students (Rich, 1980, p. 66), tutors' subject
expertise remains 'academic', and can become a component of professional
superiority, rather than a basis for mutuality, identification, co/creativity.
Within such an alliance, tutors nonetheless have a specific responsibility to
become skilled in exercising power in non-coercive and supportive ways
(hooks, 1994; Collins, 1991; Hollway, 1994; Morley, 1993; Watt and Cook,
1991). Failing to do this by, for example, using theory to justify non-
intervention or acceptance of oppressive, prejudicial and damaging behaviour
from or between students – in the name of respecting difference, or acknowledging different and competing narratives – is in itself an intellectual and
political standpoint, likely to produce an ethical void into which we all fall. Val
sums up her position:

I am me, but not a natural me . . . Like a robot I am wired for sound,
which, without batteries, fails . . . But as a human being, I have feelings, breathe, have loves, likes, worries and problems, but without a
culture or community, I am a placeless nomad.

Here are our common needs and rights, without which we languish and falter.
We all need cultures and communities in order to 'be ourselves'. But the
boundaries of the identity we forge within these must also remain provisional
and permeable, otherwise we acquire a 'purity' which is defined in terms of
someone else's 'impurity' as 'other': the 'victim' who makes us uncomfortable
with ourselves, especially as we move on / up / out. Dialogue and alliance are
not technical matters. As black American poet and activist, June Jordan,
advised: 'The ultimate connection cannot be the enemy. The ultimate connection must be the need we find between us' (Jordan, 1989, p. 144).

Conclusion

Self-recovery and politics are inextricably joined for women, and combine to
redefine education and the academic in relation to lives. Andrew Sparkes has
demonstrated the transformative possibilities of autobiographical material,
'to provoke people to make emotional connections to themselves and each
other', even in academic contexts (Sparkes, 1995, p. 98). In this process, issues

of profound intellectual significance regarding what it means to be a researcher arise, which bear on issues of validity and authenticity within research, reading and writing (*ibid.*). This also holds for pedagogic practice. Jo Spence has described how, in her educational work, she began to drop 'the masquerade of being in a position of "knowledge" and work[ed] rather through the shamanistic idea of visibly "sharing my wounds", thus offering the framework for an egalitarian relationship' (Spence, 1995, p. 163). This has been a feature of some of the most important and inspiring feminist activism and cultural production (art and writing, for example) outside the academy, and at least implicit in the pedagogic practices of some feminists (see Stanley, 1995). Yoking (rather than staunching) our wounds with feminist theory and politics, in contexts of mutually supportive feminist networking, provides for empowerment as co/creativity and healing, not simply as upward mobility and professional advancement.

The feminist values of responsible and contextualized reflexivity and transparency of process and structure are significant, not just in our research and writing, but also in our pedagogic practices, as students and tutors. Once pedagogy is identified as something in itself, and not simply a neutral, 'invisible' vehicle for subjects and disciplines, it becomes first a practice which *services* subjects and disciplines, then, as counter-hegemonic and anti-oppressive practice, it becomes *equal to* (but not the same as) those disciplines. Finally, as holistic practice, pedagogy can act as a model of integration of mind / body / spirit, reconnecting specialized knowledge to wider contexts of living. Holistic pedagogy owns and uses its own ambiguous and multiple origins, its hybrid, marginal identity, to resist, dilute and intercept the academy's drive for sexual polarity, purity and absolute control, working to replace these with a more tender and tentative stance, towards self and others, and our environment. Pedagogy conceived as heuristic, as co/creativity, works with and through complexity and contradiction, not to order or resolve difference, but in a movement towards a 'sense of deep affiliation' (Gablik, 1991, p. 128) which is both spiritual and political: 'beyond protest and oppositional mind to embrace reconciliation' (*ibid.*, p. 182).

A place of safety is not without risks, excitement and passion. As students and tutors, we will never be everything we need to each other, we will never be able to avoid every 'mistake', hurt or misunderstanding. But if feminist pedagogy does not variously encompass the goals of self-recovery / self-creation / empowerment / creativity, it risks becoming just another career choice, confined by and to 'Reason's Dream' (Walkerdine, 1990, p. 201), and a potentially *more* dangerous place, for some women students and tutors, than the rest of the academy. As marginals, women students and tutors need to construct a healing space in higher education, not because we conceive education as consciousness-raising or as therapy, but because if it is not a healing space, it will be yet another piece of oppression and damage. With June Jordan, we must remember and ensure that 'we are the ones we have been waiting for' (Jordan, 1992).

Notes

1 Degrees of Change is a three-year life history and peer group project, started in November 1995, which involves a group of women academics from white working-class backgrounds. See Walsh, 1995d.
2 Canterbury Christ Church College; Kings College, London; and Liverpool John Moores University, all offer opportunities for work in relation to 'holistic health and human potential' (Hill and Stears, 1995), and the new *Journal of Contemporary Health*, produced at the Institute for Health, Liverpool John Moores University, aims to foster collaboration between academics and practitioners in the fields of health, healing and human potential (*ibid.*).
3 Adrienne Rich (1977) made an analogous distinction between the experience of mothering and the institution of motherhood in patriarchal society.
4 I had worked with these students as one of a core team of four tutors on a Communication Studies degree programme, and with a minority on a social science option on gender, in various capacities and to different extents: as workshop tutor, lead lecturer, tutorial tutor, seminar tutor, photography tutor, studies adviser, project and dissertation supervisor, and course leader. They were invited to reflect on their sense of self and identity on entering and on exit, and to compare any two courses within their degree programmes in terms of contrasting methods and ethos, for example, traditional, interdisciplinary, and multi-media. The respondents were mainly women, including a high proportion of mature students and a small number of lesbians; several gay men; one student not studying in her first language; and two disabled students. There were no black students in this cohort. Names have been changed.

References

ARMSTRONG, L. (1996) 'Who Stole Incest?', *Everywoman*, February, pp. 10–12.
BACCHI, C. (1992) 'Sex on Campus – Where Does "Consent" End and Harassment Begin?', in *Australian Universities Review*, Federation of Australian University Staff Association, 35, 1, pp. 31–6.
BAGILHOLE, B. (1993) 'How to Keep a Good Woman Down: An Investigation of the Role of Institutional Factors in the Process of Discrimination against Women Academics', *British Journal of Sociology of Education*, 14, 3, pp. 261–74.
BARBER, M. and PRESTON, C. (1996) 'Teachers Lead a Revolution in Outward Mobility after the Isolation Years', *The Times Higher*, Multi-Media Features, 9 February, pp. iv–v.
BATESON, G. (1978) *Mind and Nature*, Glasgow, Fontana.
BATTERSBY, C. (1989) *Gender and Genius: Towards a Feminist Aesthetics*, London, The Women's Press.

BOHM, D. (1981) *Wholeness and the Implicate Order*, London, Routledge and Kegan Paul.

BRODRIBB, S. (1992) *Nothing Mat(t)ers: A Feminist Critique of Postmodernism*, North Melbourne, Australia, Spinifex.

BUTLER, J. (1990) *Gender Trouble: Feminism and the Subversion of Identity*, London, Routledge.

CAPLAN, P. J. (1994) *Lifting a Ton of Feathers*, Toronto, University of Toronto Press.

CAPRA, F. (1983) *The Turning Point: Science, Society and the Rising Culture*, London, Fontana.

CARTER, P. and JEFFS, T. (1995) *A Very Private Affair: Sexual Exploitation in Higher Education*, Ticknall, Derbyshire, Education Now Publishing Co-operative.

COLLINS, P. H. (1991) *Black Feminist Thought: Knowledge, Consciousness and the Politics of Empowerment*, London, Routledge.

CRAFT, M. (1996a) 'The Right Recipe for a Melting Pot: Personal View', *The Times Higher*, 9 February, p. 11.

CRAFT, M. (Ed.) (1996b) *Teacher Education in Plural Societies*, Brighton, Falmer Press.

DALY, M. (1978) *Gyn/Ecology: The Metaethics of Radical Feminism*, Boston, Beacon Press.

DAVIES, C. and HOLLOWAY, P. (1995) 'Troubling Transformations: Gender Regimes and Organizational Culture in the Academy', in MORLEY, L. and WALSH, V. (Eds) *Feminist Academics: Creative Agents for Change*, London, Taylor and Francis, pp. 7–21.

DOSSEY, L. (1993) *Healing Breakthroughs: How Your Attitudes and Beliefs Can Affect Your Health*, London, Piatkus.

DOUGLAS, M. (1966a) *Implicit Meanings: Essays in Anthropology*, London, Routledge and Kegan Paul.

DOUGLAS, M. (1966b) *Purity and Danger: An Analysis of Concepts of Pollution and Taboo*, London, Routledge and Kegan Paul.

EDWARDS, R. (1993) *Mature Women Students: Separating or Connecting Family and Education*, London, Taylor and Francis.

EVANS, M. (1995) 'Ivory Towers: Life in the Mind', in MORLEY, L. and WALSH, V. (Eds) *Feminist Academics: Creative Agents for Change*, London, Tayler and Francis, pp. 73–85.

EVANS, M., GOSLING, J. and SELLER, A. (Eds) (1994) *Agenda for Gender*, Canterbury, University of Kent at Canterbury, Women's Studies Committee.

FALUDI, S. (1992) *Backlash: The Undeclared War on Women*, London, Chatto and Windus.

FINEMAN, S. (Ed.) (1994) *Emotion in Organizations*, London, Sage Publications.

FRENCH, M. (1992) *The War against Women*, London, Hamish Hamilton.

FREIRE, P. (1972) *Pedagogy of the Oppressed*, Harmondsworth, Penguin.

GABLIK, S. (1991) *The Re-Enchantment of Art*, New York and London, Thames and Hudson.

GIBSON, L. (1995) 'Schumacher College', *The Journal of Contemporary Health*, 2 (Summer), pp. 26–7.

GOODISON, L. (1990) *Moving Heaven and Earth: Sexuality, Spirituality and Social Change*, London, The Women's Press.

GORE, J. (1992) 'What We Can Do for You! What *Can* "We" Do for "You"?: Struggling over Empowerment in Critical and Feminist Pedagogy', in LUKE, C. and GORE, J. (Eds) *Feminisms and Critical Pedagogy*, New York and London, Routledge.

GRIFFITHS, M. (1995) *Feminisms and the Self: The Web of Identity*, London, Routledge.

HANMER, J. and MAYNARD, M. (Eds) (1987) *Women, Violence and Social Control*, Basingstoke, Macmillan,

HARDY, J. (1996) *A Psychology with a Soul*, London, Woodgrange Press.

HILL, F. and STEARS, D. (1995) 'Promoting Spiritual Health: Curriculum Development Initiatives in Health Education', *Journal of Contemporary Health*, 2 (Summer), pp. 32–4.

HOLLWAY, W. (1994) 'Relations among Women: Using the Group to Unite Theory and Experience', in GRIFFIN, G., HESTER, M., RAI, S. and ROSENEIL, S. (Eds) *Stirring It: Challenges for Feminism*, London, Taylor and Francis, pp. 211–22.

HOOKS, B. (1989) *Talking Back: Thinking Feminist – Thinking Black*, London, Sheba Feminist Press.

HOOKS, B. (1993) *Sisters of the Yam: Black Women and Self-Recovery*, London, Turnaround.

HOOKS, B. (1994) *Teaching to Transgress: Education as the Practice of Freedom*, London, Routledge.

JORDAN, J. (1989) *Moving Towards Home: Political Essays*, London, Virago.

JORDAN, J. (1992) Poetry reading, Liverpool, Unity Theatre, 13 May.

KENNEDY, M., LUBELSKA, C. and WALSH, V. (Eds) (1993) *Making Connections: Women's Studies, Women's Movements, Women's Lives*, London, Taylor & Francis.

KITZINGER, C. and PERKINS, R. (1993) *Changing Our Minds: Lesbian Feminism and Psychology*, London, Onlywomen Press.

KRAMARAE, C. and TREICHLER, P. A. (1992) *Amazons, Bluestockings and Crones: A Woman's Companion to Words and Ideas (A Feminist Dictionary)*, London, Pandora Press.

LANCASTER, B. (1991) *Mind, Brain and Human Potential: The Quest for an Understanding of Self*, Shaftsbury, Dorset, Element.

LANCASTER, B. and CLAXTON, G. (1995) 'In Conversation', *Journal of Contemporary Health*, 2 (Summer), pp. 28–31.

LUBELSKA, C. (1991) 'Teaching Methods in Women's Studies: Challenging the Mainstream', in AARON, J. and WALBY, S. (Eds) *Out of the Margins: Women's Studies in the Nineties*, London, Falmer Press, pp. 41–8.

MELLOR, M. (1992) *Breaking the Boundaries: Towards a Feminist, Green Socialism*, London, Virago.

MIES, M. and SHIVA, V. (1993) *Ecofeminism*, Halifax, Nova Scotia, Fernwood Books; London, Zed Books.

MORLEY, L. (1993) 'Women's Studies as Empowerment of "Non-Traditional" Learners in Community and Youth Work Training', in KENNEDY, M., LUBELSKA, C. and WALSH, V. (Eds) *Making Connections: Women's Studies, Women's Movements, Women's Lives*, London, Taylor and Francis, pp. 118–29.

MORLEY, L. (1994) 'Glass Ceiling or Iron Cage: Women in UK Academia', *Gender, Work and Organization*, 1, 4 (October), pp. 194–204.

MORLEY, L. (1995) 'Theorising Empowerment in the UK Public Services', *International Journal of Empowerment in Organisations*, 3, 3, pp. 35–41.

MORLEY, L. and WALSH, V. (Eds) (1995) *Feminist Academics: Creative Agents for Change*, London, Taylor and Francis.

NYE, A. (1994) *Philosophia: The Thought of Rosa Luxemburg, Simone Weil, and Hannah Arendt*, London, Routledge.

RAMAZANOGLU, C. (1987) 'Sex and Violence in Academic Life or You Can Keep a Good Woman Down', in HANMER, J. and MAYNARD, M. (Eds) *Women, Violence and Social Control*, Basingstoke, Macmillan, pp. 60–74.

RICH, A. (1977) *Of Woman Born: Motherhood as Experience and Institution*, London, Virago.

RICH, A. (1980) *On Lies, Secrets and Silence: Selected Prose 1966–1978*, London, Virago.

ROSZAK, T. (1993) *The Voice of the Earth*, London, Bantam Press.

SHIVA, V. (1989) *Staying Alive: Women, Ecology and Development*, London, Zed Books.

SPARKES, A. C. (1995) 'Autobiographical Moments and the Absurdity of Validity', in *Re/Viewing Auto/Biography*, thematic issue of *Auto/Biography*, 4, 1, pp. 97–8.

SPENCE, J. (1986) *Putting Myself in the Picture*, London, Camden Press.

SPENCE, J. (1995) *Cultural Sniping: The Art of Transgression*, London, Routledge.

SPIVAK, G. (1993) *Outside in the Teaching Machine*, London, Routledge.

SPURLING, A. (1990) *Report of the Women in Higher Education Research Project: 1988–1990*, Cambridge, King's College.

STANLEY, J. (1995) 'Pain(t) for Healing: The Academic Conference and the Classed/Embodied Self', in MORLEY, L. and WALSH, V. (Eds) *Feminist Academics: Creative Agents for Change*, London, Taylor and Francis, pp. 169–82.

STANLEY, L. (Ed.) (1990) *Feminist Praxis*, London, Routledge.

STANLEY, L. (1992) *The Auto/Biographical 'I': Theory and Practice of Feminist Auto/Biography*, Manchester, Manchester University Press.

STIVER LIE, S. and O'LEARY, V. E. (Eds) (1990) *Storming the Tower. Women in the Academic World*, London, Kogan Page.

WALKERDINE, V. (1990) *The Mastery of Reason: Cognitive Development and the Production of Rationality*, London, Routledge.

WALSH V. (1994) 'Virility Culture: Academia and Managerialism in Higher Education', in EVANS, M., GOSLING, J. and SELLER, A. (Eds) *Agenda for Gender*, Canterbury, University of Kent at Canterbury, Women's Studies Committee, pp. 1–10.

WALSH, V. (1995a) 'Eyewitnesses Not Spectators – Activists Not Academics: Feminist Pedagogy and Women's Creativity', in DEEPWELL, K. (Ed.) *New Feminist Art Criticism: Critical Practices*, Manchester, Manchester University Press, pp. 51–60.

WALSH, V. (1995b) 'Unbounded Women? Feminism, Creativity and Embodiment', in JASSER, G., VAN DER STEEN, M. and VERLOO, M. (Eds) *Travelling Through European Feminisms: Cultural and Political Practices*, Utrecht, The Netherlands, WISE (Women's International Studies Europe), pp. 149–61.

WALSH, V. (1995c) 'Transgression and the Academy: Feminists and Institutionalization', in MORLEY, L. and WALSH, V. (Eds) *Feminist Academics: Creative Agents for Change*, London, Taylor and Francis, pp. 86–101.

WALSH, V. (1995d) 'Women Academics of White Working Class Origin: "Strangers" in Paradise? Or Just "Other"? And/or the Impossible Dream/er Herself?', paper presented at the BSA Study Group on Auto/Biography annual conference, Auto/Biographical Imaginations, Rome, Italy, December.

WALSH, V. (forthcoming) 'Creativity', in KRAMARAE, C. and SPENDER, D. (Eds) *The International Encyclopedia of Women's Studies*, New York, London, and Sydney, Harvester Wheatsheaf.

WARDE, A. (1996) 'The Effects of the 1992 Research Assessment Exercise', *Network* (Newsletter of the British Sociological Association), 64 (January), pp. 1–2.

WATT, S. and COOK, J. (1991) 'Racism: whose liberation? Implications for women's studies', in AARON, J. and WALBY, S. (Eds) *Out of the Margins: Women's Studies in the Nineties*, London, Falmer Press, pp. 131–42.

WEILER, K. (1991) 'Freire and a Feminist Pedagogy of Difference', *Harvard Educational Review*, 6, 4, pp. 449–74.

Chapter 15

Mothering and Education: Reflexivity and Feminist Methodology

Miriam David, Jackie Davies, Rosalind Edwards,
Diane Reay and Kay Standing

We are a group of feminist academics, all mothers, researching and writing about women in relation to families, family structures and forms such as lone-mother families, and in relation to bringing up children and their education in schools. We are concerned to explore, from a feminist perspective, whether and how mothers choose to bring their children up and their relation to their schools. We are all white, relatively privileged women, at different stages of our academic careers and at different levels in the academic hierarchy. We all have children of different ages and with different needs. This impacts upon our mothering and academic lives in different ways. As feminists we have tried to break down hierarchical structures and the power relations between us, with varying degrees of success, to write collaboratively in an educational environment which fosters individualism and competition, and which makes few allowances for the demands of mothering, either for us, or for our students. As feminists we are concerned to explore women's experiences, taking into account not only their material realities but their diversities and differences. As part of this we have looked at, on the one hand, the various *structural constraints* on mothers' experiences and, on the other hand, the various *moral dilemmas* and constraints that mothers face, as we ourselves well understand.

We have also drawn upon our own varied experiences of being both gendered parents and feminist academics to write together. Writing together is never an easy process, but it is made the more difficult for us by having also to deal with the ways in which discourses about mothering are suffused with judgments which make us all, in very different ways, feel guilty about our experiences of being mothers and being academics – perhaps the more so for being the latter, which gives us licence not only to reflect upon but also agonize about our social and intellectual endeavours. We are also trying to explore the potential incompatibility of mothering and academia, the complexities of trying to be feminist academics and 'good enough' mothers.

Beverley Skeggs makes the point well:

The despair generated by those whose demands and needs are not met can turn to hostility. The burden of guilt is enormous; and feminist students are very good at generating it. . . . The accusation that we are metaphorically 'bad mothers' who don't care about our dependents hurts. Sometimes being a Women's Studies teacher feels like (what I expect to be) motherhood: knowing that you can never achieve the standards established for you, on which you are continually monitored and monitor yourself, being exhausted and having little institutional support. As well as being 'super moms' we have to be 'wonder women', everywhere and all the time. We are also often the repository of projected desires. And there is nothing worse than unrequited desire, thwarted anxiety, and educational righteousness hitting you all at once, especially when you did not even know of its existence. (Skeggs, 1995, p. 482)

Academia does not accord well with feminists' ways of working, which are about collaboration and the dismantling of hierarchies. Higher education is not an ivory tower, it is a microcosm of wider society; one in which competition and individualism are endemic. For feminists, promoting issues which centre equity and social justice becomes inextricably bound up with self-promotion and struggles for power within academic fields. As Ladwig and Gore point out, reflexivity demands that any discussion of social privilege and power needs to pay attention to 'questions of *academic* power and privilege, competition and contestation' (Ladwig and Gore, 1994, p. 236, emphasis in original).

Discourses of mothering shape our understandings both as teachers in higher education and as feminist researchers undertaking fieldwork. Valerie Walkerdine has written about 'the contradiction and doublebind of women's position in relation to childcare' (Walkerdine, 1986, p. 64) which presents women with invidious choices. They can either be 'super mothers' ensuring everything runs smoothly, or else they can fail successfully to juggle all their responsibilities and be reconstructed as inadequate or even bad mothers. As Beverley Skeggs points out, discourses which hold women responsible for the intellectual and emotional well-being of others apply just as much to female academics without children as to those with (Skeggs, 1995). However, we would argue that it is in relation to research, particularly research that takes mothering as its subject-matter, that difficult and often painful issues about our own mothering and those of our respondents loom largest.

Reflexivity, in the sense of a continual consideration of the ways in which the researcher's own social identity and values affect the data gathered and the picture of the social world produced, has been a paramount project within feminism. It has meant that feminism has been able to offer ways of challenging 'academic power and privilege, competition and contestation' (Reay, 1996b). Feminist researchers have stressed the importance of locating themselves within their research (Gelsthorpe, 1992; Maynard and Purvis, 1994; McRobbie, 1982; Roberts, 1981; Walkerdine and Lucey, 1989). Liz Stanley and Sue Wise (1993) argue that 'recognition that who a researcher is, in terms of their sex, race, class and sexuality, affects what they "find" in research is as true for feminist as any other researchers' (Stanley and Wise, 1993, p. 228).

However, there are other social positionings that impact on the research process. Researching motherhood as full-time academics and mothers raises painful issues about the gaps in researchers' own mothering (Smith and Griffiths, 1990). We have all at different times had to contend with guilt in the research field, but our response to other mothers is much more varied than simply feeling guilty. Feelings of association and antipathy influence researchers' relationships with the researched in subtle yet powerful ways. Tales of juggling different roles and never having enough time lead to empathy and identification, while stories of full-time mothering often result in a complex mixture of envy, condescension and disbelief. Barbara Du Bois has outlined the dangers of proximity:

> The closer our subject-matter to our own life and experience, the more we can probably expect our own beliefs about the world to enter into and shape our work – to influence the very questions we pose, our conception of how to approach those questions, and the interpretations we generate from our findings. (Du Bois, 1983, p. 105)

However, while in some spheres we are dealing with the problems of proximity, in others, as we have indicated above, we have to negotiate differences. Our very commitment to feminism means that often our interpretation of the social world is very different to those of some of the mothers we interviewed. As Joan Acker, Kate Barry and Johanna Esseveld (1991) highlight, there are difficult ethical dilemmas confronting feminist researchers faced with women whose interpretations of their lives diverge radically from their own. Janet Holland and Caroline Ramazanoglu state that:

> By treating coming to conclusions as a social process, we can show that interpretation is a political, contested and unstable process between the lives of the researchers and those of the researched. Interpretation needs somehow to unite a passion for 'truth' with explicit rules of research method that can make some conclusions stronger than others. (Holland and Ramazanoglu, 1994, p. 127)

As feminists we have all struggled to adopt the principles they suggest in our own research practices. However, there is an inherent problematic in making clear a feminist epistemological position and recognizing our role in the research process. Too often it is read as bias within the malestream research world. Within academia, feminist researchers are constantly working with, and caught up in, malestream epistemologies which give primacy to male views of the world. Far from challenging the system, all too often we find ourselves inevitably colluding with it.

The difficult choices that we face as feminist academics are magnified for mothers in the sphere of parental involvement. Neither mothers' involvement in their children's education nor mothering more generally are seen as worthy substantive or theoretical topics by academics working in the mainstream. For them – mostly men – the issues are about ungendered parents. The higher education ethos, in which we are situated as we carry out our research, is characterized by individualistic competitiveness for academics and institutions, and individualistic consumerism for students. Similarly, in the British schooling system, government policy emphasizes ungendered, unclassed and 'unraced' parents as individual consumers of their children's schooling in the market place. The detailed twists and shifts in public policy discourses as they affect individuals with respect to access to and involvement in education at home and in schools, the curricular offer and forms of assessment, provide the backdrop to our presentation of parents' experiences of the processes of education and schooling. The public policy discourses of choice are mere rhetoric and hide a range of policy intentions which serve in the maintenance of inequalities in access to and benefit from schooling, and which, moreover, constrain individuals in their freedom to equal access to or outcomes from quality education – what we call structural constraints.

In other words, we argue that choices take place in particular socially and economically structured contexts, which means that all individuals are to some extent constrained from being entirely free to choose. This can be as much the case for ourselves, as feminist academics, as it is for those whose lives we study. Such constraints have not only to do with social and economic location within families and wider communities, but also to do with forms of moral and social 'education' in the broadest sense. That is to say, we learn from our families and communities as well as schools what we come to believe are the right ways to bring up children – the next generation – and in what kind of family context. This is what Edwards and Duncan (forthcoming) call 'gendered moral rationalities', with reference to the ways in which lone mothers think about paid employment with respect to having young and pre-school children (a point to which we return).

Unpacking 'Choice' and 'Constraint'

'Choice' is an increasingly widely used concept and practice in many areas of service provision, and one which also increasingly affects women as mothers – as they become mothers (e.g. choice in maternity care and childbirth services) and as they carry out their mothering. This is particularly the case in their interactions with public sphere service provisions on behalf of their children. As many of those analysing and explaining women's lives have pointed out, it is principally mothers who hold responsibility for linking and coordinating children's and other family members' needs with services' and agencies' provisions and requirements (for example, in addition to our own work, Graham,

1984; Balbo, 1987; Smith, 1987; Ribbens, 1994). It is also so in relation to their 'choice' to study or work, in the form of paid employment in the public sphere of the labour market – although in Britain this choice is privatized in terms of a lack of coherent commitment to provide publicly funded childcare. While mothers generally are viewed as free to choose whether or not they go out to work, if they do so they must deal with the consequences as a private responsibility (New and David, 1985). We too, as academic workers who are also mothers, have faced such private consequences.

Indeed, the relevance of choice to mothering is also often the case in the more 'private' aspects of childrearing within the domestic sphere. Parents – by which we mean mothers, for it is they who are still largely responsible for rearing children – more and more are concerned with bringing up children to shape their own biographies; struggling to balance their own needs with those of their children, and to provide their children with the skills to negotiate their own life choices – although there are social class variations in the adoption of this form of childrearing (see Everingham, 1994; Andenaes, forthcoming; Dahlberg, forthcoming). This modernist 'individualism' places enormous responsibility on mothers for how their children 'turn out', and while, as academics, we may theorize about and deconstruct such issues, as mothers we are not immune to their force. We envisage constraints as they relate to mothering, especially mothers' involvement in their children's education, as operating on two levels: structural and moral.

Structurally, mothers do not make their choices under the same conditions; they do not have the same resources. Mothers do not all live in the same area or in the same standard of housing, they do not all have the same levels of education, the same social networks, the same amount of income, the same position in the labour market, the same family structure and roles, the same race/ethnicity, the same physical and mental health and ability, and so on and so on. Crucially, the fact that mothers are not all making their choices under the same circumstances has the effect that they are not all making the same, if any, choices.

Morally, there can be gendered constraints on mothers' choices. Indeed, the whole concept and model of 'choice' is gender-blind and emotion-free, with its concentration on autonomous, empowered and asocial rationality. It is, however, crucial to take account of the fact that mothers have to negotiate particular socially 'gendered moral rationalities' (Edwards and Duncan, forthcoming) that are very different from the moral rationalities to which fatherhood is subject. In other words, our continuing patriarchal society influences the evaluations that men and women place on their positions. These gendered moral rationalities can operate as a constraint on mothers' choices, and can vary by social group and social setting.

Generally, then, the conditions under which mothers make choices are hedged around with constraints that are derived from sources outside themselves, including those from (albeit contradictory) official public policy discourses. These impinge upon their lives, and may become part of their moral psyche.

Choices as the Product of Particular Contexts and Constraints

Choices are the products of a particular context and set of structural and moral constraints. That context sometimes means that the preferred choice is not available to a mother. Official discourses on choice ignore the constraints trammelling many mothers' options (DFE, 1992). Academic discourses, while touching on the constraints, frequently underplay their influence. In contrast, our research indicates that for many mothers it is the constraints rather than the opportunities that overshadow their relationship to their children's schooling (Reay, 1996a; Standing, 1995). Lone mothers, mothers surviving on benefit and those trying to make ends meet on income support and, from inside and outside of these groups, black women, all operate within contexts characterized by structural and moral constraints.

There are issues of power for us as feminist academics and mothers – even those of us from working-class backgrounds – interviewing black and white working-class mothers, especially as we are all involved in education, and mothers may assume that we share the dominant discourses. Awareness and acknowledgment of the diversity of mothers' experiences is not enough, and we address the fact that social differences are often grounded in unequal and asymmetrical power relations (Olson and Shopes, 1991) in which we are implicated. Linked to this is the issue of how we can step outside of dominant discourses on mothering, if we take, for example, Kum-Kum Bhavnani's definition of feminist research:

> any study whose main agent is a woman/women and which claims a feminist framework should not reproduce the researched in ways in which they are represented within dominant society – that is, the analyses cannot be complicit with dominant representations which reinscribe inequality. (Bhavnani, 1994, p. 29)

How can we present a feminist analysis which represents our understandings of mothers' understandings of their lives, even when their understandings are shaped by / in agreement with the dominant discourses? In order to make sense of these conflicting and contradictory viewpoints, Donna Haraway (1990) suggests feminist research adopts 'situated knowledges', a partiality of vision, in order to account for multiple 'truths' whilst still retaining a sense of structural inequalities. The issues constraining mothers' relationships to their children's schooling were often those of poverty. The everyday costs of schooling, travel, uniform, books and equipment, constrain mothers' choices of school when operating in a context of low income. We present these illustrative examples from mothers' accounts.

> If you're a lone parent with not much money then you can't afford the things that would help with your children's education, computers etc. I'm aware that if we had a computer indoors then some things would be easier for her to do. Reports, it would be a lot easier if she could word-process 'em, and I'm sure she'd get better marks as well, but we can't afford one. (Jane, white, working-class, lone mother)

> When I was on income support I got some allowance for school uniform. It was a joke amount, like £25. I think it was £50 or £75 when Isobel went to secondary school. But that's supposed to last you for years. Now, who in their right mind, I had to allow, I'm guessing now, about £200 for Louise just to get her to that school. No one gave me a penny towards that . . . I know I'm maybe not the worst off person, but I live on that, just above the poverty line, you know what I mean. All my money's accounted for. (Marie, white, working-class, lone mother)

Many of the women in our various research studies chose secondary schools that were some distance from their homes, because local discourses informed them that the 'best education' was elsewhere, a moral dilemma for them. For some mothers, however, the cost of travel was a constraint. In particular, operating in a context of having insufficient money can drain women's emotional energy to the extent that it is difficult to do anything (Smith and Noble, 1995). More specifically, black mothers often have to take into account additional, essentially moral, factors linked to their social positioning as black in a predominantly white society.

> There are some schools over here I wouldn't let Rosetta go to because they're racist. I don't want her to ever go to a school where she's called racist names. So I'd have to go to the school first to check it's not racist. I'd have to find someone who's got a kid at that school and who isn't white. It's no good asking a white person about racism. It's a waste of time going up to a white mother or a white child and saying 'How does your child get treated?', 'How do you get treated at school?', because they won't know what you're talking about. (Denise, black, working-class, lone mother)

For another mother, Helen, her choice of school was linked to her structural position as a black mother in a white society, and her own experiences of racism at school, so that her choice of education for her sons was one that would be qualitatively different from hers, in which racism would not be an issue.

For working-class black and white women, issues of social class position-ing in choosing schools have to be taken into account. For working-class women there may be a conflict between their high educational aspirations for their children and their children's happiness, a factor which is often neglected in the literature on school choice. Constraints on choice are not simply mate-rial and financial, or what we call 'structural', but linked into a range of what we would consider 'moral' discourses about appropriate education for working-class children. Grainne, for example, was in the process of choosing a school for her eldest daughter at the time of the interview. The factors influ-encing her decisions were both the best possible education, and that both her daughters attended the same school. Her choice however, was constrained by her class position. What she thought was the 'best' school academically was rejected because of the feeling that her daughter 'would not fit in'.

Despite the impression created in a majority of the texts on both choice and parental involvement, individuals act in specific circumstances, not in a vacuum. For mothers, these circumstances include their financial resources, social positioning, marital status, and, where there is a partner, the contribu-tion they make, if any. As a consequence, issues of class, ethnicity and division within households have a power that prevailing discourses on choice ignore.

Mothers' involvement in schooling is a continual process of choice-making within constraints. While much of the literature on parental choice focuses on choice at key stages in a child's educational career, women are making choices about their children's education on a daily basis (David *et al.*, 1993). Mothers are balancing the efficacy of different responses to difficulties children experience in schools, making judgments about whether to intervene, or simply weighing up the pros and cons of investing scarce time and energy in various aspects of involvement on a regular basis. There are minutiae of choice which only become apparent within a gendered analysis of parental involve-ment, which examines the different ways in which mothers and fathers are involved in their children's education. Such an analysis reveals the complex details of maternal choice-making. For example, while some mothers may decide to calm a child down by talking through their feelings of upset about being ostracized by the peer group, others may choose to go into school to talk to the teacher, and yet others decide that the best course of action is to approach other children's mothers. Mothers can be seen to be engaged in a daily process of weighing up, evaluating and choosing between options, a process their male partners are rarely involved in (Reay, 1995).

However, family dynamics do also have a part to play in these various considerations about choice, particularly of school, say at age 11. Overall, we wish to argue that mothers take the main responsibility for choices about schools (even if not the major responsibilities as seen in the public world). They all operate within varying individual constraints of limited resources in one way or another, but they share the constraint of working within a patriar-chal society. This leaves them unsupported in the 'choosing process' and introduces the intervention of men at other stages. They also work within the constraints of ambiguous government policies and promptings which heighten maternal guilt. In another of our studies (funded by the ESRC), we asked parents of year 6 primary school children to talk with us about secondary school choices and who had overall responsibility for choosing the school. Three-quarters said both parents were involved in choosing a secondary school (80 per cent were in two-parent families). In very few two-parent households were fathers completely without involvement. The choice of a secondary school is an important decision which fathers often want to control and not allow women to dominate. Therefore, when inevitably the logic of the various options clash, it is the mother who bears the moral responsibility.

Women are allowed to have greater control when decisions can be defined by men as being less important. Just as those working with younger children are less well paid, have lower social status and are more often women, so the role of the mother is greater with younger children. When asking the same parents of year 6 children who had chosen the primary school, it was half and not three-quarters who reported that it was both parents. When we asked parents of reception class children to say who chose the primary school (with again 80 per cent being in two-parent families) over half said the mother had been the sole chooser. When we asked these reception class parents who had had the main responsibility of choice, the mother had taken the main responsibility in two-thirds of the families (and if the occasions when one looks at how often the mother is at least one of those responsible, the percentage rises to over 90). When asking these reception parents about pre-school, the role of mothers was clearly even greater and in some families the father seemed very unsure about what had happened pre-school. One mother qualified her husband's lack of involvement in choices of his two children at primary school. When asked who had the main responsibility for Frankie's educational activities she said:

> Me. It's my role. It's expected of me. I'm the one at home. Don thinks I'm doing a reasonable job and doesn't interfere.

It is a constraint (and at least a 'moral' one) on mothers that they are expected to make decisions with little support from fathers about the 'minor' issues, and our interviews showed fathers having very little involvement in anything but the 'major' decisions. The hidden agenda is the sexual division of labour between parents within the household:

> You've got to be joking, Vassos (my partner) does not get involved. Well he may tell me what to say to the teachers and if I'm lucky he'll drop me off at the school gate but I don't call that getting involved in your children's education.

School brochures are often read by both parents but usually obtained by the mother. So the mother is doing what we call the 'leg work' (David *et al.*, 1994). We found that although family dynamics played a part, mothers found themselves in the position of having to weigh up the options and present the information to the rest of the family. However, in the case of parents of children at private school, where money is involved, schooling is viewed as more important, therefore the father takes a greater interest and control in middle-class households. In the small number of cases where children were said to have a key involvement in making the choice, it was more often girls than boys. Some mothers felt that this was because they had the maturity to take responsibility. This may also be early evidence of girls growing into a mothering role. Indeed, in some families children could exercise a 'veto' on the choice, being only willing to go to a school 'with friends'. This was more often the case with working-class households than middle-class ones, where parents tried to exercise a greater influence. But for the most part, mothers felt that they did not have a 'free' choice, being constrained by locality, money, transport and information or lack of it. In other words, the main burden of responsibility for childcare and early childhood education clearly falls on mothers, whatever their socio-economic and family circumstances.

However, there may be limits that mothers place on their emotional and practical responsibility in relation to their children's schooling. Many of the mothers we interviewed were ambivalent about assuming what they perceived to be an unfair degree of responsibility for their children's educational learning in the classroom. Although all of the mothers operated with a model of home-school relations which was premised on the child's best interests, and frequently resulted in the mothers taking action when they felt this interest was not being served, maternal action was accompanied by complex negative emotions. Reactions to the existing division of labour between mothers and school staff ranged from disquiet and guilt through to resentment and, in a few cases, open expressions of anger.

The subtexts in maternal understandings of school expectations are the mothers' own expectations of what they should be doing. Much of the dissatisfaction expressed revealed a link between perceived gaps in what the school was providing and the consequences for maternal work. Mothers got angry when they felt the school was delegating large areas of educational work to them:

> I think they expect too much of you as a parent. I really do. They expect you to . . . I mean OK, I expect to actually read and that to the kids to make sure they can read and write, but the teachers tell you to. I mean why should they tell you when it's their job? You do help your kids at home. I mean everybody tries to help their kids the best they can. But some people have got big families like me. I don't have time to sit down every night with all of them. I have five kids I have to cook for, get clean clothes ready for. I have to clean and the teacher told me, she said 'Can you try and teach him at home' and I said 'I do try and work with him'. (Julie, white, working-class, married mother on income support)

For some mothers, living under the constraints of poverty and lone mothering had implications for the amount of maternal work they could do at home, and consequently, they felt 'blamed' for their children's performance at school and which feelings could be linked to their family form:

> I had this little thing at St Michael's primary school when Louise was there, I got the impression that if she wasn't doing well it was my fault . . . I don't mind spending half an hour, and I do resign myself to fifteen minutes, half an hour a night on each of them, but I did take umbrage at the fact that they, it was like my fault if they weren't getting on . . . If you don't do it, it's going to affect them, so you were feeling guilty . . . Because I'm a single parent, I was in a position where I was less likely to give my time to them. Now if two parents had been there, it would've been easier for them, in theory. I'm not saying the dad's around all the time, but in theory I felt, um, a bit put out and angered by the fact that everything was on me, it was my fault if they weren't doing well, cos I didn't spend enough time with them. (Maria, white, working-class, lone mother)

But they also expressed anger when they identified areas of educational work which they felt the school was not covering adequately and were quick to spell out the consequences for their own time and labour:

> It's Sophie's last year before entrance exams but there's still all this focus on frills. They spend so much time on Art activities. I find myself working with Sophie every evening on basic maths. (Clare, white, middle-class, lone mother)

We do not want to idealize the notion of motherhood, rather to subject it to careful and critical scrutiny and to raise the level of debate about the characteristics of motherhood which may then influence our varied range of activities. We are deeply conscious that the various discourses around motherhood are either implicitly or explicitly evaluative. These themselves have great consequences for all our activities and are suffused with moralisms such that maternal guilt is ever present. But the dominant discourses on women have shifted over the past hundred years from ones which see women primarily in terms of being a wife to ones which centre on motherhood. The invention of motherhood is very historically and geographically specific. Also, the discourses about motherhood may be from professionals, such as social services or doctors and health workers, or from educationalists, teachers and those professionals increasingly involved with work with children.

All mothers are invidiously trapped inside dominant 'good-enough mothering' and 'parental involvement' discourses. Nevertheless, white middle-class women (such as ourselves) occupy a different position in relation to dominant discourses than do black and white working-class women, because our experi-

ences are more likely to approximate to the theoretical norm. The consequences are very different forms of oppression. This said, though, from our
various research projects, we know that guilt appears to be a theme that
overrides differences between mothers, suggesting that being middle-class is
no more protection against the 'good enough' paradigm than being black and/
or working-class. While women rework discourses on mothering and parental
involvement in children's education, they still have very little room for manoeuvre. 'Normal' mothering seems to operate within very narrow param-
eters. Merely asking mothers about what they do in relation to their children's
education, both within the home and the school, invokes judgmental and
evaluative discourses for the mothers that we interview, and also for ourselves,
such that they (and we) cannot help but feel, to a greater or lesser extent,
inadequate. The discourses around parental (read maternal) involvement are
so dominant and 'naturalized' that we have little space to step outside them
and ask mothers about what they do without implying what they should be
doing, and implicitly evaluating both them and ourselves in terms of the
dominant discourses. They and we are likely to end up feeling not 'good
enough'. However, it is also the case that dominant discourses are contested,
adapted and reworked. Feminism provides one means of constructing alternatives to the guilt-ridden 'good enough' and 'parental involvement' discourses.

If we are critically to interrogate these and produce a feminist version, we
need a methodology which allows feminist researchers to 'work both from
outside and inside the (mothering) discourse to reshape it' (Griffiths and
Smith, 1987, p. 100); quite how to achieve such plural positionings is another
matter. It is a relatively easy step to see the need to reshape the discourse so
that those subjugated within it have a voice. It is a much more difficult venture
to accomplish such a reshaping or reworking.

As we have discovered, a feminist interpretation is not an automatic
consequence of being a feminist. It has to be struggled for in tension with
exisiting epistemologies which privilege male versions. Women's interpretations of both our past and our present are inevitably inscribed to an extent in
dominant discourses. Patriarchal, classist, racist and heterosexist discourses all
influence our understandings of the social world and our experience of motherhood. Ann Manicom suggests that:

> beginning with experience is not straightforward, because we have to
> deconstruct experience to show both its social and its ideological
> nature. . . . We cannot develop a feminist critique of how official
> forms of knowledge are produced without looking at the production
> of our personal knowledges. We cannot claim the importance of
> beginning in personal knowledge and experience, without attending
> to the character of this knowledge. (Manicom, 1992, p. 374)

We see these discursive constraints clearly in our research with women as
mothers. However, the ways in which they impinge powerfully on our work as

teachers and researchers in the academy is something we have been far more reluctant to address. Within the individualistic, competitive ethos of higher education, owning up to being a mother seems almost like a confession of weakness, a limitation which might detract from intellectual productivity. The choices we need to make about our children's education on a daily basis often seem to intrude on, and subtract from, our work as academics.

Conclusions

Discourses around parental involvement in education cast everything that mothers do as enhancing or holding back children's educational progress. There are problems here, as we have noted above, of how to ask mothers about this without conjuring up mothers' feelings and their own judgments about it. And our own feelings as researchers on mothering are inevitably implicated. We need therefore to give consideration to all these issues and to foreground particular issues to do with evaluative discourses and judgments in order to make sense of their complexity. It is clear that we cannot step outside of these discourses entirely, but we can bring them out in order to locate, understand and research them. Not to do so continues the process of denial or occlusion of the complexities.

As we have argued, changing public policy discourses of parental choice of school impinge upon mothers' and fathers' daily lives differentially, creating and regularly re-creating a changing context of family life which is itself experienced differentially. The changing balance between home and school, such a critical feature of current public policy debates, is also a changing balance between men's and women's responsibilities, and between the public and private. Despite the public rhetoric of individual choice, this is commonly experienced by women, as mothers especially, as a further tightening of the constraints, whether structural or moral, on how they live their lives and rear the next generation – a far cry from freedom of choice. There is a dissonance between public and private discourses as we ourselves, as not dispassionate researchers, have experienced and here reflect on. These balancing acts that absorb mothers' time and attention have also absorbed our time and attention, in part as researchers and in part as mothers, and yet again, as Beverley Skeggs (1995) puts it so evocatively, as feminist academics. The fact of being, or having the potential to be, a mother suffuses all our daily lives and provides the backdrop to our passionate feelings about the correct, collaborative ways of living our lives and bringing up our sons and daughters for the future.

References

ACKER, J., BARRY, K. and ESSEVELD, J. (1991) 'Objectivity and Truth: Problems in Doing Feminist Research', in FONOW, M. M. and COOK, J. A. (Eds)

Beyond Methodology: Feminist Scholarship as Lived Research, Indianapolis, Indiana University Press, pp. 133–53.

ANDENAES, A. (forthcoming) 'Challenges and Solutions for Children with Two Homes', in BRANNEN, J. and EDWARDS, R. (Eds) *Perspectives on Parenting and Childhood: Looking Back and Moving Forward*, London, South Bank University.

BALBO, L. (1987) 'Crazy Quilts: The Welfare State Debate from a Woman's Point of View', in SASSOON, A. S. (Ed.) *Women and the State: The Shifting Boundaries of Public and Private*, London, Hutchinson, pp. 45–71.

BHAVNANI, K-K. (1994) 'Tracing the Contours: Feminist Research and Feminist Objectivity', in AFSHAR, H. and MAYNARD, M. (Eds) *The Dynamics of 'Race' and Gender: Some Feminist Interventions*, London, Taylor and Francis, pp. 26–40.

DAHLBERG, G. (forthcoming) 'Negotiating Modern Childrearing and Family Life in Sweden', in BRANNEN, J. and EDWARDS, R. (Eds) *Perspectives on Parenting and Childhood: Looking Back and Moving Forward*, London, South Bank University.

DAVID, M., EDWARDS, R., HUGHES, M. and RIBBENS, J. (1993) *Mothers and Education: Inside Out? Exploring Family-Education Policy and Experience*, London, Macmillan.

DAVID, M., WEST, A. and RIBBENS, J. (1994) *Mother's Intuition? Choosing Secondary Schools*, London, Falmer Press.

DEPARTMENT FOR EDUCATION (DFE) (1992) *Choice and Diversity: A New Framework for Schools*, Cmd. 2021, London, HMSO.

DU BOIS, B. (1983) 'Passionate Scholarship: Notes on Values, Knowing and Method in Feminist Social Science', in BOWLES, G. and KLEIN, R. D. (Eds) *Theories of Women Studies*, London, Routledge and Kegan Paul, pp. 105–16.

EDWARDS, R. and DUNCAN, S. (forthcoming) 'Rational Economic Man or Lone Mothers in Context? The Uptake of Paid Work', in BOROLAIA SILVA, C. (Ed.) *Good Enough Mothering: Feminist Perspectives on Lone Motherhood*, London, Routledge.

EVERINGHAM, C. (1994) *Motherhood and Modernity*, Buckingham, Open University Press.

GELSTHORPE, L. (1992) 'Response to Martyn Hammersley's Paper on Feminist Methodology', *Sociology*, 26, 2, pp. 213–17.

GRAHAM, H. (1984) *Women, Health and the Family*, Brighton, Harvester.

GRIFFITHS, A. I. and SMITH, D. E. (1987) 'Constructing Cultural Knowledge: Mothering as Discourse', in GASKELL, J. S. and MCLAREN, A. T. (Eds) *Women and Education: A Canadian Perspective*, Calgary, Alberta, Detselig Enterprises, pp. 87–103.

HARAWAY, D. (1988) 'Situated Knowledges: The Science Question in Feminism and the Privilege of Partial Perspective', *Feminist Studies*, 14, 3 (Fall), pp. 575–600.

HARAWAY, D. (1990) 'A Manifesto for Cyborgs: Science, Technology, and

Bibliography continued

Socialist Feminism in the 1980s', in NICHOLSON, L. J. (Ed.) *Feminism/ Postmodernism*, London, Routledge.

HOLLAND, J. and RAMAZANOGLU, C. (1994) 'Coming to Conclusions: Power and Interpretation in Researching Young Women's Sexuality', in MAYNARD, M. and PURVIS, J. (Eds) *Researching Women's Lives from a Feminist Perspective*, London, Taylor and Francis, pp. 124–48.

LADWIG, J. G. and GORE, J. M. (1994) 'Extending Power and Specifying Method within the Discourse of Activist Research', in GITLIN, A. (Ed.) *Power and Method: Political Activism and Educational Research*, London, Routledge, pp. 227–38.

MANICOM, A. (1992) 'Feminist Pedagogy: Transformations, Standpoints and Politics', *Canadian Journal of Education*, 17, 3, pp. 365–89.

MAYNARD, M. and PURVIS, J. (Eds) (1994) *Researching Women's Lives from a Feminist Perspective*, London, Taylor and Francis.

McROBBIE, A. (1982) 'The Politics of Feminist Research: Between Talk, Text and Action', *Feminist Review*, 12, pp. 46–57.

NEW, C. and DAVID, M. (1985) *For the Children's Sake: Making Childcare More Than Women's Business*, Harmondsworth, Penguin.

OLSON, K. and SHOPES, L. (1991) 'Crossing Boundaries, Building Bridges: Doing Oral History among Working Class Women and Men', in GLUCK, S. B. and PATAI, D. (Eds) *Women's Words: The Feminist Practice of Oral History*, London, Routledge, pp. 189–204.

REAY, D. (1995) 'A Silent Majority: Mothers in Parental Involvement', *Women's Studies International Forum*, 18, 3, pp. 337–48.

REAY, D. (1996a) 'Contextualising Choice: Social Power and Parental Involvement', *British Educational Research Journal*, 22, 5.

REAY, D. (1996b) 'Dealing with Difficult Differences: Reflexivity and Social class in Feminist Research', in WALKERDINE, V. (Ed.) *Feminism and Psychology: Special Edition on Social Class* 6, 3, pp. 443–56.

RIBBENS, J. (1994) *Mothers and Their Children: A Feminist Sociology of Childrearing*, London, Sage.

ROBERTS, H. (Ed.) (1981) *Doing Feminist Research*, London, Routledge and Kegan Paul.

SKEGGS, B. (1995) 'Women's Studies in Britain in the 1990s: Entitlement Cultures and Institutional Constraints', *Women's Studies International Forum*, 18, 4, pp. 475–85.

SMITH, D. E. (1987) *The Everyday World as Problematic: A Feminist Sociology*, Boston, North Eastern University.

SMITH, D. E. and GRIFFITHS, A. (1990) 'Coordinating the Uncoordinated: Mothering, Schooling and the Family Wage', *Perspectives on Social Problems*, 24, 1, pp. 25–43.

SMITH, T. and NOBLE, M. (1995) *Education Divides: Poverty and Schooling in the 1990s*, London, Child Poverty Action Group.

STANDING, K. (1995) 'Just One of the 20 Per Cent: Lone Mothers' Dissatisfaction and Local Action in Education', paper presented at the British Sociological Association Annual Conference, University of Leicester, 10–13 April.

STANLEY, L. and WISE, S. (1993) *Breaking Out Again: Feminist Ontology and Epistemology*, London, Routledge.

WALKERDINE, V. (1986) 'Poststructuralist Theory and Everyday Social Practices: The Family and the School', in WILKINSON, S. (Ed.) *Feminist Social Psychology: Developing Theory and Practice*, Milton Keynes, Open University Press, pp. 57–76.

WALKERDINE, V. and LUCEY, H. (1989) *Democracy in the Kitchen: Regulating Mothers and Socialising Daughters*, London, Virago.

Notes on Contributors

Elizabeth Bird is Staff Tutor in Sociology and Head of the Department for Continuing Education at the University of Bristol. She is the coordinator of the MSc in Gender and Social Policy and teaches the Culture and Education option in that programme. Her research interests/expertise span: cultural theory, with specialized interests in film, television, media and visual arts; gender and employment, with special reference to women returning to the labour market; women's studies and Europe; theory and practice of adult and continuing education.

Miriam David is Head of Research , Professor of Social Sciences and Director of the Social Sciences Research Centre at South Bank University. Her research interests are in the area of family, gender, social and educational policies and women's studies. She has published widely and has an international reputation for her feminist scholarship. Her publications include *Parents, Gender and Education Reform* (Polity Press, 1993), *Mothers and Education: Inside Out? Exploring Family-Education Policy and Experience* (Macmillan, 1993, with Rosalind Edwards, Jane Ribbens and Mary Hughes) and (with Anne West and Jane Ribbens) *Mother's Intuition? Choosing Secondary Schools* (Falmer Press, 1994). She is co-editor, with Dulcie Groves, of *The Journal of Social Policy*. She is the lone mother of two teenage children and remains fascinated by the relations between family and education at all levels, especially the professional/academic.

Jackie Davies comes from a 'typical' white, middle-class, two-parent family. She went to university after finishing 'A' levels and at 20 gained a BA in History. She spent ten years doing 'women's' jobs (mainly secretarial). In her late twenties she enrolled as a part-time student at Birkbeck College to study for a BSc in psychology while working as a PA. During this four-year period she became a mother. Her final-year dissertation was on cognitive changes during the transition to motherhood. After graduating from Birkbeck in 1993 she worked in a residential project for mothers and babies. There followed two years as a research fellow on an ESRC-funded project, 'Parental Choice, Involvement and Expectations of Schools', directed by Miriam David and Anne West.

Máiréad Dunne is a Research Fellow at the University of Sussex Institute of Education. Her PhD, completed at Birmingham in 1994, was an ethnographic study focusing upon the construction of mathematical ability. Her current research interests include the sociology of education, social justice issues, social class and cultures of schooling. Currently she is working with Barry Cooper on an ESRC project concerned with pupil performance and interpretations of Key Stage 2 and 3 mathematics test items.

Rosalind Edwards is a Senior Research Fellow at the Social Sciences Research Centre, South Bank University. Her research interests broadly encompass mothers' interactions with social institutions for themselves and on behalf of their children, as well as feminist methodologies. She has published widely in these areas, including *Mature Women Students* (Taylor and Francis, 1993). She is about to become a grandmother, and is constantly amazed at the shifting relations between professional/academic and familial/mothering 'ways of knowing' in her life.

Ruth-Elaine Gibson is an Equal Opportunities Officer and part-time lecturer in human resource and personnel management at The Nottingham Trent University. Becoming deaf at 13, she attended the Royal School for the Deaf in Derby. Much of her work revolves round training, providing support and advisory services to all levels of staff, policy development and implementation of a range of equal opportunities issues, monitoring statistical data and teaching undergraduate and postgraduate students on equal opportunities topics within human resourcing and personnel management.

Breda Gray left Ireland in 1984 and has lived in Canada and England since then. She is currently researching Irishness, gender and migration at the Centre for Women's Studies and Department of Sociology, Lancaster University.

Christine Heward is a historical anthropologist with interests in gender, the history of childhoods and primary schooling in the developing world. She has published extensively on masculinities including *Making a Man of Him: Parents and their Sons' Education at an English Public School 1929–1950* (Routledge, 1988) and masculinities in families in *Understanding Masculinities: Social Relations and Cultural Arenas* edited by Mairtin mac an Ghaill (Open University Press, 1996). She is Senior Lecturer in the Institute of Education at the University of Warwick, UK and is presently working on a book on gender and the professions for Longman.

Pat Hornby is a senior lecturer in Applied Psychology at the University of Central Lancashire. Prior to this appointment she was an ESRC Mangagement Teaching Fellow at The Manchester Metropolitan University where she taught on diploma and masters management and HRM courses. Her research concerns are in the area of social networking and decision-making and in organizational research methods.

Notes on Contributors

Maggie Humm is Professor of Women's Studies at the University of East London, Britain's first full-time single honours degree in Women's Studies. She is the author of nine books, notably *Border Traffic* (Manchester University Press, 1991) which looks at strategies of contemporary women writers, *Feminisms: A Reader* (1992), *The Dictionary of Feminist Theory* (2nd edition, Harvester Wheatsheaf, 1995) and *Practising Feminist Criticism* (Harvester Wheatsheaf, 1995). She is currently a Subject Editor of the *International Encyclopedia of Women's Studies* and is completing *Feminism and Film* for Polity Press.

Alessandra Iantaffi is currently a first-year research student and a teaching assistant at Reading University, in the Education and Community Studies Department. She holds a *Laurea* (equivalent to a British MA) in English, German and Linguistics, gained at the III University of Rome, Italy, and a Postgraduate Diploma in Deaf Studies and Sign Language Communication for Higher Education by the University of Reading. Among her research interests are women's issues and feminist research, disability, deafness, sign language, bilingual education of deaf children, and equity in higher education.

Jane Kettle is a Senior Lecturer in Housing Studies in the Faculty of Design and the Built Environment at Leeds Metropolitan University. She spent nine years in housing practice in a number of London Boroughs, after which she job-shared the post of Access and Equal Opportunities Officer at Leeds Metropolitan University. She moved to her current position in 1994. Her main interests are in housing policy, housing and social welfare, and inequalities in housing. She has recently been involved in developing a cross-university MA in Feminist Studies. She has two children.

Meg Maguire works at King's College, London. Previously she taught in inner-city primary schools. Her publications include work on women in education and initial teacher education.

Louise Morley has recently joined the Institute of Education at the University of Sussex. She was previously at the University of Reading. Her research interests focus on gender, equity and change in professional and higher education. She has published widely on policy, pedagogy and empowerment, in particular relation to the micropolitics of women's studies and feminism in the academy. Recent publications include *Feminist Academics: Creative Agents for Change* (edited with Val Walsh, Taylor and Francis, 1995).

Liz Price works as a Senior Lecturer in Human Resource Management at Oxford Brookes University. She has a particular interest in women's employment and is currently involved in a research project exploring women's employment in four European countries. She has been a member of the University's Equal Opportunity Action Group since 1993 and was appointed as the half-time Head of Equal Opportunities in 1995.

Judy Priest works as a staff and educational developer at Oxford Brookes University. She has a particular interest in support staff. She was a member of the University's Equal Opportunity Action Group from 1993 to 1995.

Diane Reay is a Research Associate at King's College, London, engaged in research on social justice and education. Her doctoral research explored the influences of social class and 'race' on mothers' involvement in their children's primary schooling. Prior to undertaking a PhD she worked for twenty years as a primary teacher in inner London.

Catharine Ross completed an MA in Industrial Relations at Warwick University and then worked at the Local Government Management Board before becoming a lecturer at the University of Central Lancashire, running a project to improve the representation of black people in the personnel profession. She is currently a lecturer in Business Management at Worcester College of Higher Education.

Louise Ryan graduated from University College, Cork, with a PhD in 1992. Since then she has taught sociology and women's studies in England. Her book *Irish Feminism and the Vote: An Anthology of the* Irish Citizen *Newspaper* (Blackwater Press) will be published in 1996.

Sue Shaw is a Course Director/Senior Lecturer in Personnel Management at the Manchester Metropolitan University for the MA/PG Diploma in HRM. Additionally she contributes to a wide range of masters and postgraduate diploma programmes including the MBA, MSc in action learning and DMS. Her research interests are in women and management and international HRM.

Kay Standing is a Research Scholar at South Bank University in the SSRC. Currently she is writing a PhD on lone mothers' involvement in their children's education. She is interested in exploring the intersections of power relations and how working-class lone mothers construct their identities and negotiate their relations with various institutions under structural and moral constaints. She is from a white, working-class background. She graduated from Lancaster University (CF Mott Campus) and has an MA in Women' Studies from the University of Kent. She returned to study for a PhD after several years of travel and work outside higher education. She has a 1-year-old daughter.

Val Walsh is a freelance writer, researcher, editor and teacher, with many years' experience of equal opportunities activism, consultancy and teaching interdisciplinary and multi-media courses in higher education. She co-edited, with Mary Kennedy and Cathy Lubelska, *Making Connections: Women's Studies, Women's Movements, Women's Lives* (Taylor and Francis, 1993) and, with Louise Morley, *Feminist Academics: Creative Agents for Change* (Taylor and Francis, 1995). In 1995 she set up a life history and peer group project involving women academics from white, working-class backgrounds. Her abiding concern is women's creativity as both self-care and politics.

Index